The Last Generation

A History of a Chesapeake Shipbuilding Family

Geoffrey M. Footner

Axia

Collection of Leslie L. Youngblood.

Axia, ex-Mike, *Recipient of Mystic Seaport Museum Certificate of Excellence for 1989. See page 162.*

The Last Generation

A History of a Chesapeake Shipbuilding Family

Geoffrey M. Footner

Calvert Marine Museum Press
Solomons, Maryland
1991

First published in 1991 in Solomons, Maryland
by Calvert Marine Museum Press,
P.O. Box 97, Solomons, Maryland 20688

Library of Congress Cataloging-in-Publication Data

Footner, Geoffrey M. (Geoffrey Marsh), 1923-
    The Last Generation : a history of a Chesapeake shipbuilding
family / Geoffrey M. Footner.
        p.   cm.
    Includes index
    ISBN 0–941647–10–2 (alk. paper)
    1. Shipyards—Maryland—Solomons Island—History. 2. Davis,
Clarence E., 1883–1936. 3. Davis family. I. Title.
VM299.6.F66 1991
338.7'62383'0975244—dc20   91-3667
                                                            CIP

Manufactured in the United States

Dedication

I dedicate this book to W. H. F., who was, in a very modest fashion, much more than just an adventurous writer.

Acknowledgments

My principal debt is to the library of the Calvert Marine Museum under the direction of Paul L. Berry. Paul Berry is one of those rare people who loves to help others even as he seeks cover in the shadows of his bookshelves. The Mariners' Museum, the Mystic Seaport Library, the National Archives, and the Documentation Section of the United States Coast Guard are other institutions and agencies that enthusiastically support the researcher. Many others have been helpful, too: the Historical Societies of Calvert and Dorchester Counties, the Enoch Pratt Library, the Maryland Historical Society, the Easton Public Library, the Peale Museum, the John F. Kennedy Library, and the Boston, Chicago, and New York Yacht Clubs. The former employees of M. M. Davis and Son, the Davis family, the citizens of Solomons, and Kay Assenmacher, librarian of the Paul Hall Library at the Harry Lundeberg School of Seamanship, Piney Point, Maryland, have also helped.

This book includes the story of a handful of great yacht designers who guided yachting to its peak of popularity in the twentieth century. I particularly want to thank Olin and Rod Stephens, Jr., for their interest in this work, and Philip L. Rhodes, Jr., and Mrs. John Hanna for their assistance. I thank through acknowledgment the writers and publications I used in the preparation of the Davis story by referring to them in my endnotes. Individuals who should be specifically mentioned for their contributions are Thomas G. Skahill, Cathy Stanton, Kenneth Kroehler, Samuel M. Clarke, and Charlie Sayle of Nantucket. I am enthusiastic, too, in my thanks to Christine V. Durham, who not only corrected and computerized this work, but who survived the abuse of my labor agonies as we learned our way.

In the design and publishing of this book, effort has been made to produce a book a peg or two above the ordinary. Special thanks to the following contributors to a fund that supplemented the Calvert Marine Museum's budget: Jean King Grier, Dorothy Davis Hank, Rolf Graage, Steven Ambus, Kenneth Kroehler, and Mr. and Mrs. Peter Johnson.

Contents

List of Illustrations

Cover: Murray Yorke, *Manitou*, oil on canvas
Photographer: Kenneth Kroehler.

Introduction

My title, *The Last Generation*, refers to the life and work of Clarence E. Davis, a fine shipwright, who was one of the last generation of wooden boat builders. Davis died at the age of fifty-three, in 1936, so he missed the actual close of the era which was during and immediately following World War II.

The Last Generation also outlines the work of four generations of the family that preceded Clarence Davis and built wooden vessels from the immediate post-Revolutionary War period to the age of leisure in which yachting became one of the principal pleasures of prosperous Americans, almost 150 years after John Davis built his pilot schooners.

1

Sandy Island

In the decades between the two World Wars, Maryland's Route 2 meandered down the crooked backbone of Calvert County to its terminus at Solomons Island. The narrow roadbed with a sharp crown and accommodating curves around bordering farms made the trip slower than the straight route today. As travelers left Annapolis behind, the modernness of the then less-modern world of the early 20th century fell away like the bow wave of a speeding ship. It was not a pretty trip, for the charms of the peninsula were hidden behind forests of scrub pine and skirts of high grass. There was no view of the beautiful Chesapeake Bay or the winding Patuxent River at any point on the highway until the traveler rounded the last curve into Solomons. At that point, an incredible scene filled the car windshield. Off to the right in the nearby cornfield, or so it seemed, were four giant ships, German prizes from the first World War. Without warning, and with no visible water, the vast dark hulls with their immense stacks and masts loomed into the traveler's vision. A local writer wrote about the ships:

First to come were *Kronprinzessin Cecile* and her sister ship, *Kronprinz Friedrich Wilhelm*. These in their day were the queens of the North Atlantic, and they were still among the most beautiful of steamships with their sheer bows and four big raking funnels. They are now called *Monticello* and *Mount Vernon*. Later came the *America* (ex-*Amerika*), a still bigger ship, more economical of funnels and less beautiful; and finally the famous *George Washington*, biggest of the four, which carried President Wilson and the Peace Commission to Europe. They have been lying there close to shore, for years now, bring[ing] a strange flavor of a busy world to our simple countryside.[1]

Once past the ships, which were actually anchored in deep water in the curve of Point Patience, the road straightened as it approached Solomons. In the gaps between the houses and the school, Back Creek and the Patuxent River could be seen for the first time as the land narrowed to the edge of the road before it passed over a small bridge onto the island itself. On the island the choice homesites were along the "Avenue" facing the mouth of the Patuxent River where the Episcopal rectory and the doctor's house were located. The rest of the homes, mostly modest white clapboard, were scattered among gear sheds and mounds of oyster shells. At the many small piers were the charter fishing boats that carried a steady flow of city folks out to the mouth of the Patuxent River and well beyond to find the rockfish and the

The Dark Ships   Maryland State Archives (MSA SC 908–05–497).

At that point, an incredible scene filled the car windshield. Off to the right in the nearby cornfield, or so it seemed, were four giant ships, German prizes from the first World War.

blues. The center of activity was Cook Webster's store, a squat, characterless building that spread out in the little hollow between the bank building and Rekar's Hotel, the only lodging house with the mettle to call itself a hotel.

Clarence E. Davis, owner of M. M. Davis and Son, lived on the rise beyond the bank in the island's most pretentious house which anywhere else would hardly have been noticed. A visitor looking for the shipyard would be told he could either retrace his steps back up Route 2 about five miles to the Olivet Road, and take a right turn down the rut-filled Rousby Road, or he could roll up his pants legs and cross the creek in a skiff to the shipyard, a distance of about a half mile. The Davises had expanded the yard to the Mill Creek location just before the United States entered the first World War when they started receiving requests for bids from the federal government related to the military build-up.

In 1925 Clarence Davis, Cook Webster, and others persuaded the county to build a new school for the islanders. Honored guest at the school's opening ceremonies was one of the island's first teachers, Molly Hawkins, who had arrived at Solomons in 1878. She married the island's doctor, William H. Marsh. Mrs. Clarence E. Davis, who later taught in the island's grammar school, was her daughter. Clarence Davis wrote about the island's progress in 1925:

> In the past ten years, conditions at Solomons have very much improved, to give you an idea of the improvements that have been effected in this period: $25,000, Bank, $22,000, Ice Plant, $33,000, High School, boat station built by Standard Oil Co., and a number of new stores, boarding houses and private homes running way in excess of $100,000. In our business, ten years ago,

2

M. M. Davis and Son Shipyard

The Davises had expanded the yard to the Mill Creek location just before the United States entered the first World War...

we thought that $30,000 was a good year, the year, 1918, we did one-million and a half, of course, that was during the war, but our business now runs from $100,000 to $150,000 per year.[2]

The price of oysters fell after the stock market crash, and in 1932 the bank failed, wiping out most of the locals' savings. That same year the Chesapeake Biological Laboratory dedicated its first permanent building, bringing a new breed of people to the island. In 1933 a great hurricane cut 40 feet off the bank in front of the "lab," as it came to be known, and the state rushed in to build a seawall from the steamboat wharf to the curve in the "Avenue" in front of Dr. Marsh's house.

World War II brought the Navy back to Solomons. With it came inflated shipyard contracts, waterwell and sewage problems, and, practically speaking, the end of the isolation which had contributed to the special character of the island. The rough, natural attractiveness of the setting now seemed to lose some of its beauty, as Navy sheds marred the beaches, Navy airstrips cut across the green woods, and Navy ships and planes buzzed the river.

Just after the War Between the States the village of Solomons started with a boom not unlike a Colorado mining town or any temporary town along a railroad's route west. The prize was oysters. Dealers from Baltimore to New England descended on the remote island much as they did across the Chesapeake Bay at Crisfield and other waterman towns. Almost overnight the small island of Solomons changed from a farm to a commercial and manufacturing community. The oyster-canning factory built by Isaac Solomon in 1869 had the greatest impact on the area.

Before the cannery, there had been just one house on the island. Quickly the land was measured into lots for workers from Baltimore, watermen from St. Mary's County and Virginia, and ship carpenters from the Eastern Shore. Soon houses dotted the land and an oyster fleet filled the harbor, sometimes rafted across the creek from shore to shore.

There were no historians at Solomons Island in 1870 to document early events. The destruction of Calvert County's records by fire in 1882 puts the past in shadow, lighted only by the sparks of legend. No doubt these years were filled with the excitement growing out of the boom, and then the burst of the oyster bubble, and by the dream that Solomons would become a deepwater port to rival Baltimore and Alexandria.

In 1868 the Baltimore and Drum Point Railroad Company was granted a charter. Governor Bowie, in his message to the legislature that year, said:

> Drum Point has long been known to the shipping interests as one of the safest and most commodious harbors in the country, and has for many years been looked upon by many intelligent merchants and shippers as a point which would prove a valuable adjunct to the commerce of Baltimore, if connected by railroad with that city, affording as it does the deepest water, never liable to any obstruction by ice or otherwise, and within an easy run of the Capes.[3]

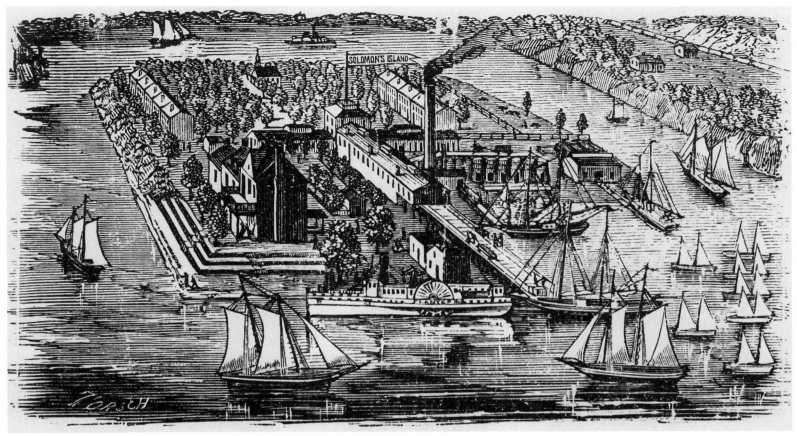

Isaac Solomon's Oyster Cannery

The oyster-canning factory built by Isaac Solomon in 1869 had the greatest impact on the area.

The story involves the intertwining lives of Isaac Solomon and Frederick L. Barreda and a railroad that was never completed. It begins before the Civil War in a time when speculators dreamed of a great new port at the mouth of the Patuxent River.

The Barreda family of Peru held the export rights to that country's guano supplies, a prized product in agriculture before the days of manufactured chemical fertilizer. Frederick Barreda, the family's United States representative, had established his American headquarters at Baltimore before the Civil War. After a few years, Barreda, a man of great charm, decided it would be more appropriate to his important position in commerce and society to relocate to New York City. Baltimore remained an important receiving port for shipments of guano, so upon his departure he gave Richard B. Fitzgerald, principal in the firm of Fitzgerald, Booth & Company, his shipping agents, a power of attorney.

Captain Fitzgerald, as skipper of the brig *Canada*, had become familiar with the west coast of South America and the guano trade. He formed the partnership of Fitzgerald, Booth & Company with Washington Booth, his half brother. Booth became the company's representative in Lima, Peru. As the U. S. agents for Barreda Brothers, the firm prospered. Fitzgerald, Booth & Company owned and operated several vessels, including the ship *Susan L. Fitzgerald*, named for Captain Fitzgerald's wife.

Although it was not until the post-Civil War period that the planned railroad to Drum Point received a charter from the Maryland legislature, individuals had been continuously promoting the project since the 1850s. Richard B. Fitzgerald was one of these promoters and he had backed his dream by buying land around the mouth of the Patuxent River, both in Calvert and St. Mary's counties.

Guano cargoes into Baltimore generated large cash receipts which passed through Fitzgerald's firm, and he probably used a portion of these funds to speculate in land. His purchases included Drum Point Farm, Rousby Hall, Solomons Island (then called Sandy Island), and several other farms around Drum Point and across the river where the Drum Point Railroad would link up with another line projected for St. Mary's County down to the Potomac River. While evidence of the land records is concrete, the source of Fitzgerald's funds is conjecture. If he did not use the guano receipts, then there is no logical explanation as to how Frederick Barreda became the owner of over 2,000 acres of land in Calvert County, including the Drum Point Farm.

Richard Fitzgerald's dream was dashed as the Civil War brought its special set of problems to the United States and economic ruin to the Chesapeake Bay region. There are only thin threads of evidence to follow as one picks up the scene around Sandy Island in the early postwar years. Isaac Solomon bought the island in 1865 from the trustees of Richard B. Fitzgerald, now legally adjudicated insane and a ward of the court. On June 10, 1871, R. S. Stewart, a landowner in Anne Arundel County and promoter of the Drum Point Railroad, wrote to Barreda in New York "on a matter of business interesting to myself and many other landowners in Maryland, and probably to yourself, as one of them—as I have lately learned you now own the landed estates formerly belonging to Mr. Fitzgerald and Co."[4] Barreda must have discovered his losses when the guano trade to Baltimore was disrupted by the war, and he began to call in his funds. After Fitzgerald panicked and his health broke, the court-appointed trustees dealt with Barreda and passed to him the title to Drum Point and surrounding farms.

Frederick Barreda had homes in New York and Newport,

Rhode Island. At Newport he built Beaulieu, one of the great showplaces which later became a summer home of the Astors and the Vanderbilts. The Barreda family was distinguished, and held extensive economic and political power in Peru. Their exclusive rights to the profits of the export of guano gave Barreda ample funds to invest in the bustling American economy. Unfortunately, his background had not prepared him for the pitfalls that await the unwary in finance, and his many absences set him up as an easy mark for promoters.

At the same time, Maryland's canning industry was growing swiftly. The preserving of fruits, vegetables, and oysters was an $8,000,000 industry by 1868, a figure that would grow to $30,000,000 by 1880. In peak years, as many as 20 million cans of cooked oysters were shipped from Baltimore to points all over the United States. Approximately 14,000 watermen caught and transported the oysters as well as agricultural produce to Baltimore.

Isaac Solomon had become an exuberant leader in the canning industry even before he came to Solomons Island. The city directory of Baltimore in 1865 listed Solomon as a dealer in oysters. He was a man of great plans and grandiose schemes who could make startling, intuitive moves. He lived to speculate, a man who was clever, inventive, charmingly persuasive, and, in failure, a helpless baby for others to rescue. Solomon came to Baltimore to buy oysters for his family's interests prior to 1850, for he was known to be living in the city during that year. He was 31 and married to Sarah Chandler, who enjoyed the pleasures of her husband's successes and paid the costs of his mistakes.

The first Isaac Solomon lived in Wilmington, Delaware, in 1740 where he operated a fat-rendering and candle factory. His

Frederico Lucino de Barreda, c. 1865   F. Barreda Sherman Collection.

Frederick Barreda had homes in New York and Newport, Rhode Island. At Newport he built Beaulieu, one of the great showplaces...

descendants in the 18th and 19th centuries extended the family's interests and wealth by marrying the daughters of influential men outside of the Jewish faith. The later Isaac Solomon had married Sarah Chandler, a woman of independent wealth. His second son, Charles, moving to Calvert County, married Eloise Sommervill, daughter of Alex Sommervill, whose family included prominent landowners who once held title to what was now called Solomons Island.[5]

One of Isaac Solomon's early schemes was a partnership with Thomas Smith in 1852, described as "an oyster business." Smith owned extensive acreage on Elliott Island in southern Dorchester County, at the northern end of Tangier Sound. Evidently the two men had plans to develop the island as the oyster catch increased, and Solomon proceeded to add to his land holdings by purchasing additional acreage in 1852 and 1853. It is estimated that at one time he owned 600 acres on the island, either outright or jointly with Smith. Much of the land was deeded to the partnership for development and they proceeded to sell an occasional half-acre lot.[6]

Elliott Island is so remote that almost no one outside Dorchester County has ever heard of it, and almost no one in Dorchester County has ever been there. A single-lane road winding through scrub pine and endless miles of marshes is the only land connection to the rest of the world. It is located 19 miles southwest of Vienna near the point where the Nanticoke River and Fishing Creek join and quietly lap its shores.

At first glance the Elliott Island venture may seem unsound, yet behind it was a strategy. Eastern Shore watermen had been hammering at their legislators to pass laws that would open up county waters to oyster scrapes. These were the protected waters of Tangier Sound between the mainland

and Hooper, Holland, and Bloodsworth Islands, where the oyster beds are too deep for hand tongs. It was widely anticipated that the Maryland Legislature of 1854 would open to dredging these bars situated within the waters of Dorchester, Talbot, and Somerset counties. When the session was over, however, only the watermen of Somerset County could scrape for oysters in their portion of Tangier Sound. The bars below Elliott Island in Dorchester were not opened to dredges until 1870, years after Solomon had lost his gamble.

Isaac Solomon lost Elliott Island in 1856 when the Court of Common Pleas of Baltimore accepted his plea of insolvency. Nonetheless insolvency for Solomon was a temporary setback, for in 1860 he was operating an oysterpacking and canning plant in Baltimore. The canning trade credited him with developing a process of adding calcium chloride to the tanks of boiling oysters and water. The process raised the boiling point of the mixture, thereby reducing cooking by several hours per vat. The canning journals of the day reported that his brainstorm revolutionized the industry. In fact, while it is true that this process greatly increased production, profits, and even product quality, it was not actually Solomon's invention. Napoleon's armies had used canned foods processed with calcium chloride, and the process was most probably developed by an Englishman, Sir Humphrey Davies.[7]

As the War Between the States ended, watermen of the Chesapeake were working the oyster bars again, trying to satisfy the nation's appetite for oysters. From his office at 309 West Lombard Street in Baltimore, Solomon monitored the legislature intently as the clamor mounted once more to open the bay to dredging. He fixed his eyes on Sandy Island, the land that would soon bear his name. True, there were no roads leading to it, but it was perfectly situated in relation to the great oyster beds. In November 1865 he purchased it from the trustees of Richard B. Fitzgerald. After 1869 watermen began delivering their catch to "Solomons."

The oyster boom was on and Isaac Solomon was moving to the heart of it. Frederick Barreda's interest in the promotion of a railroad to Drum Point was growing. Both men were now on parallel courses.

On Sandy Island, Isaac Solomon's new facilities opened in April 1870. They consisted of a cannery, a shipyard and marine railway, and a general store. His two sons moved to the island and were placed in charge. William, the elder, ran the cannery, while Charles managed the store and marine facilities. Isaac Davis, the son of George Davis of Taylors Island, was brought in to run the marine railway and to build new ships at the yard. In 1871 he was made a partner in Solomon & Son and Davis, as the marine activities were then named.

Isaac Solomon invested over $80,000 in the new facilities. The company owned ships and barges which hauled canned products and supplies between Baltimore and Solomons. The fleet included the schooners *Sallie Solomon* and *Arthur S. Sampson*, and the pungies *Mary*, *American Eagle*, *Dove*, *Daniel and Augustus*, *Exchange*, *Carpenter*, *Father & Son*, and *Isaac Solomon*. After a year of operation, cannery assets totaled more than $100,000 and the profitable marine facilities were valued at more than $20,000.[8] Oysters were brought to the cannery by local tongers who worked the bars of the Patuxent River and from a steady line of bay craft that were now legally dredging the deeper bars of the Chesapeake Bay. They included dozens of pungies, among them *John Henry Davis*, built on James Island in 1869 by John Henry Davis, grandfather of Clarence Davis.

Isaac Solomon's cannery opened two years after the railroad received its charter. He must have been beside himself with enthusiasm as the cannery was rushed to completion. From his second floor office, Solomon could gaze over the masts of the arriving oyster-laden sloops, pungies, and canoes to Barreda's Drum Point Farm and visualize the smoking locomotives and the ships at the cargo piers with the great warehouses behind. Solomon's influence was everywhere. He had himself appointed railroad commissioner to sell its bonds. He bought estates in St. Mary's County—Esperanza, St. Richard's Manor, Poorhopes—which was being surveyed as the connecting point for the railcar floats of the Baltimore and Drum Point Railroad and a connecting service south to the Potomac River and north to Washington, D.C. A speculative fever gripped Solomon as he threw himself into the promotion of the railroad.

Frederick Barreda returned to the United States in 1871 after serving as Minister to Great Britain for Peru. He had reached the pinnacle of financial and social success. He hobnobbed with the movers and doers in finance and commerce in New York, then joined them for the social season at Newport.

With the arrival of R. S. Stewart's letter of June 10, which related that "it has been long known that near Drum Point there is one of the finest harbors in the U. S.," the direction of Barreda's life would change drastically. He threw most of his energy into the promotion and planning of the Baltimore and Drum Point Railroad. Barreda, who probably had never visited his Drum Point estate when he first heard of the railroad from Stewart, and was, therefore, unaware of the potential value of his property as a railroad terminal and port, was hooked by the vision of potential wealth before Stewart's second letter arrived. It was sent on June 21, 1871, and stated:

It is now 12 years since I first moved in this business but the war and its subsequent events put a stop to our efforts. Since then two new [rail]roads have been commenced and are on the way to be perfected. One is the Western Md. Railroad. Some of the heavy monied men of New York are largely interested in this, I believe, solely, to benefit the lands and mines they own in Allegany County. This is the road that could be the great artery for our Road. The only hope I have is to show all parties interested in the coal business and its transportation by land and by water, that money can be made by such a road and such a place of shipment from Drum Point. The whole peninsula, 60 miles long, is a fine agricultural country, for wheat, corn and tobacco. It will afford very considerable travel and transport of produce. It will take coal for local use, much needed supplies, the mails and passengers could be quickly carried to Norfolk by this route. A small town will soon grow up there already the

oyster business has created a concentration of labour and the proprietor [Solomon] is in favour of our plan.[9]

Barreda was contacted by D. R. Magruder, a county judge from Calvert County, who was also a promoter of the Baltimore and Drum Point Railroad. He informed Barreda that in addition to Stewart, Henry M. Warfield of Baltimore and James Briscoe of Calvert County were on the railroad's executive committee, and that he, as secretary, was looking for a chairman. In his letter dated June 30, 1871, he gave Barreda details of the railroad's organization, costs, and needs:

Your aid would be most opportune and would give us great strength—for you are known to be a gentleman of means as well as of enterprise and business capacity. A good subscription from you would be worth several times its amount in the effect on others. The oyster trade will become a very large one at that point. Mr. Solomon at the island just above Drum Pt. has already shown what can be done in oyster packing. With a railroad, the amount of oysters shipped to the West would be immense and other packing houses would spring up. Now there are not proper facilities as the steamboats are not sufficient and do not run at all in the winter.[10]

On a visit to Drum Point organized by the directors Barreda was given a royal tour, probably in August 1871. From that time on Barreda was continually involved in the affairs of the railroad as surveys were made and money raised. He subscribed heavily in the railroad's bonds, became chairman of the executive committee, and was in constant touch with the men who were hired to build the railroad.

By the end of 1872 the roadbed was graded all the way to Drum Point. Barreda hired engineers to plan the docks at the terminal, and materials, rails, and piles were purchased. It looked as though the first train would ride the rails in just months. For construction, the railroad received $152,000 from the state of Maryland, $200,000 from Anne Arundel County, and from Calvert County, $100,000. Barreda was one of the individual contributors who together pledged an additional $221,000, buying 500 shares at $10,000. There seemed to be no obstructions. Terminals were built in Baltimore, right-of-ways obtained, and connecting track acquired from Baltimore to Annapolis. The roadbed was graded from Annapolis to Drum Point at a cost of $742,000.

In 1872, Solomon opened a Baltimore office for the railroad. By that time, the cannery had been operating just two years and its ledger recorded that Isaac Solomon's personal drawing account was in excess of $30,000,[11] a vast sum for a new company to cover. Yet there seemed to be nothing to worry about, as grading was complete to the water's edge and only tracks and equipment were needed to operate. A bonanza for Solomon appeared imminent. Yet that which seemed so sure was never to happen. The tracks of the Baltimore and Drum Point Railroad were never laid. What occurred was the "Panic of 1873," the first financial crisis in the United States caused by the inability of bankers and stock brokers to cover the value of stock and bonds placed on the market. There was not enough money in America, or Europe, to cover the issues. *Harper's Magazine* wrote:

> From the hour this discovery was made, it was inevitable that certain great unfinished railways, which were large absorbers of money, and had not yet begun to yield

refunds on the investment, must go to the wall. With the first approach of monetary stringency, railroad acceptances with bankers endorsement became unsaleable.[12]

The market crash rendered the unfinished Drum Point Railroad's bonds worthless. The public screamed that the crisis was the fault of speculators.

Isaac Solomon's passion for Solomons Island dissipated as his debts mounted. In the bleak winter of 1874 he knew that no railroad would be built to serve his factory and to inflate the value of his lands. He spent the next few years frantically bailing his sinking ship. Money to cover his debts was provided by his wife, Sarah, and his brother, Joseph. By 1877, Solomon had retreated once again to Baltimore to face a bankruptcy court.

The Barreda family, rendered penniless, moved to Drum Point after the Wall Street collapse. Frederick Barreda lost everything except his remote Maryland home which was saved for him by an older brother. Mrs. Barreda wrote to a friend:

> The view from the house is lovely as it faces the bay [that is, the Patuxent River's great harbor] which, being well-protected, is always full of ships, large and small, coming to shelter in it. And that, as you can imagine, gives a great deal of life to the place, which is not at all lonely as I had expected.[13]

Isaac Solomon's sons, William and Charles, stayed on after the crash of 1873 to operate the cannery and store. Solomon & Son and Davis continued to build new vessels and canoes, including the bugeye *Clyde*.[14] *Clyde* was titled to E. L. Solomon

Drum Point House

"The view from the house is lovely as it faces the bay [that is, the the Patuxent River's great harbor] which, being well-protected, is always full of ships, large and small, coming to shelter in it."

in an effort to hide her ownership from company creditors—E. L. Solomon being Mrs. Charles Solomon. The end came as the decade closed. In 1879, Thomas Moore and John S. Farren purchased all of the Solomon family interests on Solomons Island.

Isaac Solomon's oyster-canning factory put Solomons Island on the charts, and it continued to be a regional transfer point for oysters and a harbor-of-haven for great fleets of dredgers and tongers. In 1884 the oyster catch of the bay peaked at about 15,000,000 bushels. But by the end of the century the annual haul dropped to about 5,000,000 bushels. The island's boatyards had become the backbone of its economy.

Five Generations of Shipwrights

2

The demand for oyster dredgers took up the slack at Solomons Island after the cannery failed. The first boat-yard was Solomon & Son and Davis, located between the steamboat landing and The Narrows. Under Isaac Davis's management, the first vessel constructed was the pungy *Zephyr*. Pungies were deep-keel boats, the last surviving version of the Chesapeake pilot schooner. *Isaac Solomon*, a pungy, was built in 1872, and in 1873 the tug *Joseph Zane* was built for Edward Wilson of Baltimore. (A painting of this tug is on exhibit at the Calvert Marine Museum.) The following year, Isaac Davis built the coasting schooner *Stephen J. Fooks*, a vessel of 430 gross tons, measuring 135 feet long with a beam of 34 feet and a depth of 11.6 feet. She had three masts, and her owners put her in the Atlantic coastal trade.

Solomons Island expanded its shipbuilding capacity. Thomas W. Elliott and J. J. Saunders, ship carpenters, and William Kopp, an immigrant blacksmith, were employed by Solomon & Son and Davis. Elliott and Saunders were soon self-employed shipwrights. Other independent builders were Robert T. Allinson and James T. Marsh. Marsh, one of the most respected builders on the bay, was a New Yorker who arrived at Solomons in his own boat, *Mystic Shrine*, about

1872. Marsh built schooners, sloops, and the yacht, *Leatha*. In 1879 he built the frame bugeye *Carrie*. The bugeye was replacing the old expensive pungies.

The working life of the bugeye as an oyster dredger was full but short. In wide use after 1875, the craft was the last of its species, the final version of a line of oyster boats that had changed in size, layout, accommodations and rigging, but not in basic design or materials. It had developed from the original single-log canoe, the coasting canoe, and the brogan. As many as nine logs were used, with boats changing in size as conservation laws changed over the years. The increasing difficulty in locating large pine trees forced shipbuilders to change to the more expensive frame-and-plank construction after 1877. Marsh and his brother Charles, a blacksmith who invented deep-water oyster tongs, played key roles as Solomons became a center for bugeye construction.

Isaac Solomon's financial problems did not immediately affect Solomon & Son and Davis. Isaac Davis's daybook has survived, revealing the work of a fine shipwright. He was constructing framed bugeyes (which he called "canoes" in his records) at least two years before James T. Marsh built

13

Pungy *Isaac Solomon*   Photographer: Percy Budlong, The Mariners' Museum Collection.

Carrie, generally credited by marine historians as the first framed bugeye. On May 29, 1877, according to his daybook, Davis commenced work on a framed canoe, *Clyde*, a truly historic craft in the Chesapeake Bay's history.[1] The book's final entry was on July 16, 1878. By that time the name of the facility had been changed to Alex Sommervill's Marine Railway, apparently an attempt to confuse Isaac Solomon's creditors, since Sommervill was Charles Solomon's father-in-law. When the yard came under Thomas Moore's control in 1879, Moore used the marine railway to repair his oyster fleet, leasing the area reserved for constructing new vessels to various ship carpenters. The first of these was John Henry Davis, father of Marcellus Mitchell Davis and grandfather of Clarence E. Davis.

The years that Isaac Solomon owned the island had been evolving years for Solomons, and in a way for the Davis family, too. Isaac Davis found himself in quicksand as Solomon's empire crumbled. Mrs. Davis closed her account at Charles Solomon's store on July 3, 1878.[2] John Henry Davis arrived as cousin Isaac Davis departed for Maryland's Eastern Shore.

Pungies were deep keel boats, the last surviving version of the Chesapeake pilot schooner.

While information has been accumulated about Isaac Davis the shipbuilder, little is known about Isaac Davis, the man. His relationship to the other Davises has never been absolutely established. Nothing is known of him before his appearance at Solomons in 1870 except his age, 49 years, and that his wife's name was Henrietta.

The shipyard that Isaac Davis established on East Cambridge Creek operated for many years. In 1894 it was called Richardson, Davis and Company. The principals were William C. and William W. Davis and Webster Richardson, a descendant of the famous family who built ships at Church Creek prior to the Civil War. James Richardson, who in modern times built the replica *Maryland Dove* and in 1985 the bugeye *Jenny Norman*, identified Webster Richardson as a great uncle whom he met in Cambridge in 1916 and knew as "Long Neck Web."

Ship carpenters were skilled artisans, but they frequently lacked formal education and a "business head." There were frequent insolvencies but few formal bankruptcies. One way these builders reduced their risks and at the same time stepped up their construction schedules was to form partnerships. These were informal in the legal sense and existed only during the period that a particular boat was being built. One can understand the need for these associations because of the high percentage of skilled labor used throughout the construction period. One ship carpenter could not easily build a large schooner alone.

These factors made the trade an itinerant one, for when a Richardson or a Davis completed the work at hand, he moved on to the yard of a cousin who had just received a new contract and was looking for skilled assistance. For the

historian, there is much frustration over the lack of information. Many of the records of the old yards have been lost—in some instances destroyed by fire—or may never have existed beyond the half-model from which the builder took his plan. The survival of the records of Solomon & Son and Davis has made it possible to reconstruct much of the history set forth in this chapter.

John Henry Davis moved his family to Solomons after settling legal problems in Cambridge. The family members are listed as residents of Solomons in the federal census of 1880. John Henry Davis probably learned of Thomas Moore's acquisition of Solomon's shipyard and came to work with Moore after a court decision the preceding fall that had stripped him of his home and shipyard in Dorchester County.[3] John Henry Davis stayed at Solomons two years. Several vessels built during that time could have been built by him, although documentation is incomplete. His short stay raises questions: Was his health declining? Had he been shattered by his losses in Cambridge? Had he found Thomas Moore too difficult to work with?

Clarence Davis's wife Edna wrote years later that the origins of the Davis family in Maryland derived from seven brothers who arrived together from Wales to seek their fortunes. Unfortunately, she never knew their names and never mentioned their date of arrival. By the 19th century, there were numerous Davis families in Maryland, many of whom traced their roots back to the early days of the colony. For example,

Thomas Davis lived at the "Cliffes" in Calvert County in 1660 and was a neighbor of Thomas Taylor, an early surveyor for the Proprietor and the man who gave his name to Taylors Island in Dorchester County where John Henry Davis was born. There was Walter Davis, who lived on Taylors Island in 1680 and entered the history books as the man who overcharged the king of the Choptank Indians two skins for a trip across the bay. He gave his name to Davis Creek which, in 1832, was the site of John Henry Davis's father's home and boatyard.

The Davis who was living and working in St. Michaels in Talbot County in 1800 is of special interest for it is possible that this John Davis was the first of the five generations of shipwrights that ended with Clarence Davis. John Davis was one of that talented group of shipbuilders working in St. Michaels at the end of the 18th century and into the period of great ship building activity that peaked with the War of 1812.

Thanks to the work of John Goldsborough Earle of Easton, who has extensively researched the shipwrights of Talbot County, it is known that John Davis built a schooner on the Miles River near St. Michaels in 1804. This was *Flying Fish*, for Robert F. Hay of Talbot County. Davis built other schooners, including *Experiment* in 1806 and, in 1808, *Hope*.[4] *Experiment* was built for packet service between Queenstown and Baltimore.

The names of the ships John Davis built appear in the customhouse records, but his personal records are less clear, as only the names of heads of families appeared in the census tabulations before 1850. His sons George and Isaac, the second generation, would have been ages 20 and 10, respectively, in 1810. John Davis had two sons of comparable ages in the census of that year.[5] There were also three sisters. The

family owned two slaves, indicating that they were reasonably well off. Later that same year John Davis, shipwright, was incarcerated in a debtors' prison.[6]

Local records place George and Isaac Davis, ship carpenters, in Dorchester County in 1819. Most probably these are the sons of John Davis, driven out of Talbot County because of their father's financial failures, and into Dorchester where an expanding shipbuilding industry existed.[7]

The cause of John Davis's financial problems is unclear but may have resulted from the war fever that was already high by 1808, the year that he completed *Hope*. On June 22, 1807, the frigate *Chesapeake* had been attacked at the entrance to Hampton Roads by the British ship HMS *Leopard*. American reaction to the *Chesapeake* affair was intense as public opinion grew increasingly strong against the British and culminated in open warfare in 1812. The demand for larger vessels rose sharply, placing the small shipyards of St. Michaels under financial stress as vast outlays were required in labor and materials. Some shipwrights joined together to form stronger organizations. The Harrisons, the Kemps, and the Spencers were able to finance and construct the fleet of large pilot boat schooners, later to be called Baltimore Clippers, which sailed out to harass the British merchant fleet during the War of 1812. Others, like John Davis, fell into debt, victims of a shipbuilding boom they could not finance.

After the war the shipbuilding industry crashed. There was a fall in demand for the fast, sharp-built schooners and brigs that had successfully challenged the British fleet. The Baltimore Clipper became the preferred craft of men working outside the law—those unsettled captains of privateers who became the haulers of human cargo in the African slave rade or who sold the services of their ships and crews to nations in revolution. The shipbuilding industry which had brought so much glory and wealth to St. Michaels fell upon hard times. Ship carpenters of the town began to seek other occupations and other places to provide a living. Then, too, good timber had become scarce locally.

John Davis sold his personal effects in May 1810. Placed on the auction block were his furniture, food, tools, oakum, and his two slaves, Robin and Nan.[8] From this time on he was continually harassed by creditors.[9] In 1816 he was once again forced to sell his possessions,[10] and was placed in a debtors' prison.[11] There was no future for the Davis family in Talbot County.

In January 1818, George Davis, then 28, prepared to move to Dorchester County where forests were still standing and land was affordable. He purchased furniture for the new homestead[12] and settled in early that year, marrying Levina Pagan of Dorchester County on October 17, 1818.[13] His brother Isaac was with him, while his father moved to Queen Anne's County. By 1832, both George and Isaac Davis had acquired substantial homesteads on Taylors Island. George's farms were Risdon's Beginning and Locust Neck. Isaac's farms were Pilgrim's Rest and Aaron's Folly along Davis Creek that flowed into the Little Choptank River near the entrance to Slaughter Creek.[14]

The postwar lull in shipbuilding on the Eastern Shore lasted until the 1820s when the demand for coastal freighters and bay craft picked up. George Davis's first known schooner was *Orizenbo* built in 1822.[15]

In the northern states, oysters had been consumed since colonial days. By the time the nation was founded, however, northern oyster beds were barren, so the New England packers ordered their schooners south into the Chesapeake to maintain the flow of oysters to market. Yankee dredgers scraped the bars in Virginia waters until 1810 when that state's government passed laws reserving the catch for its citizens. Yankee boats then moved farther up the Chesapeake into Maryland waters. Had the northern packers let the local tongers fill the cargo holds of the Yankee buyboats, there would have been a chance for the arrangement to succeed. But as the demand for oysters exceeded the catch offered by the tongers, the northern packers sent vessels equipped with the dredge, a contraption never seen before locally. The storm of protest that swept up the bay to Annapolis resulted in the Maryland legislature prohibiting oyster dredging in the state's portion of the bay. While this act curtailed the legal use of dredges, it was the law's second section that created demand for baycraft on the Eastern Shore, as the act also curtailed the transportation of local oysters by other than vessels registered in Maryland for one year.[16] Packers and shippers from Philadelphia, New York, and Connecticut opened packing plants at Baltimore. One of the largest was C. S. Maltby of Fairhaven, Connecticut, which sent wagons, then rail cars of oysters west to Ohio and into the great cities of the northeast. Isaac Solomon established his facility in Baltimore around 1850 and participated in the expanding production of bay oysters.

There is no exact count of the number of sloops and schooners built in Dorchester County between 1820 and the Civil War. Surviving carpenter certificates at the National Archives indicate that more than 50 shipwrights were building vessels in that county at the time. This was the period the 11 Richardson brothers built ships at Church Creek and George and Isaac Davis worked on Taylors Island. It also included the Mitchell family of James Island who later sponsored the early work of John Henry Davis. It was the prelude to the great boom that came after the Civil War, a boom in which Crisfield and Solomons were created and Cambridge became the leading oyster shipping center of the middle Eastern Shore.

While George Davis is credited with building several bay schooners, his brother Isaac, John Henry's father, has been positively identified as a builder of only one, the schooner *Miranda*, built in 1842.[17] She was 45 feet, 3 inches at the keel and a broad 20.5 feet. On January 18, 1842, Levi Travers, Justice of the Peace on Taylors Island, issued a warrant for Isaac Davis on the complaint of James A. Stewart, to collect an unpaid account.[18] As there is a carpenter's certificate at the National Archives for the schooner *Sally Ann*, built by two men identified only as Stewart and Davis, the warrant was probably related to Isaac Davis's collaboration with Stewart. As a result, Davis lost his property on Davis Creek and moved to Fishing Creek. He died in 1869.[19]

The supply of oysters continued to fall behind the demand, and there was great pressure brought upon the Maryland legislature to allow dredging or scraping of the deeper bars of Tangier Sound. At this time Isaac Solomon bought extensive tracts of land on Elliott Island in lower Dorchester County at the northern rim of the Sound. This was also when John Henry Davis built his first schooner, *Jamestown*. The year was 1852, and Davis was 22.

John Henry Davis wrote well and spoke eloquently, and was a master shipwright. He became a leader in his community's Methodist church[20] and an active member of the local debating society known as the Taylors Island Lyceum.[21] These qualities brought him to the attention of Marcellus Aaron Mitchell, who helped his early career and whose sister Cornelia, Davis married. Cornelia's father, Solomon Mitchell, had been a builder and owner of ships. His home was on James Island, the seat of the Mitchell family.[22] This property eventually came to John Henry Davis who, though related by marriage only, was the lone male member of the family in Dorchester County. John Henry Davis named his first son Marcellus Mitchell Davis in honor of his patron who had moved to Baltimore and owned several ships in the coastwise trade.

Following the death of Solomon Mitchell in 1863, John Henry Davis moved from Taylors Island to James Island. That year he built two vessels, the schooner *Corredor*, in which Davis kept one-fourth interest, and the hermaphrodite brig *Nellie*. *Nellie* had two decks, two masts, and was 100 feet in length, 25 feet in breadth, and 8 feet, 11 inches in depth. This ship, which measured 200 tons, was built for Marcellus Mitchell's fleet.

After the close of the War Between the States, the Chesapeake Bay prospered once again. Trade was restored and the demand for oysters grew, fostered by increasingly efficient transportation systems. Maryland oysters in sealed cans reached Europe and fresh oysters carried by the railroads were on the menus of fancy restaurants of Chicago and other inland cities.

John Henry Davis built two ships on James Island in 1869, the pungies *John Henry Davis* and *Levin A. Insley*. He continued to build at least one vessel a year, including the pungy *L. C. Spencer* for Thomas Moore in 1870.[23] On August 29, 1871, John Henry completed work on the hull of the schooner *Augusta* and turned it over to her owners.

Augusta's original owners, Travers, Travers, and Pattison, placed her in service in September 1871, and her first voyage took her to Baltimore with 53 cords of wood at a freight rate of $2.00 per cord. Over the next year and a half she was worked principally within the Chesapeake Bay. There were also at least two voyages to Philadelphia with cord wood which paid the vessel $4.00 per cord. Overall, *Augusta* made 37 voyages for the original owners, hauling in addition to cord wood, grain (five cents per bushel), coal ($1.50 per ton), and lumber ($1.50 per 1,000 feet). Her total freight earned was $5,444.35. After vessel-voyage expenses totaling $1,073.32 were deducted, the remainder was divided equally among the master and the owners. The captain paid his crew out of his share and the owners were responsible for vessel upkeep. In April 1873, *Augusta* was sold for $5,000 to Caleb C. Wheeler.[24]

In 1900 *Augusta* was sailing out of Baltimore, operated by Webster and Ford, oyster commission agents engaged in dredging, buying, and hauling oysters and freight on the bay. T. Preston Webster, who had been raised on Solomons Island, was the managing owner. *Augusta* returned to Solomons in the 1930s where Clarence Davis, grandson of the builder, performed maintenance work on her at M. M. Davis and Son.

After one particular overhaul he wrote that he had found her galvanized iron fastenings sound after almost 60 years of service.[25]

The old bay schooner continued to serve her owners until 1936 when she was taken to Curtis Creek (near Baltimore) and scuttled in this graveyard of ships. Robert H. Burgess wrote, "I saw the *Augusta* sunk in Curtis Creek, her masts jutting above the surface. I recovered two big blocks from her upper rigging."[26]

When supplies of timber and logs became scarce on Taylors and James Islands, John Henry Davis bought 55 acres on Todd Neck for what seemed to be a lot of money at the time—$3,000.00. Records reveal he built only two schooners there, stayed just four years, and moved again, this time to Cambridge.

Cambridge in the 1870s had pretty streets and comfortable homes which shared their water views with spreading hotels and commodious lodging houses located on the west side of Cambridge Creek. It was the terminus of the Dorchester and Delaware Railroad and an important call for several steamboat lines serving the area. When the Davis family moved to Locust Street, Cambridge was the commercial and social center of the Eastern Shore. With excellent transportation connections and lumber supply houses, it was the obvious location for a shipbuilding industry. As center of the oyster trade for the region with several hundred watermen living in the area, Cambridge was John Henry Davis's choice for his new boatbuilding enterprise.

Marcellus Mitchell Davis, Clarence's father, was 20 years old and at his father's side when John Henry moved to Cambridge. Davis, the father, entered into a partnership in June 1877 with Joseph H. Johnson, purchasing from him half interest in

Schooner *Augusta*

Photographer: A. Aubrey Bodine, The Mariners' Museum Collection.

Augusta's original owners, Travers, Travers, and Pattison, placed her in service in September 1871, and her first voyage took her to Baltimore with 53 cords of wood at a freight rate of $2.00 per cord.

the land and facilities of the Cambridge Shipyard and Marine Railway located on the harbor at Gay Street. Johnson was not a shipwright. He had gained prominence in Cambridge as owner of the *Dorchester Democrat and News*.

Davis was ruined financially when a judgment was brought against him in September 1878 by Charles E. Hayward, representing several creditors. The court records fail to reveal the cause of his financial collapse. Before Davis had moved to Cambridge from James Island he had been successful. His partnership with Johnson had been set up in June 1877 and in just over one year he was forced to sell his interest in Davis and Johnson.[27] He was also forced to sell the family property on James Island, and his new home on Locust Street. Certainly the world had crashed down upon him. Amazingly, he had completed three ships in the short period he operated the yard: the schooners *Joseph H. Johnson* and *Alwildina C. Eaton* and the steam tug *Anna C. Burdsall*.

It was not surprising that John Henry Davis chose to move his family to Solomons Island to make a new start. Years later, Clarence Davis said in conversation and in letters that his grandfather had come to Solomons at the request of Thomas Moore and that he had built one or more vessels for Moore before leaving the island for Annapolis in 1882.

The Davis family arrived on Solomons Island in 1879, the year Moore and John S. Farren purchased Isaac Solomon's interests there. The family, including son Marcellus Mitchell, now aged 22, moved into one of the rental properties built several years earlier for the shipyard and cannery workers.[28] John Henry Davis was the master shipwright Moore needed to build oyster dredges and runners for his expanding fleet. Davis had always been a self-employed boat builder and it

seems logical, in view of his circumstances, that he would have leased a portion of the Solomon & Son and Davis shipyard, now owned by Moore.

Two schooners were built in Solomons in 1880 and 1881 by John Henry Davis. The pungy *Early Bird* was enrolled as a new vessel at the Town Creek Customs House on December 10, 1880, with Thomas Moore, her owner. Typical of the schooners built by John Henry Davis in Dorchester County, her length on deck was 75 feet, beam 22 feet, and her depth was 6 feet, 4 inches. The second Davis-built boat was *James A. Garfield*, one of seven vessels built in 1881 that were named for the president assassinated that year. While she is listed in Brewington's work as a bugeye,[29] Clarence Davis confirmed that she was, in fact, a pungy.[30]

John Henry Davis left Solomons for Annapolis in the spring of 1882 to build the bugeye *Bessie Tankersley*. His son, M. M. Davis, or "Cell," as he was known, married Emma Norwood of Solomons that year and joined his father in Annapolis. John Henry Davis died there in November 1882, and Cell Davis returned to Solomons.

By 1882 Solomons Island was enjoying a boat-building boom. James T. Marsh was busy building his famous frame bugeyes; Thomas Moore's railway was repairing his fleet; Thomas W. Elliott, J. J. Saunders, and Robert T. Allinson were building sloops and bugeyes. The young community at the mouth of the Patuxent River owed its rapid growth to its location—not that Drum Point harbor held the same attraction for watermen it had for Isaac Solomon and Frederick Barreda a decade earlier. What watermen needed was a safe harbor in which to unload their oysters and repair their oyster fleet.

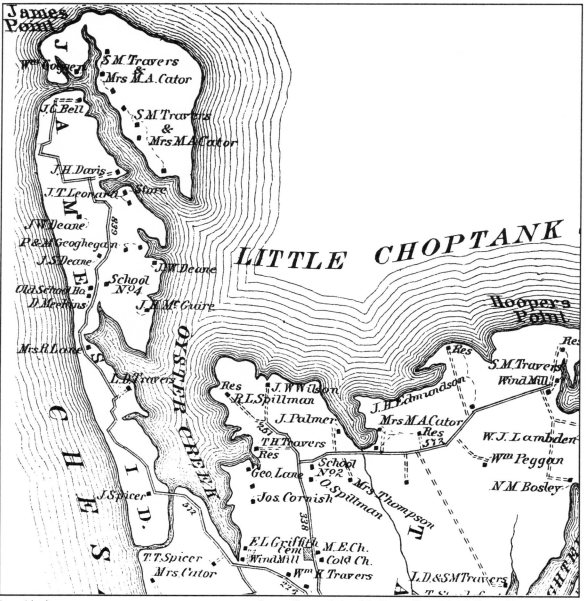

James Island

From an illustrated atlas of the Eastern Shore. Lake, Griffing and Stevenson, 1877.

The Patuxent River lies west of a vast network of water routes and inland waters that extend from the Little Choptank River to Holland Island. Dozens of watermen communities were located in this range of protected waters that served as the highways for the fleet of 1000 or more baycraft. The course to Solomons Island from most of these points was open water, a prevailing fair wind, and no shoals. Nothing suits a sailor more. Bay captains have related that the roughest, meanest parts of the Chesapeake Bay lie from the wide mouth of the Potomac River easterly through Hooper Straits and Tangier Sound. Storms are usually accompanied by winds out of the north clear around the compass to the southeast and they mean trouble for the captain who must beat upwind. The safest heading was, and is still, to the mouth of the Patuxent—truly the waterman's harbor of refuge. The transfer of the catch from dredge boat to runner could be accomplished at no better place, and for the heavy schooners laden with oysters for Baltimore, there was the usual southerly wind to push them to market.

His home was on James Island, the seat of the Mitchell family.

Survivors

The Chesapeake Bay was the domain of the watermen who sailed out of coves and from islands spotted around the bay. To these isolated communities, the bay's oyster bars, over which they sailed and tonged from their skiffs and log canoes, were theirs to work without interference. The demand for oysters continued to grow throughout the nineteenth century. After the Civil War, packers such as Isaac Solomon rushed to reopen their packing houses. The demand pushed the existing conservation laws aside initiating the great oyster bonanza of the last quarter of the century.

The feverish demand for the Chesapeake oyster could not be satisfied by a few hundred tongers. Unemployed Yankee dredgers became instant Marylanders. Crews of immigrants released from quarantine and sailors staggering drunk from bars along the waterfront were pressed into the fleet. Blacks, recently freed, formed crews as the demand for their service overcame the nation's prejudices. Investors, gamblers, widows, and thieves joined the hunt. With speculators rushing in to order vessels for dredging, new shipyards sprang up at Baltimore, St. Michaels, Cambridge, Madison, all over Somerset County, and of course at Solomons.

Production of sloops, schooners, and a new type of boat—the bugeye—rose dramatically as outside money flowed into these new shipbuilding centers.

At Solomons, shipbuilders James T. Marsh, Thomas Elliott, William Allinson, J. J. Saunders, and M. M. Davis, the fourth generation, were attempting to fill the great demand for oyster "drudge" boats. The log canoe and the brogan, both undecked boats, were unsuitable for dredging in the bay. The bugeye, with its planked deck, greater size, and increased sailing power, was the shipwright's answer. Centerboard schooners and sloops were also built in great numbers for the oyster industry. Big pungies were equipped to dredge or became runners, the haulers of oysters to market, connecting communities such as Solomons with the great processing and shipping centers of Baltimore, Crisfield, and Cambridge. Eventually, the sloop and the bugeye became the favored dredge boats of the watermen as the pungy passed out of use.

At the beginning of the exploitation of the Chesapeake's oyster beds by the northern packers, the first contacts of the watermen from the bay's isolated communities were Yankee trader captains sent down to buy and haul oysters back to New England. At the time these remote communities began peeling off the layers of isolation that had shaped their lives over the preceding century and a half. While much has been written about their log canoes, little has been written about the men who built them. One of the waterman's early prejudices was against formal education. Watermen have left few written records of their early communities and have become footnotes in the books written about the craft they created.

Soon after the first colonists reached the Chesapeake region, its islands and marshy isolated peninsulas were occupied by the disenfranchised settlers of Virginia—men and women of English stock who migrated north to escape the oppression of Royal Virginia. By deciding to live in these water-bound communities, they chose a life out of the mainstream of developing America. Other pockets of settlers developed in mountain regions west of the rich tidewater plantations. These were small groups who, like the Native Americans they replaced, lived in isolation reinforced by self-sufficiency. While they may not have lived like American Indians, they favored an existence that placed its foundation on the bounties of nature, so abundant in the 150 years before the War of Independence.

A few miles away, yet beyond the range of the watermen's small canoes, the main community of settlers lived and worked toward a society closely resembling mercantile Europe. Emphasis was placed on the growth of trade and the accumulation of land and wealth. Tobacco and grain were the backbone of the region's commerce. To the smaller farmers who failed or who were bought out by large planters, there were means for survival on the water. First war, then the rising demand for oysters pushed the watermen's communities into the mainstream. The natural result was social change, some violence, exploitation, and finally, participation in the great oyster boom of the 1870s and 1880s.

When M. M. Davis started construction on his first bugeye, *Katie and Ella*, at Solomons in 1882, the oyster catch was about to peak. Ironically the bugeyes that he was to build under the name of Hayward and Davis, then as M. M. Davis and Company, and finally as M. M. Davis and Son, were built in years of declining oyster production. The construction of the framed bugeye *Katie and Ella* was started by Cell Davis upon his return to Solomons from Annapolis following his father's death. Young Davis received the commission from Thomas A. Tankersley, the owner of *Bessie Tankersley*, the bugeye that Cell's father completed just before he died. It is possible that in the hard, unsentimental world of the greedy oyster boom, Tankersley was showing his appreciation and concern for a now rootless family by giving the young Davis a start. Cell completed *Katie and Ella* in the spring of 1883.

A number of important events occurred that year. Cell Davis completed his first vessel and his first son, Clarence, was born. Cell's wife, Emma, was the daughter of Richard Norwood who had arrived at Solomons about the time of the opening of Isaac Solomon's cannery and had stayed on to operate a general store. Norwood was an early lay preacher for the Methodist Church conducting services at the cannery and later at the church that was built next to his house on lot number 1. Norwood was owner of one or more oyster boats and a sense of humor. When requested to state his occupation for the federal census of 1880, he responded, "speculator."

Frederick Barreda died in 1883 in San Francisco, where he had entered the coffee business after losing his Drum Point estates. The title to those properties had passed to his brother, Felipe, two years before. At Drum Point in 1883, the Lighthouse Service built a screw-pile, cottage-type lighthouse.

The oyster boom was at a feverish pitch. The demand for bugeyes and sloops kept the local shipyards buzzing. Following the delivery of *Katie and Ella*, M. M. Davis formed a partnership with George W. Hayward, Thomas Moore's son-in-law. Moore was prepared to place every ship built into his fleet, which some have estimated at 100 vessels, but was in fact far less according to the records compiled at the local customs house at Town Creek across the river in St. Mary's County. Hayward ran a store and ship

Bugeye *North State*, ex-*Willie A. White*   Photographer: Frank A. Moorshead, Jr., The Mariners' Museum Collection.

The latter was renamed Agnes C. Leonard, *and now is* North State, *working out of Port Norris, New Jersey.*

chandlery, and was an ideal partner for young Davis. The firm was called Hayward and Davis, according to the business directories of the period. Three bugeyes have been identified as being built by Marcellus M. Davis while a partner of Hayward: *Fannie E. Hayward*, *Freddie Hayward*, and *Willie H. White*. The latter was renamed *Agnes C. Leonard*,[1] and now is *North State*, working out of Port Norris, New Jersey.

In 1884 and 1885 the sloops *Carrie P. Gambrill*, *Mattie*, and *Maud R.* were built at Solomons for either Moore or Hayward. They most likely were Davis-built boats as Hayward and Davis existed until August 1, 1885.

After Hayward and Davis broke up in 1885 Cell Davis bought a site for his own yard from Thomas Moore, in The Narrows on lot number 6. Davis left Hayward for the same reason the preceding generations of Davises had set out on their own—to satisfy a need to be self-employed builders of fine craft. The break was not bitter, as Davis built the bugeye *M. Blanche Hayward* for Hayward in 1886.

Provided the oyster fleet did not block his view, when Cell Davis looked up from his work he could see across the harbor to the busy yard of James T. Marsh. To his right, Davis could watch the activities of the Thomas Moore Marine Railway as well as the arrivals and departures of his fleet sloops, bugeyes, and pungies carrying heaping cargoes of oysters to market in Baltimore. Between Davis and Moore's yard, Robert Allinson and J. J. Saunders were turning out bugeyes for their neighbors. From the Methodist Church to the steamboat landing, the island was alive with activity. A new school, post office, homes, and the stores and marine chandleries of the Norwoods, Crocketts, and Haywards completed the picture. In 15 years "Sandy Island" had been transformed into a busy, prosperous community.

Historians tend to fix beginnings. Jim Richardson, the renowned boat builder of Lloyds in Dorchester County, suggests that Chesapeake Bay shipyards generally evolved and were not born. With this in mind, the beginning for M. M. Davis was the construction of *Katie and Ella* in 1882, and all vessels built after under his supervision were M. M. Davis's; the names of the companies were unimportant.

The Calvert County Courthouse records reveal that M. M. Davis bought lot number 6 from Thomas Moore on August 1, 1885.[2] There is no record of his having built a house there. Perhaps he was living with his father-in-law, Richard Norwood, or renting one of the small homes originally built for cannery workers. In 1885, M. M. Davis took back two mortgages on sloops built that year. Though documentation has not been located for *Little Maud* and *Raymond* (the name of Davis's second son, born in 1885) he would not have financed them had he not built them. The following year he built three bugeyes, *Claudy May*, *M. Blanche Hayward*, and the well-known *Col. R. Johnson Colton*. There are no records of any Davis-built vessels in 1887, but between 1888 and 1890 he built sloops, several bugeyes, and the schooner *Ada C. Shull*.[3]

Cell Davis worked on many schooners under the watchful eye of his father, but not until 1888, six years after the death of John Henry Davis, did the son's small yard launch its first schooner, *Ada C. Shull*. The owner, John Shull of Cumberland County, New Jersey, watched his new vessel slip down the greased ways and scowled as *Ada*, named for his daughter, stuck fast before it hit the water. This is a sign of hard luck, and Joseph R. Lore, son of Ada C. Shull Lore, says that the vessel had her share.

Through good and bad times, *Ada* survived years of oystering in New Jersey and Virginia, until 1910, when she was sold to New England owners. Charlie Sayle, mariner and historian of Nantucket, recalls that Captain Henry Long bought the schooner and sailed her to Nantucket where he set up the Island Service Co. in 1917 to handle cargoes of lumber, cordwood, coal, and, later, petroleum products for the islanders. A 40-horsepower Wolverine engine was installed to supplement her sails.

In her final years *Ada C. Shull* was skippered by Captain Ed Barrett and was used to haul coal for the school and paving oil for the roads of Nantucket. Each spring Captain Barrett would row his skiff under the bow, lay down his oars, and pick up a crowbar which he would thrust like a harpoon into her planking. In 1937, the steel bar hit the timbers and kept on going up to the hilt. Captain Barrett hauled her up the harbor off Joe Folger's place to die, 49 years after M. M. Davis had built her.[4]

By 1890, M. M. Davis and Company was solidly established. Cell Davis, a key man in Solomons' tight little community, had been appointed justice of the peace, a position he held until 1898. A new shipyard was

Two-Masted Schooner *Ada C. Shull*   Photographer: C. F. Sayle, Calvert Marine Museum Collection.

In her final years Ada C. Shull was skippered by Captain Ed Barrett and was used to haul coal for the school and paving oil for the roads of Nantucket.

Solomons Harbor, circa 1900

In years that followed, Davis built many bugeyes, along with Solomon Island's other builders, making the town a center for these famous oyster boats.

established on the backside of lots 12 and 13, on the shore in The Narrows. On the river front, Davis built a fine house which stands today as strong as the day it was built. In years that followed, Davis built many bugeyes, along with Solomon Island's other builders, making the town a center for these famous oyster boats.

Between 1890 and 1898, M. M. Davis and Company built at least 16 bugeyes, a couple of schooners, and in 1896, the first tug built at Solomons since *Joseph Zane* was built by Solomon & Son and Davis back in 1873. The steam tug *James O. Carter* was the first of several built for the Taylor brothers (A. J. and W. F.) of Washington, D. C.

Davis's ability to diversify lengthened his career at a time when many yards disappeared as the needs of the oyster trade declined. Yet, in spite of having contracts to build tugs and at least two bugeyes, the M. M. Davis Marine Railway Company declared bankruptcy in 1898. The marine railway had been built in 1892 and a new corporation, separate from M. M. Davis and Company, was organized to finance it. The incorporators and stockholders were Davis, Dr. William H. Marsh (Clarence E. Davis's future father-in-law), James W. Northam, and two Baltimoreans, Charles S. Waples and William H. Whiting, the owner of a marine supply company.[5] The formal corporate structure

Bugeye *Florence*

Florence *was a big bugeye, 73 feet long on deck. As with many of her sisters, she ended up as a yacht.*

Tug *M. Mitchell Davis*

The Peale Museum Collection.

The tug M. Mitchell Davis *was later chartered to the Baker-Whiteley Coal Company where she had a long career working large freighters into their berths at the Port of Baltimore.*

with demanding stockholders, inexperience with accounting methods, and hard times among the oyster fleet probably produced a crisis resulting in its failure. The property and fixtures were sold at auction on June 19, 1899.[6]

Unlike the simple facility generally required for construction of small vessels such as bugeyes and tugs, a marine railway is a permanent construction requiring extensive labor, equipment, and materials. A significant investment is required. The M. M. Davis Marine Railway Company stockholders pledged $12,000, a large sum at a time when the labor rate for repairs was between 25 and 30 cents per hour. It would take a busy railway to turn a profit.

With the company failure in 1898, M. M. Davis and his family moved to Baltimore but there is no record of his activities in that city. His sons attended Baltimore public school during the two-year period which ended when the Davises returned to Solomons in 1900. M. M. Davis took up where he had left off at the location on The Narrows behind his house, building *Florence* during the summer of that year.

Florence was a big bugeye, 73 feet long on deck. As with many of her sisters, she ended up as a yacht. The high point of her career was an appearance in the movie *The First Kiss*, filmed in Oxford, Maryland, in 1928. *Florence*

30

was one of several bugeyes, schooners, and skipjacks used as props in this unfortunate, forgettable movie—a film so undistinguished that the Chesapeake Bay Maritime Museum of St. Michaels' search for a copy in Hollywood has been fruitless. It was an important film, however, for two future superstars, Fay Wray and Gary Cooper. They had their first leading roles in the film. In a review by one New York film critic the movie was described as "the quintessence of corn."[7]

After *Florence*, M. M. Davis and Company built steam tugs in the main for the next ten years. One of these, the tug *M. Mitchell Davis*, was built for A. J. Taylor and Bros. of Washington. It was the second tug named for the builder. The first one, built in 1897, also for the Taylor brothers, had been sold to a towage company in Maine.

The second *M. Mitchell Davis* was launched in 1902, and for several years was used in the vessel-towing services operated by the Taylors. She was a powerful steam tug, 100 feet in length overall. Fred and Jack Taylor had her built to make the run from Washington down the Potomac River, sometimes as far as the Capes at the entrance of the Chesapeake where tugs were used to tow the great schooners to and from Alexandria, Georgetown, and Washington. These three-, four-, and sometimes five-masted schooners carried cargoes of ice and granite from Maine to Washington and returned with coal. The long tows up and down the river made big profits for firms like the Taylors, but often turned the long voyage of the schooner into a losing one. Other cargoes hauled into the port areas of Washington were lumber, building products, and fertilizer for the tobacco fields of Southern Maryland. The tug *M. Mitchell Davis* was later chartered to the Baker-Whiteley Coal Company where she had a long career working large freighters into their berths at the Port of Baltimore. In 1933 the heirs of Alexander J. Taylor sold her to the Harper Towing Co. of Baltimore which used her in its towing services on the Chesapeake Bay.

In 1954 her useful life was cut short by a bizarre accident. The tug had survived a devastating fire in 1948. Rebuilt, she had passed her annual inspections with ease. In the latter part of November 1954, government inspectors appeared at the *M. Mitchell Davis* berth unexpectedly and found her boilers cool. Rather than postpone her annual inspection, a decision was made by the crew to fire up the boilers, who then, with the federal inspectors, recessed to "Dougherty's Pub" to pass the time while she built up steam. One drink led to another until the group finally left the bar; as they approached the tug, they heard her screaming valves change to deadly moans as her boilers cracked. She was sold for scrap in early 1955.[8]

It is unusual that four vessels built by Marcellus Mitchell Davis should carry his name. Two of these were the previously mentioned tugs built for the Taylor brothers. The very first vessel so named was the bugeye *M. M. Davis*, built in 1890 at Davis's new facility located behind his house. The fourth vessel to carry the name of its builder was a fishing trawler built in 1911 for the menhaden fleet of the C. E. Davis Packing Company of Fairport, Virginia. (There is no evidence of any link between the two families.)

The C. E. Davis Company was managed by John Armistead Palmer, Jr., who became well-known in the menhaden industry. During World War I, Palmer sold the trawler *M. M. Davis* to the United States Navy and she was converted into a minesweeper serving on patrol duty with the North Atlantic fleet. Her name: USS *M. M. Davis*.

Bugeye M. M. Davis

The very first vessel so named was the bugeye M. M. Davis, built in 1890 at Davis's new facility located behind his house.

Little is known of M. M. Davis, the man who built so many fine vessels and who was the leader of his community for many years. Other than the usual legal notices and records of lands bought and sold, births and deaths, new companies and the end of existing ones, there is little information about the man himself. Old timers describe him as a competent man, a fair employer, and as a justice of the peace compassionate to local watermen appearing before him, yet firm with outsiders who entered local waters to take oysters protected from dredges or on private beds. Dorothy Davis Hank, his granddaughter, remembers him as the beloved senior figure in her family who shouldered his responsibilities with grace and ease.

Clarence E. Davis was 21 years old in 1904. The occasion was noted by the formation of a partnership between father and son. The new company was called M. M. Davis and Son.[9] Whatever prior success there was, it palled when measured against the quality, diversity, and the number of ships and yachts built in subsequent years. Two partnership agreements existed between the father and son, the first written in 1904 and the second in 1921.[10] They contained the wisdom of partners who place the continuity of the company above their monetary needs. Particularly in the last agreement, Cell Davis recognized the need to leave his son unencumbered with family squabbles and specified

Gladys Marsh with Clarence E. Davis

Calvert Marine Museum Collection.

Clarence E. Davis was 21 years old in 1904. The occasion was noted by the formation of a partnership between father and son.

33

that at his death everything concerned with the shipyard—capital, profits, and plant—would pass to Clarence, his partner and first son.

Changing needs at the beginning of the 20th century altered the types of vessels that M. M. Davis and Son was hired to build. The supply of oysters had declined. The demand for bugeyes and other vessels for the oyster fleet disappeared as watermen were forced to use cheaper and more efficient craft. The tongers were beginning to convert their canoes to power. By 1900 the construction of the simpler skipjack rigs had replaced the sloops and bugeyes with their higher initial cost and larger crews. The single-masted skipjack or "bateau" was a vessel that could be constructed along any creek or in a waterman's backyard, but was seldom built by an established boat yard. A number of builders closed down during those years. Others, such as James T. Marsh and his son, John Henry Marsh, and the Davises carried on.

M. M. Davis and Son continued building tugs, an occasional baycraft, and in 1911, the motor yacht, *Condorth*, was built for the Davis family. It was the second motor yacht built by M. M. Davis and Son. In 1908 the firm had built the steam yacht *Gadabout*, designed by E. B. Schook, a well-known naval architect. Her owner was Edward M. Fulton, of Catonsville, Maryland, who had an agency for the sale of small steam engines. He had *Gadabout* built as a demonstrator for his engines. William Hulbert Footner, a newcomer to Solomons then, signed on as cook for her maiden voyage. He described Fulton as childlike and unstable, for the steam engine had gone out of use in small boats some years previously.

Gadabout had a galley forward in which there were pipe berths for the crew. Aft of the galley was a small stateroom with two more berths. The midship space was entirely taken over by the boiler and steam engine. On her stern was a saloon. About her maiden voyage, Footner wrote:

> The skipper was with child to cast off; there was no test, no trial run, and a hundred details were still unfinished when we steamed out of the harbor. Off Little Cove Point the engine stopped and no effort could get her going. Nothing on the damned boat would work. The steam mounted higher and higher in the gauge, and we waited for the safety valve to pop. It didn't pop when it ought, and after a period of hideous anxiety, we drew the fire in panic and dumped it overboard.[11]

A storm came up and when *Gadabout*'s anchor dragged, two of the crew frantically rowed ashore to Cove Point Lighthouse for assistance. A tug from Solomons was dispatched to rescue the yacht and the crew still on board. Footner wrote:

> This adventure drew us so close together that when the *Gadabout* was repaired, I not only shipped to Baltimore in her, but (since the crew approved of my cooking) continued on a longer cruise down to Norfolk, up the Elizabeth River, through the Great Dismal Swamp, and down the Pasquotank to Albemarle Sound.[12]

They never did sell any steam engines.

After this experience with their first yacht commission M. M. Davis and Son made no aggressive moves to build more. Except for *Condorth*, the company did not become involved with yachts again until after World War I.

M. M. Davis and Son built the tug *America* in 1907, *Advance* for the the Navy in 1911, and at least six tugs for the U. S. Government in 1918 and 1919: *Artisan*, *Craftsman*, *Custodian*,

Guardsman, *Progress*, and *Woodman*. After the war, *Progress* was sold to the Bethlehem Steel Company which used her for berthing the giant ore ships that supplied their Baltimore mill. Later, *Progress*, under her new name *Joseph H. Moran*, became a familiar sight in New York harbor.

The last bugeye built by M. M. Davis and Son was *Leroy Woodburn*, built for J. Cook Webster and Harry Woodburn in 1913. She is one of the last working bugeyes built on the Chesapeake. Renamed *J. Hammitt Lake* when she was bought in 1929 by the state of New Jersey, she was used as a police service boat for several years on the Delaware Bay. Early in the 1950s, powered by a 96-horsepower engine and without her sailing rig, *J. Hammitt Lake* reverted to private hands. Ever since she has been an oyster dredge boat in the Delaware Bay. Her present home port is Dorchester, New Jersey.

As World War I evolved into a pattern of inconclusive battles of the trenches, American life was increasingly affected. The demand for vessels increased as the United States moved closer to war. Yards such as M. M. Davis and Son became bustling centers of activity as the federal government ordered wooden vessels to relieve the high demand for steel in a nation preparing for war.

One of the last commercial vessels built by M. M. Davis and Son before World War I

Bugeye *Leroy Woodburn*; *Condorth* in Foreground

The last bugeye built by M. M. Davis and Son was Leroy Woodburn, built for J. Cook Webster and Harry Woodburn in 1913.

was the wooden freighter *Sarah Weems*. It is assumed that she was placed under the control of the U. S. Shipping Board for wartime service. Launched in December 1917, the ship measured 206 feet at the waterline, by far the largest vessel built at Solomons. A newspaper of the time described the launching:

> The *Sarah Weems*, one of the first, if not the first of the new wooden steamers to be built on the Atlantic Coast, was launched recently at the yard of M. M. Davis & Son, Solomons, Md. The vessel is owned by the Baltimore & Carolina Steamship Company, of Baltimore, and was named by Miss Matilda Weems Williams, sister of the president of the Company. The vessel has a length of 212 feet between perpendiculars, an extreme beam of 38 feet, and a dead-weight capacity of 1,200 tons. She has triple expansion engines, with a working pressure of 180 pounds.[13]

After the war, *Sarah Weems* continued in commercial service, though hundreds of other wooden ships were tied up to rot or eventually burned. Renamed *Sarah Weaver*, and finally *Southland*, the largest ship built by Davis continued to serve various owners in New England and New York. On December 3, 1930, she burned in Massachusetts Bay.

M. M. Davis and Son bought several acres of land along Mill Creek across from Solomons in 1910. Larger vessels such as the menhaden trawler, *M. M. Davis*, were built at the new yard which was continually expanded as World War I approached. *Sarah Weems* was built there as were the large barges and tugs that the yard built during the first World War. The old yard on The Narrows continued to operate as a repair facility for smaller vessels until after the war.

There were no roads to the new Mill Creek facility and even after an all-weather road was built into Solomons in 1913, most of the supplies for the yard came by water. With the completion of the highway, trucks began to haul freight into Solomons, and from there it was transported across Mill Creek by boat. Clarence Davis traveled back and forth to work by boat as did most of his men who lived at Solomons, Dowell, and Olivet.

The partnership between M. M. Davis and Clarence Davis was dissolved in favor of a corporation during the war years. The supposition is that the father and son management team again needed outside capital to land the large government contracts which were offered, evidently without bidding, as the need for vessels was great. Certainly the Davises also had in mind limiting their liability as they expanded to meet the needs of a country at war.

The work done by M. M. Davis and Son in the war was summed up in a newspaper article that appeared in 1920:

> M. M. Davis & Son, Inc., at their yard in Solomons, Md., have made an Atlantic Coast record in construction of wooden vessels, their figures showing that from January 1, 1918, to November 1, 1920, they successfully launched and delivered thirty-five boats, an average of one launching every four weeks. The list includes one 1,700-ton barge for the Northern Transportation Company, one 133-foot seagoing tug for the Bethlehem Steel Corporation, one 600-yard mud scow for the Sanford & Brooks Company, fourteen 600-ton barges for the Quartermaster Department, U. S. Army; eight 133-foot seagoing tugs for the Shipping Board, and ten 1,000-ton pontoons for the Bethlehem Shipbuilding Corporation, Ltd., for the Fore River Plant, the last of which has just been delivered. The company is now constructing a 1,700-ton

Steamship *Sarah Weems*

Launched in December 1917, the ship measured 206 feet at the waterline, by far the largest vessel built at Solomons.

World War I Barges

Calvert Marine Museum Collection.

"The company is now constructing a 1,700-ton barge for its own account, ..."

barge for its own account, which will probably be completed and launched by the latter part of this month. Present prospects are for several large contracts in the spring. In the construction of each of the Bethlehem Company's pontoons 260,000 feet of Oregon pine and approximately twenty-five tons of galvanized fastenings were used.[14]

The resident inspector for the U. S. Government at the shipyard was Captain Leonard S. Tawes, the well-known master of the coasting schooner trade. In his journal he wrote that he held the job one-and-a-half years, until April 1920.[15]

Marcellus Mitchell Davis was 63 years old in 1920. More and more his son Clarence's hand controlled the helm. Cell Davis's wife Emma died in 1921, and he married his nurse, Pauline Vaughan, who survived him for many years. Marcellus Mitchell Davis died in 1924. Each year at Easter Clarence Davis sent funds to his stepmother in Baltimore for flowers which she placed on the graves of his parents.

M. M. Davis had been an exceptional shipwright. His work was more diversified than the work of his father, John Henry Davis. Each generation of the family shared equally an ability to teach their sons to build boats better than they had been trained themselves.

Yachting on the Chesapeake

Pleasure craft were scarce on the Chesapeake Bay before the 20th century. Few Marylanders had the time or the money to participate in pleasure boating. The bay, dominated by the thousands of watermen fishing its waters and fighting each other for the catch, was not viewed as friendly or even civilized by most of the population. There were no yachting facilities prior to 1900 and only a couple of small yacht clubs existed at the turn of the century. On the Eastern Shore's Tred Avon River between Easton and Oxford, and under Federal Hill in Baltimore, small sailing clubs held regattas during summer weekends. Racing log canoes had started years before at St. Michaels. All of these activities were enjoyed by very small groups of men considered odd by other Marylanders who were involved with hunting and horses and other sports then popular with gentlemen.

Large schooners, fast sloops, and steam yachts, popular around New York and Boston, were not seen very often on the waterfront of Baltimore, in the basin at Washington or in the Hampton Roads. At the great yacht clubs or at any of the many major races up north, spectator boats vied with the competitors in such numbers to cause the scene to be described by the Boston *Globe* as a situation where "one cannot jibe his main boom without hitting a millionaire. It is a long purse that wins a race." Maryland was just recovering from years of economic disruption caused by the Civil War and there were no clusters of the very rich comparable to those in Boston and New York.

There were exceptions. Alexander Brown IV owned the 148-foot steam yacht **Ballymena**, built in Rhode Island by the Herreshoff Manufacturing Company in 1888. Henry Walters's **Narada**, at 491 tons, was one of the mightiest yachts afloat; and T. Harrison Garrett's yacht **Gleam**, also built by Herreshoff, was the victim of a tragic collision with the bay steamer **Joppa** in 1888 that cost Garrett his life. But the yachts of these wealthy Marylanders were more often seen at anchor in Florida waters, in the Mediterranean Sea, or at a New York Yacht Club station than at a dock in Baltimore.

On occasion a northern yacht would venture through the Chesapeake and Delaware Canal into the bay. Feeling brave and very much like an explorer, the yachtsman was usually en route to the sunny south and was not in the Chesapeake to gunk hole in its coves or sightsee the likes of Solomons Island or Crisfield. Most northern yachtsmen had little interest in what they conceived to be the unfriendly waters of the bay populated with locals in homemade pleasure boats and warring watermen whom they heard sometimes shot guns to make a point. The sophisticated yacht club member from Long Island Sound or from any one of the fine clubs between Boston and Marblehead was closer to his British counterpart sharing an interest in the trendy new designs of each other's naval architects and comparing performances of their schooners and sloops.

British yachtsmen were avid racing competitors and, seemingly, were linked forever to the New York Yacht Club by the frustrating defeats inflicted by their American cousins. From the time of the victory of the schooner *America*, participating in the Hundred Guinea Cup Race around the Isle of Wight in 1851, New York sailors have been obsessed by an apparent need to extend the string of victories. From that year forward the world of yachting centered on New York and Britain, with Boston and Eastern Canada playing satellite roles. In the press the America's Cup series dominated all racing news. New York journals became mesmerized by the victories of the New York Yacht Club members' yachts, whose chances were blatantly boosted by race rules written by the host club.

Reviewing the contents of the newspapers and journals of the period between 1880 and 1910, one is struck by the dearth of yachting news outside of New York and New England. Items from the Chesapeake Bay appeared from time to time, usually describing some tragic or ridiculous event. One of the most prominent publications was *Forest and Stream*, a weekly magazine for sportsmen that became the yachting bible under the editorship of W. P. Stephens. While this magazine printed little about yachting events south of Philadelphia, exceptions occurred when there was something negative to report. The magazine reported on the tragic accident of *Gleam* in several issues. It printed a letter from a New Yorker who did not get his boat built by the spring of 1888 because of "the stupidity of the Baltimore builder."[1] Another reader wrote that yacht racing at Baltimore was not quite dead.[2] A captain reported that he "got out of the Chester River just ahead of the Oyster War."[3] Collisions and capsizing were written about infrequently, but when one occurred on the Chesapeake it was likely to be reported by *Forest and Stream*. The following is from their issue of June 16, 1891:

> On July 4th, the death trap *Otto Duker*, by courtesy a cabin sloop yacht, capsized in a moderate breeze near Baltimore, with a large party of ladies and children aboard.[4]

The negative tone of the reports on conditions on the Chesapeake continued into the 20th century, and the bay and its tributaries became known for tasty oysters and unfriendly cruising grounds.

Leatha, built at Solomons in 1874 when highways were rutted oxen trails and steamboats were the only link to the outside world, was one of the first great yachts launched on the Chesapeake Bay. Her builder, James T. Marsh, a New Yorker, arrived on the island in 1872/73 and established a shipyard several years before John Henry Davis and his family arrived from Dorchester County. According to legend, Marsh's arrival was cloaked in mystery and secrecy. He was supposed to have in his pocket a commission to build an America's Cup defender for a New York yachtsman.

Marsh built the 56-foot yacht *Leatha* for General W. W. Sanford who sailed her north. After one year, Sanford sold her to Smith Ford, a member of the Brooklyn Yacht Club, home club of several America's Cup contenders. A search of the entries and results of the cup trials of 1876 reveals no mention of Marsh's *Leatha*. Over her 40 year life she was rebuilt twice, her hull lengthened, and her stern changed from square to round. When she was acquired by a Boston yachtsman, a keel replaced her centerboard and her name was changed to *Kathleen*. There is no record of her ever entering a race.[5]

Since Baltimore was a major shipbuilding center in the latter part of the 19th century it was not unusual that someone from out of town would come to one of the shipyards to have a yacht built. Mrs. Lucy Carnegie, a member of the Pittsburgh steel family, had a 120-foot yacht built by the Maryland Steel Company in 1894, and an excited press reported on this rare instance of a woman commissioning such a vessel:

> Among the new steam yachts of the year, the steel steam yacht *Dungeness* possesses a special interest from the fact that she has been designed and built to the order of a lady, and also that she will be the first yacht enrolled in the New York Y. C. under the name of a lady member, as permitted under a recent amendment of the constitution. The yacht was designed by Mr. George B. Mallory of New York, and was constructed under his supervision at the works of the Maryland Steel Co. of Sparrows Point, Md.[6]

The largest yacht built in Maryland was launched in 1880 at the yard of Malster and Reaney in Baltimore. She was the bark-rigged, steam-powered yacht *Bretagne* built for Mr. Leon Say. Her length was 240 feet overall, 31.5 feet in the beam, and 20 feet depth of hold. She was built of wood, the frames of white oak and plankings of Georgia yellow pine. All fastenings below the waterline were copper. *Bretagne*'s boiler was designed to develop eighty pounds pressure and she consumed twenty tons of coal a day; and her brass propeller was thirteen feet in diameter. *Lloyd's Register of American Yachts* listed her as the second largest yacht in existence at the time she was launched.

Malster and Reaney built the steam yacht *Chronometer* for William O'Sullivan Dimpfel in the 1880s. Dimpfel, who came to Maryland from Philadelphia, could be called the "father of yachting on the Chesapeake Bay" as he owned several early yachts and was an amateur designer. He was a charter member of the Baltimore Yacht Club in 1878. Later, after moving to the Eastern Shore, he became a founder and first commodore of the Chesapeake Yacht Club which celebrated its hundredth birthday in 1985.

Wm. Skinner and Son built a couple of yachts, and another firm, Beacham Brothers, built the schooner *Rena* for the members of the Baltimore Yacht Club. She was 75 feet overall and at the time she was probably the only major sailing yacht out of Baltimore. She was launched in 1880.

In a small but profound manner the Chesapeake Bay affected the American yachting world. The schooner *America*, designed

Kathleen, ex-Leatha

Photographer: N. L. Stebbins, The M.I.T. Museum, Hart Nautical Collection.

*Marsh built the 56-foot yacht
Leatha for General W. W.
Sanford who sailed her north.*

by George Steers, was modeled after the Chesapeake Bay pilot schooner. This topsail schooner, Chesapeake Bay 's most important contribution to vessel design, first appeared before the Revolution. It was used on the bay as small pilot boats, ferries, and as baycraft hauling grain into the port of Baltimore, and it was the prototype for the Baltimore Clipper, the pungy boat, New York and Boston pilot boats, and most of America's early yachts.

America was the yacht to which most New York writers linked the birth of yacht racing as a sport in this country. Her last berth was at Annapolis at the U.S. Naval Academy where over the years she was allowed to deteriorate until it became necessary to have her broken up in 1945, six years short of her 100th birthday.

The Gloucester fishing schooners of the 19th century and the fleet of yachts that came later from the drawing boards of the naval architects of the Boston area, including John G. Alden, owe something to *America* and the Chesapeake Bay schooners that preceded her. In still another way, Alden and others are indebted to the craft of the Chesapeake Bay. At one time or another, each has admitted a debt to the bugeye and its predecessors, the log canoe and the brogan. In the case of John Alden, his change from the gaff rig to the triangular sails of his later schooners and ketches came after seeing the bugeye perform.[7] This graceful boat, built to dredge oysters in winter and to carry produce in summer, caught the eye of the yachting public and held it for years. In 1915, *Heather II* was built in Cambridge for a member of the New York Yacht Club. M. M. Davis and Son built *Orithia* for a member of that club in 1930. In between, many other yachts were built from the bugeye design. Over the same period, many of the working bugeyes were converted to yachts. On August 6, 1885, *Forest and Stream*, New York's yachting weekly, had taken notice:

> A Chesapeake Buckeye—One of these peculiar craft has lately been cruising about the Sound, **S. E. Walters**, Dr. R. M. Weed of New York, owner. Her foremast is longer than the main, giving her an odd appearance.[8]

This less than enthusiastic commentary nonetheless focuses attention on the continuing affair between yachtsmen and the bugeye. Admiration for the bugeye is not just an instance of old sailors caring for traditional craft, but an honest and enduring interest that started when the bugeye was young and queen of the Chesapeake workboat fleet. In fact, in 1885, **Sarah E. Walters**, as she was originally named, had been built only seven years before by Sam Somers of Crisfield for the oyster industry. The earliest bugeye is thought to have been built in 1867 in Somerset County, and construction of the type did not reach a peak until the year that Dr. Weed's yacht was seen on Long Island Sound.

It was not a passing fancy, for as long as a single bugeye exists there are sailors willing to spend years and fortunes to bring it up to yacht condition. In 1986, *Little Jennie*, a graceful bugeye built by James T. Marsh at Solomons Island 104 years earlier, was restored by her owner to take part in the celebration of the 100th birthday party for the Statue of Liberty in New York harbor.

Little has been written about the sailing qualities of the bugeye. As he sailed from New York to Norfolk in 1889, Captain Lutes of the yacht *Leona* wrote: "The buckeye is the prevailing boat here; they range from 18 to 60 feet long, and sail very fast and will live in almost any kind of sea."[9]

J. T. Rothrock, a keen observer who cruised the bay in 1884 wrote of his encounter with a bugeye:

> Alongside of us came a Chesapeake bugeye of light draught, but long and narrow. We saw her start from Tolchester Beach and creep up on us swiftly and surely. We were laboring; she was moving along without effort, going not only faster, but working more to the windward. At the very time this 40-foot bugeye was leaving us, we ourselves were distancing a large coasting schooner. The bugeye careened over very little, went easily through the water, made no pounding or splashing, and looked almost into the wind. Thus she proved herself as possessing every requisite of a first class sea-goer.[10]

The Davis yard built the bugeye *Blue Wing* in 1893 and the *Calvert Journal* announced in its August 1893 issue that M. M. Davis had built a bugeye yacht for Theodore Harrison of Philadelphia. The following year *Blue Wing* was registered in Baltimore as a working bugeye, throwing doubt on her prior description. If she was actually built as a yacht, this fact would make her among the first bugeyes built for a yachtsman. As such she becomes the first yacht built by Davis.

Several M. M. Davis and Company-built bugeyes were converted to pleasure boats. An early conversion was *Lula and Sadie*, built by Davis in 1892. Her owner (before she became a yacht) was Captain Charles E. Leatherbury of Shadyside, Anne Arundel County, one of the bay's best-known watermen and a boatbuilder himself. *Lula and Sadie* was renamed *Frances* by her yachtsman owner, E. M. Padeford of Washington, D. C.

Among the other Davis-built bugeyes that were converted to yachts were **North State**, **Florence**, **Col. R. Johnson Colton**, and **Florence Northam**. Each of these vessels had her moment of glory: *Florence* briefly appeared in a Hollywood film, as described in Chapter 3; *Col. Colton*, a yacht for more than 40 years, in the 1940s was home to the writer Nathaniel T. Kenney; *Florence Northam*, a frequent entry in the yearly workboat races of the 1920s and 1930s, won the bugeye race held off St. Georges Island on the Potomac River in 1930. Of the 14 bugeyes competing that year, seven were built at Solomons.

Edwin W. Bietzell, in his book *Life on the Potomac*, relates a story told to him by R. Johnson Colton II, son of the colonel. According to the younger Colton, the bugeye was ordered by Colonel Colton for Taylor Green, a black waterman whom Colton held in high regard. Green named the vessel for his patron. According to Bietzell, Green used *Col. Colton* to transport oysters to Washington, since bugeyes were not generally used to dredge oysters on the Potomac River.[11] However, surviving official documents and licenses for this bugeye, including a copy of its original license issued at the Town Creek Customs House on November 5, 1886, do not agree. According to these documents her first owner was not Green but a man named Long; and in 1887 she was owned by Captain J. J. Gibson on the Potomac River.

Another story about **Col. R. Johnson Colton** is provided by Nathaniel Kenney who wrote that Colonel Colton was a Virginia tidewater judge. When her crew of Maryland watermen was hauled into his court for apparently illegally dredging Virginia oysters, Judge Colton threatened to throw the book at them. Kenney quotes Colton and the skipper:

> "You are desperate dangerous criminals. I am going to halt forever the stealing of Virginia oysters by you

blasted half-yankees. What ship are you from?"

"The **Col. R. Johnson Colton**," the skipper replied. "Case dismissed," said Judge R. Johnson Colton, colonel in the Virginia militia.[12]

Other bugeyes converted to cruising yachts include *Bee* (a familiar sight at the yacht clubs around Hampton Roads and the upper bay), *Brown Smith Jones*, a former police boat, and *Sallie L. Bramble*, built in 1890 by Otis Lloyd in Salisbury. *Little Jennie*'s home port was New York in 1988 and *Sallie Bramble*'s, Boston. *Maggie E. Smith* became the yacht *Gypsy*. She is now in the collection of the Mariners' Museum at Newport News.

According to the younger Colton, the bugeye was ordered by Colonel Colton for Taylor Green, a black waterman whom Colton held in high regard.

Bugeye Yacht *Col. R. Johnson Colton*

John G. Earle Collection.

Bugeye Yacht *Brown Smith Jones*   Photographer: Morris Rosenfeld, ©Rosenfeld Collection, Mystic Seaport Museum, Inc.

Another of the early bugeye conversions was *E. F. Terpie*, built by Thomas McCoster of Baltimore. An early yacht of bugeye design at Solomons was *Retsilla*. This yacht was the work of M. P. McDonough who arrived in Solomons in 1898 from parts unknown and leased a portion of Thomas Moore's marine yard and shed. As the production of oysters fell in the late nineteenth century, Moore leased his ways to at least three boatbuilders: McDonough, Samuel Tingstrom, and in 1904, to George Dawson.

Retsilla was a well-known yacht because she was built for Francis W. McAllister, one of the Chesapeake Bay's yachting pioneers. He owned several yachts, including *Gaetina*, which had been designed in 1883 by William O'Sullivan Dimpfel, previously mentioned.

Retsilla was described by the Barrie brothers during a cruise of the bay in 1899. They were in company with Dimpfel who at that

Other bugeyes converted to cruising yachts include Bee *(a familiar sight at the yacht clubs around Hampton Roads and the upper bay),* Brown Smith Jones, *a former police boat, and* Sallie L. Bramble, *built in 1890 by Otis Lloyd in Salisbury.*

time owned the yacht *Panola*. After a night anchored with *Retsilla* they wrote:

During the night the bugeye yacht *Retsilla*, of Baltimore, belonging to Mr. McAllister, came in, and about ten o'clock we made an official visit. The *Retsilla* is not a regular out-and-out bugeye, as she has an overhanging stern. We were interested in her, as ever since the skipper and I first went to the Chesapeake, we have been talking of having a bugeye, but it will be an out-and-out one, with a sharp stern.[13]

Retsilla was just under 62 feet on the deck. Her beam was 17.3 feet, and she had a handsome profile. Her cost was $1,500. She was renamed *Afjen* by a later owner, Thomas H. Barrington of New York.

The shipwright E. James Tull, maybe the only shipbuilder rivalling the Davises in quantity and diversity, built the bugeye yacht

"During the night the bugeye yacht Retsilla, *of Baltimore, belonging to Mr. McAllister, came in, and about ten o'clock we made an official visit. The* Retsilla *is not a regular out-and-out bugeye, as she has an overhanging stern."*

Retsilla

Maryland Historical Society Collection.

47

Condorth

Dorthy Davis Hank Collection, Calvert Marine Museum.

The Davis family built
Condorth *for their enjoy-*
ment and for transportation
between the yard at Solomons
and their second location
across Mill Creek at Rousby.

Dixie for Thomas Dixon at Pocomoke City in 1899. Dixon, a lawyer and a Baptist minister as well as an author, gained entrance to many encyclopedias by authoring the *Clansman*, a glorification of the Ku Klux Klan. Episodes from the book were developed into the landmark movie, *Birth of a Nation*.

Tull built the beautiful bugeye yacht *Hasse* in 1924 at the end of his long, successful career. She was designed by the famous naval architect Charles Mower, who in 1915 had designed the bugeye yacht *Heather II*. *Hasse* is presently owned by Ed Farley of Bosman, Maryland.

In 1907 George Dawson built the sailing yacht *Gertrude* at Solomons and J. T. Marsh & Sons built the three-masted schooner yacht *Vanessa* for Dr. Morton R. Peck of New York. It was also the year that M. M. Davis and Son built the motor yacht *Condorth*. The Davis family built *Condorth* for their enjoyment and for transportation between the yard at Solomons and their second location across Mill Creek at Rousby.

The Davises were aware of the increase in yachting on the bay because Solomons was a stopover port for yachts traveling between the North and southern waters. Yet observing John Henry Marsh build the schooner *Vanessa* across the harbor, they knew she was only the third or fourth yacht built at

Solomons in 35 years. To the practical Davis family Solomons was far too isolated from the yachting world. It didn't seem likely that the clubby northerners would come to them to build their fancy yachts. These self-trained shipwrights were certain they did not speak the language of the worldly yachtsmen.

In August 1907 M. M. Davis and Son became the second Rudder Station on the Chesapeake Bay. The first had been the Nilson Yacht Building Company of Baltimore which had signed up several years earlier. A Rudder Station was a yard or marine facility selected by *Rudder* magazine to serve its yachting readers as mail drops and service stations on cruises beyond home waters. Later, the Davises often said they operated the oldest marina on the Chesapeake Bay south of Baltimore.[14]

When Clarence Davis received a commission in 1929 to build the bugeye yacht *Loretta*, there were no surviving records or models of the many bugeyes the family had built. The yard had been destroyed by fire at least twice, the most recent in 1928 when the

When Clarence Davis received a commission in 1929 to build the bugeye yacht Loretta, *there were no surviving records or models of the many bugeyes the family had built.*

Loretta

Photographer: Hughes of Baltimore, Maryland Historical Society Collection.

49

main shed and office burned. By 1929 Clarence Davis was very much involved in yacht construction and closely associated with Philip L. Rhodes, the yacht designer. Davis wrote to him about *Loretta* on February 9 of that year:

On arrival at office this morning looked through files and found the Bugeye dope that you sent me some time ago. I only wish that I had thought of this, as it would have saved me a lot of work in making up sketches. The boat designed by Mower called the *Hasse* seems to be about what I worked out. This boat has spent a good deal of time at Solomons and has always impressed me as being a pretty good design with some modifications. Owing to the additional length of this boat can get much more interior accommodations, however, it will all tend to help us in working out our job, and I repeat I feel like kicking myself for not remembering that you had sent me this stuff.

Yesterday morning I went down to the fish wharf in Washington and saw a typical sharp stern bugeye 61 ft. long, on deck and 18-ft. beam. I took some measurements as to location of the well, which are noted in sketch attached. The spars on this boat, foremast 61 ft. above deck and mainmast 53 ft. above deck.[15]

M. M. Davis and Son's price for *Loretta*, built for Frank Reagan of Baltimore, was $11,050, f.o.b. Solomons, complete except for the engine, shaft, and a propeller supplied by Reagan. When the yacht was ready for delivery, Davis submitted an additional bill for $2,672.69; this was for extras of yacht quality, such as sails, trim, rigging, and various gear which replaced items of commercial quality originally specified on the contract.

The publication of *Loretta*'s lines and photographs in yachting magazines produced many inquiries, but only one additional contract. Haliburton Fales, the first member of the prestigious New York Yacht Club to come to M. M. Davis and Son for a yacht, fell in love with the bugeye lines as had so many yachtsmen before him. For his bugeye, only slightly larger, Fales chose teak decks, double-planking of the hull, outside ballast, and many frills that ran the cost up to $18,500. His yacht *Orithia* was completed in April 1930.

What is rather surprising about *Loretta* and the larger, more refined *Orithia* is that both owners came to Clarence Davis for a traditional bugeye design. Davis prepared and sent Philip Rhodes rough drawings after he examined an old working bugeye in Washington. However, the yachts drawn by Rhodes bore little resemblance to the hull of the traditional bugeye.

The round stern bugeye *Norma* was built in 1905 by Otis Lloyd who founded the Salisbury Marine Construction Company. She very closely resembled the designs created 30 years later by Philip Rhodes for *Loretta* and *Orithia*. From the broadside the resemblance of the hulls and rigging is remarkably close. The Rhodes yachts, however, had long trunk cabins. The other distinctive difference was that Rhodes's yachts were given counter sterns rounded only on the corners while *Norma* had a graceful, rounded stern. *Norma* and the Rhodes yachts did copy the full bilge of the traditional bugeye, which, when combined with a wide beam, made them stable under sail. *Norma*'s lines appeared in *Rudder* in 1905; those of *Loretta* were reproduced in the same magazine in 1929.[16]

One other bugeye yacht was built by M. M. Davis and Son. This was *Ko-Asa*, completed in 1936, the year in which the yard was also building *White Cloud* and the yawl *Manitou*. Clarence Davis's death on November 15, 1936, came just about the time *Ko-Asa* was delivered. It is a notable reflection on the bugeye design that the first vessel built by Marcellus Mitchell Davis in 1882 was the bugeye *Katie and Ella*, and the last boat completed by his son, Clarence, 54 years later, was the bugeye yacht *Ko-Asa*.

Ko-Asa was designed by the naval architectural firm of Henry J. Gielow, Inc., for George Marshall Allen. The yacht was designed in 1931, but Allen delayed her construction until 1936. The original contract specified that M. M. Davis and Son was to take Allen's presently owned bugeye yacht, *Hasse* (also named *Ko-Asa* by Allen), in trade. On July 1, 1931, Davis wrote to Paul Nevin, his contact at the Gielow firm, concerning the boat:

> We received yesterday your letter on the 29th with specifications dated June 26th #827 for an 80 ft. Bugeye. We haven't had time as yet to go over those very carefully, but will do so and if we find anything not in line with our general understanding will advise you. We do, however, see that you specify Yellow Pine in two lengths for Keel. We are afraid that we will not be able to get this out of stock and it will have to come from Southern Mill, so in view of this and to save delay would like to have option to use Fir. This will

Loretta's Cockpit

Photographer: Hughes of Baltimore, Maryland Historical Society Collection.

...the yachts drawn by Rhodes bore little resemblance to the hull of the traditional bugeye.

Orithia

Photographer: Morris Rosenfeld, ©Rosenfeld Collection, Mystic Seaport Museum, Inc.

Haliburton Fales, the first member of the prestigious New York Yacht Club to come to M. M. Davis and Son for a yacht, fell in love with the bugeye lines as had so many yachtsmen before him.

make a good job and we used it on the two last bugeyes that we built. Suppose that nothing further can be done until you hear from Mr. Allen. In the meantime, we will be going over specifications, very thoroughly.[17]

Very little information has been found about *Ko-Asa*. She was overshadowed in the yachting press by **White Cloud** and **Manitou**; and as noted, her completion came close to the day of Clarence Davis's death. The bugeye was 82.5 feet overall. Coast Guard records indicate she was 73.5 feet on deck and 70 feet at the water line. According to *Lloyd's Register of American Yachts*, she carried 1,978 square feet of sail on two masts plus a jib. In 1942, *Ko-Asa* was sold to the War Shipping Administration and assigned to the navy for antisubmarine duty. Following World War II, she had various ports of registry in Florida; she went out of documentation in 1975.

The first full-time yacht builder in Maryland was Leonard J. Nilson who founded the Nilson Yacht Building Company in Baltimore in 1899. Nilson arrived in that city from the North by way of Washington. Most information about him is traced through his yachts.

In 1894 Nilson built the 50-foot auxiliary cutter, *Altrurian*, in Washington, D. C., for F. A. Haight, a member of the New York Yacht Club. A half-model was displayed in the New York Yacht Club Model Room for years, but has now been lost. Nilson came to Baltimore in 1895. After selling *Altrurian*, he went to work for Joseph Thomas and Son, a lumber dealer who was setting up a marine construction division. Nilson lived with his brother, Julius, a ship carpenter, at 1332 S. Hanover Street. The two brothers worked for Thomas for about four years building *Chilhowee*, a steam yacht owned in Baltimore for many years; *Agnes*; *Lesbia,* and the schooner *Lucile* built for another member of the New York Yacht Club. By 1900 Nilson had set up his own shop and yard at Ferry Bar in Baltimore, and that year he built the yawl *Dione* and the centerboard schooner *Ciconia*.

Nilson never built a yacht that won an important race, yet a surprising number of his yachts were sold in New York and New England. Yachting was spreading to the Chesapeake Bay at this time, and a number of Nilson boats were built for Marylanders. The yard turned out launches, steam yachts, and all types of sailing yachts. In 1903 he built the yawl *Idelon* for a Baltimorean, William E. Heiser. That year he also built *Ednada*, a 110-foot schooner. In addition to the many sailing yachts that slipped down the ways into the Patapsco River, Nilson built such steam yachts as *Ruff House* for Payne Whitney of New York and the well-documented launch *Natomah*, built for King Upton, who founded the power squadron of the Boston Yacht Club. Despite his noteworthy accomplishments little is remembered about his yard, personal story, or his yachts. His designs appeared occasionally in *Yachting* and *Rudder* magazines. In an interview given to the Baltimore *Sun* on April 21, 1935, Mr. Nilson related that he came to Baltimore toward the end of the century, and that he built approximately 200 vessels at Ferry Bar. He told

how, after a disastrous fire destroyed his yard, "I started in again too big and failed. I couldn't swing it. But those were the days. I remember that in one year I built three 100-foot schooners. One of them, *Nemaha*, is now a quarantine ship at the Panama Canal."[18]

One Nilson-built yacht of special interest to this narrative was *Inquirer*. She was owned by Albert S. Crockett who cruised into Solomons and wrote about his experiences in *Forest and Stream* in its issue of October 1, 1910. What makes his story different is its ring of truth, for Crockett was coming home. He was the son of William and Ada Crockett who kept store on the island. Albert had left Solomons to become a writer, achieving success first as the Paris correspondent for the New York *Herald*, and later as a publicist for the Waldorf Hotel in New York. Crockett's homecoming cruise started at Riverside, Connecticut, on July 21, 1910. He said in part about it:

> One of the most delightful cruises which owners of motor boats in the vicinity of New York, or in fact anywhere on the Atlantic Coast, can make is to Chesapeake Bay and the Maryland rivers. It seems strange so few owners take advantage of that beautiful stretch of water which is particularly adapted to early spring or late fall cruising.

Crockett describes his yacht in the article although he never mentions that she was built in 1904 in Baltimore by the Nilson Yacht Building Company. *Inquirer* was a cabin cruiser.

> Her heavy construction gives her a displacement of 9 tons and her 25-horse-power motor can drive her 10 miles per hour. She is divided into three compartments; the wheel house, which has two extension berths, the main saloon, which has two more berths, and the engine

room and galley, 12 feet long, which has one berth. It is a low [cabin trunk] yacht, but has more than six feet of head room.

Crockett stayed a week at Solomons. He wrote:

Solomons Island is the biggest place on the Chesapeake Bay between Annapolis and the Potomac River, and even at that it has not over 700 inhabitants. Every twenty years or so they talk about building the Drum Point Railroad, from Baltimore down, and once they got so far that they actually graded the road all the way through Calvert County. More recently, have been making efforts to have Congress put a dry dock in the harbor, which naval officers have pronounced one of the largest and finest anywhere and which was the scene of the tests made with the dry dock *Dewey* before it was sent to the Philippines.

When *Inquirer* arrived, a fleet of submarines with a tender were anchored off the shore.

In spite of inconveniences, the harbor is so excellent and it is possible to purchase provisions so cheaply that yachtsmen from Baltimore and Philadelphia usually make a stay of several days or a week at the place, for behind the island is Mill Creek, which is a perfectly safe little haven almost landlocked. Chickens may be purchased at from 25 to 30 cents a piece, eggs at 15 to 20 cents a dozen, and excellent fresh country butter, if you know where to go, at 25 cents per pound. The place is dry, but across the river, two miles, is Millstone, where you can get wet goods of all descriptions.[19]

From Nilson's time forward there was at least one full-time yacht yard in Maryland. At just about the time that Nilson

failed, Otis Lloyd began building pleasure boats at Salisbury. This yard continued in one form or another until the 1980s, although no yachts have been built there since before World War II. Lloyd, one of the Eastern Shore's finest shipwrights, bought the yard and railway of A. F. Parsons and renamed it the Salisbury Marine Construction Company. He built his famous round-stern bugeyes until demand fell off around 1910 when he started building yachts. J. Murray Watts and Thomas D. Bowes, naval architects and yacht designers of Philadelphia, sent their clients to this yard for the next 25 years—though Lloyd only operated it until 1914. One of the first yachts built by Lloyd was the centerboard schooner *Transient*, 78.5 feet overall, designed by Bowes and Watts.

In 1913 John Smith was a principal in the Sharptown Yacht Company on the Nanticoke River. After that company dissolved, he formed a partnership with Norman L. Williams and purchased the Salisbury Marine Construction Company, which they renamed Smith and Williams. One of the first yachts built by the new company was the 85-foot bugeye yacht *Sonsy*, designed by Gielow and Orr and built for Frank M. Carnegie. Smith and Williams operated the yard until their bankruptcy in 1929. The yard built fine sailing yachts and cruisers, most designed by Watts or Bowes. These included *Tondeleyo*, *Quita*, *Lismore II*, and *Jesting II*, all large schooners. Perhaps the most famous motor yacht built there was the cruiser *Blue Heaven II*, built for the popular singer Gene Austin in 1929, shortly after Smith and Williams lost their yard to the local bank.

▶

The first full-time yacht builder in Maryland was Leonard J. Nilson who founded the Nilson Yacht Building Company in Baltimore in 1899.

Adrea, ex-Ednada

Jesting II

Much like other shipyards on the Chesapeake Bay, M. M. Davis and Son expanded tremendously during World War I. New marine railways, sheds, and ship-construction facilities were built on Mill Creek. At the end of the war, Clarence Davis recognized that his yard's survival would depend on the construction of pleasure boats. Before the early 1920s, his contact with yachts had been principally repair and maintenance work. Yacht construction would be new to the company.

These included Tondeleyo, Quita, Lismore II, *and* Jesting II, *all large schooners.*

Sherwood Gets His Man

The house that Clarence and Edna Davis built still sits on the highest point on Solomons Island. The view from the front porch encompasses the sweeping panorama of the harbor. Clarence would walk down to the water's edge each morning and board his launch to cross the harbor to the shipyard. One summer day in 1923 he would see the yawl *Freda* at Webster's Wharf and other yachts at anchor in the harbor and realize that yachting had arrived on the Chesapeake. More Maryland yachts were calling at Solomons during the summer months, their numbers exceeding those traversing the bay in fall and spring between northern and southern waters.

Davis recognized that the future of his yard depended on his ability to lead it into the yacht building business. While demand for commercial wooden ships continued, particularly for tugs and fishing trawlers, orders were decreasing. Soon there would be too few to supply the amount of work needed to keep his skilled force together.

In addition to new construction, many baycraft were being converted from sail to power. A large business in marine repair work continued for the yard throughout the 1920s as Clarence Davis worked to diversify. By the end of the decade the yard had such a high percentage of yacht building work that Davis was no longer concerned with the declining level of commercial construction.

The first known commission received by the yard after World War I was a motor yacht for Robert C. Roebling in 1924. Roebling was a very young member of the famous family which had designed and built the Brooklyn Bridge—a marvel of beauty and function recognized as one of the engineering wonders of the world. John A. Roebling's Sons' wire ropes were originally used in mines and later for suspension bridges. The company also had a long association with the yachting world as Roebling wire was widely used for marine rigging. William H. Whiting & Company was the Maryland distributor of Roebling wire rope and Mr. Whiting was probably responsible for introducing young Robert to Clarence Davis.

Robert Roebling's finances at the time were controlled by trustees. Through detailed contracts and frequent inspections the trustees supervised the construction of the young man's motor yacht. She was designed by Clarence Davis without the assistance of a naval architect. Her name was *Ballantrae*. She was not pretty. Photographs taken of her at Solomons and on the Chesapeake Bay reveal a heavy, bulky yacht of a design not much different from the army vessels built by Davis during World War I. She was 61 feet, 6 inches overall, and she was powered by a Fairbanks-Morse four-cylinder gasoline engine. The Roebling trustees specified that the yacht must be capable of making 8.68 knots for a minimum of 168 hours. Presumably, they wanted to be certain that their ward would never run out of gas between stations.

Robert Roebling sailed *Ballantrae* for three years after she was launched in 1924. He was a charming young man, well remembered by yard workers. In 1927 he donated *Ballantrae* to the Boy Scouts of America in Trenton, New Jersey, and came back to M. M. Davis and Son without his trustees but with plans of his own for his second yacht, *Bonhomie*, about which more is written later.

Orders for yachts came slowly. In 1925, the Gibson Island Club, representing several owners, ordered six Star class boats from M. M. Davis and Son. The Star class boat is an open cockpit sloop under 23 feet overall. The racing craft was designed by Francis Sweisguth, working for the naval architectural firm of William Gardner. The first 22 were built in 1911 by Isaac E. Smith of Port Washington, Long Island.

When M. M. Davis and Son built the Gibson Island fleet, fewer than two hundred existed. The class is still popular and thousands are raced throughout the world.

The contract for the Stars, dated March 12, 1925, specified a price of $700 per boat, less keels, with the order to be completed by May 15. Two additional boats were added to the order. According to the yearbook of the International Star Class Racing Association, Davis built one additional Star class boat in 1926. The Davis family owned still another, *Tarpon*, Star class boat No. 183, built by the New England Boat Works and acquired, in part, for the purpose of duplication, as at that point M. M. Davis and Son's experience in yacht construction was minimal.[1]

Not until 1926 did the yard receive a commission for a sailing yacht. She remains a mystery, as Clarence Davis never listed her among the yachts he built and she did not appear in company records. It was not until the 1950s that an auxiliary ketch named **Miss Patsy** appeared in *Lloyd's Register of American Yachts* with the information that she was built in 1926 by M. M. Davis and Son. The yacht register also states that she was designed by Clarence Davis and that her original name was *Gadfly*. Company files of the period indicate that Davis quoted prices rather frequently on motor and sailing yachts, but this boat is never mentioned.

Gadfly has never been documented with the Coast Guard, making impracticable any attempt to trace her original owner. The ketch's measurements were 37 feet, 6 inches at the waterline, 11 feet, 6 inches extreme breadth, and with her centerboard up, she drew 3 feet, 6 inches. She last appeared in *Lloyd's* in 1961, her owner then being William Howard Fisher of Perth Amboy, New Jersey.

Ballantrae

Her name was Ballantrae. *She was not pretty.*

Star Class Boats

Photographer: A. Aubrey Bodine, Calvert Marine Museum Collection.

In 1925, the Gibson Island Club, representing several owners, ordered six Star class boats from M. M. Davis and Son.

John G. Hanna, the naval architect, had been developing a design for a double-ended ketch since 1921 when *Orca* was built. With *Neptune* in 1923, Hanna's double-ender design appeared in *Rudder* magazine. Then in 1926 Dr. Charles D. Lucas contracted with M. M. Davis and Son to build *Carcassonne*, a thirty footer, basically of the same design as *Neptune*. *Carcassonne* became famous when Weston Farmer, editor of *Modern Mechanix*, published a series of articles in 1932 and 1933, entitled "How to Build Twenty Boats." Farmer selected Hanna's design as one of the twenty and used photographs of *Carcassonne* to illustrate the type. He wrote in *The Skipper*, August 1970, that he called the design "Tahiti Ketch" after asking Hanna to update her for *Modern Mechanix*. As a result, *Carcassonne* became the first Tahiti ketch, of which thousands of sets of the designer's plans were sold.[2]

Davis developed a working agreement with Hanna, but there is no record that any work actually developed from it. On September 12, 1928, he wrote to Hanna about a possible order. Although no order resulted, there are subjects of interest in this letter, including the information that the yard had built a houseboat for a Baltimorean in 1926. This was M. M. Davis Job 122, a 50-footer for Neville Leary. A blueprint of her profile is in the archives of the Calvert Marine Museum. The letter to Hanna is also interesting for its comparison of copper and galvanized fastenings:

In regard to copper fastenings. In my opinion it is very good for small boats where the planking and timbers are light but in heavy vessels, such as you propose, I think that it is unnecessary and a needless expense. Galvanized fastenings will last almost for a generation. As an illustration, my grandfather built in 1872 a schooner about 80 feet long in which the fastenings were all galvanized. We had an occasion about two years ago to haul this boat on our railway and the fastenings were just as good as the day the boat was built. In fact all the boats that he, as well as my father and myself have built, have been fastened with galvanized nails with exception of some small yachts, and some of them being fifty and sixty years old are still in existence and doing good work. You mentioned that if the boat was copper riveted the rivets would have to extend through planking and ceiling, this would be very unusual; in fact, I never saw it done. If your client insists on copper rivets, I would suggest that they only go through the frames with washers or burrs

Carcassonne

Calvert Marine Museum Collection.

He wrote in The Skipper, *August 1970, that he tacked on the name* Tahiti *to* Carcassonne *after asking Hanna to update her for* Modern Mechanix.

61

on the inside, then fasten the ceiling from the inside in the usual manner. There is another thing that you have to guard against in a copper fastened boat, which is electrolysis. A few years ago one of the Lightships came to Baltimore for repairs and it was found that practically all of the fastenings were eaten off between the planking and timbers, this vessel being copper fastened and copper sheathed. In 1926 we built for a Baltimore man a house boat the bottom and sides to about 10" above the water line was copper sheathed, this boat left our yard about June 1st and in three months time all the copper sheathing at the water line was eaten completely up. All sorts of tests were made by experts in effort to locate the cause, but as far as I know no definite reason was established. We did, however, find a remedy, which was by fastening zinc plates along the sides at the water line, these only last one season and have to be renewed every year. There is one thing about galvanized fastenings that I feel safe in saying, that it will last twice as long as any wood that can be obtained for either planking or ceiling and for this reason alone, why spend considerable money for copper fastenings. In my judgment it would be much better to use this money in other parts of the boat where it would serve a much better purpose.[3]

Toward the end of 1926 Robert Roebling, now of age and in control of his fortune, was back for his second yacht. A contract was worked out between Davis and Roebling for construction of *Bonhomie*. The stumbling block was a clause

stating that Clarence E. Davis be required to have one drink of whiskey at the launching of the new Roebling yacht. Davis, a lifelong teetotaler, finally conceded the point and fulfilled his contractual obligation at a gala launching party hosted by the playful Roebling. This is said to be the only alcoholic drink Davis took in his life.

Bonhomie was built from Roebling's own designs during the winter of 1927. Larger than *Ballantrae*, she was 94 feet overall though only 20 feet in width. Guests attending the launching on April 16, 1927, recall that *Bonhomie* had such a sharp bottom that when she settled in the creek her waterline was above her ports. One of the men who worked on her recorded his experiences with *Bonhomie*:

[Roebling] was a young man in college and he had a boat built down here and he used it as a pleasure boat while he was in college. But as he grew up to be some age, I don't know what age, it wasn't very old, we built another one for him. He said "I designed this boat," but its design put nothing, no super stuff on at all. No super structure. When he got the boat built, he came in putting the stuff on her and she was a failure as far as that goes. In moderate weather we went on the Patuxent on a trial trip. When we went out around Southeast Buoy and headed towards Drum Point, that boat rolled until it capsized the equipment on deck. There was a gyro compass on a big base. Can you imagine a boat right here in the river, a hundred feet long, capsizing a compass like that on deck?

I went down that trip on her to Cove Point and there wasn't white caps in the bay. When we turned to come back, got in the trough of the sea, she rolled down till water went up in her house, and her house was six feet from the side. You couldn't stand up. Terrible! Brought her back and tied her up. She was top heavy above deck because she was mean below water. She didn't have bilge enough under water to support the top structure. You can't take something just like a knife blade, put something above it and keep it up. She was real, real sharp.

He came back and we hauled her on the railway, tore all the planking off up to the waterline and built framing sufficient to hold her stable. After that she was alright.[4]

There is no record of the original cost of **Bonhomie**, but the estimate for fattening the bilges was $7,439.04.[5] Despite her bad design, **Bonhomie** eventually made it to the West Coast where she had several owners. She was scrapped in 1968.

In 1930, both Robert Roebling and his sister, Emily Roebling Cadwalader, had new yachts built, neither one by Davis. They were vastly different from each other, but both boats placed the brother and sister among the leaders of conspicuous consumption for all times. There are no records of Robert Roebling's bill for the steel three-masted schooner **Black Douglas,** 153 feet overall, but his sister spent $4,000,000 for the 407-foot **Savarona**, probably the most luxurious yacht ever built. That vessel, obsolete before she was launched in the Great Depression, will be forever as famous to yacht historians as Black Friday is to financiers.

With **Ballantrae** and **Bonhomie** Clarence Davis and his men learned to build yachts.

Bonhomie

Calvert Marine Museum Collection.

"When we went out around Southeast Buoy and headed towards Drum Point, that boat rolled until it capsized the equipment on deck."

In his book about his fishing trips Donald Sherwood describes trips of 12,000 miles by ship, airplane, railroad, riverboat and local bus to find good fishing.[6] When asked about the circumstances that brought him and Clarence Davis together, the purposeful Sherwood responded, "I sought him out."

Sherwood, formerly a Midwesterner, discussed a desire to have a yacht built in Maryland or at least somewhere along the Chesapeake's shores with his Maryland friends. They told him there were no builders of one-design yachts among the yards dotting the towns and coves of the Eastern Shore or the rivers south of Baltimore. He was not discouraged. "I told them that I could not believe that the men who built those graceful bay boats were unable to build me a sailing yacht. I set out to find one that would."[7] But before Sherwood was to find his builder, he accomplished another mission—he located that very special designer for his first yacht, a man who would eventually design an America's Cup entry and become one of a half-dozen great yacht designers of his era.

Sherwood and his friend Edward Palmer started a series of trips to Long Island Sound to look at yachts in the water. In his book, *The Sailing Years*, in which he incorporates his logs, he relates how he found the right man:

> Out on Long Island we found a beautiful little day sailer, with a graceful sheer and an air of competence which greatly impressed us. Upon inquiry we learned it was designed by a young man by the name of Philip L. Rhodes, who had designed it in his spare time at home.[8]

This was the summer of 1926, and Rhodes, aged 31, had just set up his office at 103 Park Avenue in New York City.

Sherwood disputes this, claiming instead that Rhodes was working out of his home at the time. Let Sherwood go on with his story:

> So began an exchange of letters, specifications, and visits that created in Phil's home the beautiful drawn plans for a 34-foot overall, 10-foot beam, 5-foot draft, auxiliary yawl—named *Seawitch*.[9]

Philip Rhodes had designed other yachts before Sherwood arrived on the scene. Three commissions were for Julian Cendoya, including the yacht *Westwind*, not to be confused with the yacht *West Wind* which he later designed for Edward Palmer. However, *Seawitch* commission from Sherwood put Rhodes's career in motion.

When Sherwood received his plans he started the search for his builder. On several trips along the back trails of Maryland he heard the name M. M. Davis and Son. He heard that Davis of Solomons had a fine history of building schooners, bugeyes, tugs, barges, and ships for the menhaden fleet. Sherwood says he liked their record of accomplishment, but he admits there was another fact that took him to Davis. A member of the Gibson Island Yacht Squadron, he knew that Davis had built a fleet of Star class boats for the club in 1925.

It was autumn when he headed south out of Baltimore through Maryland's tobacco counties where he said he saw more ox carts than automobiles. When asked to recall his first impression of Clarence E. Davis, he responded that "It was his sense of presence, a confidence built on the accomplishments of a yard that felt it could build out of wood anything that floats. A shy man, uncomfortable as a wet cat off his turf, and with little formal education, he possessed the assurance of a lion when the subject centered on the capabilities of his company."[10]

Donald Sherwood had his designs and had located the builder he wanted but he had yet to get Davis to agree to build his yacht. Just before Christmas, 1926, Philip Rhodes sent his beautiful prints and 35 pages of specifications to M. M. Davis and Son. But early in the new year Clarence Davis returned them to Donald Sherwood and politely but firmly declined to execute a contract for the construction. Davis told Sherwood it was impossible for him to realize a profit when bound by such a comprehensive set of specifications prepared by businessmen. Sherwood wrote about the situation he faced in a letter to his friend W. S. Galloway, who later became a Davis client himself:

> You will note in the contract that Mr. Davis' original quotation was reduced about $1300, mainly due to the fact that he said he could not build the boat for very much less using the specifications we had formulated. As a matter of fact, he was frightened at the specifications as he considered them very exacting and as he did not know either Mr. Rhodes or myself very well, he was afraid we would be very technical and take so many exceptions that the cost would be greatly increased. It was, therefore, good policy that he protect himself sufficiently. When we had explained to him that we were not arbitrary and were very confident of the type of construction he would make, he was willing to go ahead with the work at the contract price.[11]

This confrontation produces a sharply cut cameo of Clarence Davis's personality. He had been trained by a father to build boats by the rule of thumb method with no drawings and only a half-model. His customers had been his neighbors, seafaring men, watermen, or an impersonal government. To country people, businessmen were akin to gamblers, hooch drinkers, and other unsavory types who were not generally trusted. But Davis's intelligence and good judgment pushed him beyond this traditional stance. The result was survival that had been denied almost every other yard on the bay that had opened prior to World War I. He would not close the door to this new business which he knew he must master to keep the yard profitable. But he never gave up the old ways. To check the symmetry of the framing or the planking of a yacht, he would face away from the bow as it sat in its cradle and observe it upside down by dropping his head down between his legs.

The area around Solomons was still quite isolated from the rest of Maryland in 1926. However, this was changing. There was transportation by water, including the steamboat to Baltimore three times a week. The fare was low enough ($3.00 round trip) to make an occasional trip possible for everyone. Sons and daughters left for the outside world; and once in a while someone new joined the community. For the most part, existence was as it would be on any island, with the inhabitants developing their own rules of behavior. As there was little crime, there never was need for a jail.

The structured employment practices of the 20th century are different from the free flow of the craftsmen of the shipyard.

The men moved in and out with the seasons, or to the outside world to return years later. For the men who wanted it, there was a chance to learn a trade at M. M. Davis and Son. In his oral history in the archives of the Calvert Marine Museum, Orem Elliott describes how he, as a youth, was fired by Clarence Davis, then the son of the boss, and how his father took him immediately to Cell Davis for reinstatement. Although Clarence had become a partner at 21 in 1904, the authority to deal with a family problem was not passed along to him until he succeeded his father in 1924. The fired youngster stayed on at the yard for the next 30 years.[12]

Man's customs are formed by the reality of weather and other natural forces, and therefore the shipyard work was necessarily seasonal. There was no heat within the Davis yard, and electricity was not available until the 1930s. Short winter days and the dangers of open fires curtailed winter work. Fire had destroyed the entire plant in 1921.

The cyclical nature of the work in the yard played a crucial part in the life of the community. Carpenters and caulkers became watermen during the winter. The money was better than at the shipyard. The Davises played the seasons. Lower levels of activity in the yard corresponded with the lost days, the short days, and the reality that the bitter cold could be dealt with more effectively with a pair of oyster tongs pumping heat and money than would be possible in the bleak, dark shipyard.

By 1927, many changes were in process. The telephone with its party lines had already been installed at the shipyard and in some of the island homes. The fine fishing in the Patuxent River and out on the Chesapeake Bay attracted flocks of weekend sportsmen, who in their rowdy way helped lower

the walls of isolation that had held the community intact during the preceding half-century.

It is unusual for a yacht to be a pivotal event, but if ever there was such a yacht, it was Donald Sherwood's *Seawitch*. In January 1927, Clarence Davis was preparing his material and labor estimates for his forthcoming meeting with Sherwood. He was working from a full set of Philip Rhodes's beautiful drawings—prints so fine they were almost art—and a set of detailed specifications. Davis determined that he would quote no less than $8,006.63, including $3,876.73 for materials and supplies. This figure excluded the cost of the keel, the engine, and the wheel which were to be supplied by the owner. Davis estimated his labor cost at $2,250.00 and set his overhead and profit at 26 percent.[13]

Davis accepted Sherwood's contract with a price of $7,000, and construction started during the dark winter days of 1927. Rhodes's detailed specifications stated that "all materials, manufactured articles and articles of construction of whatever kind and in every department, will be of the best quality of the grades or materials specified. For fairing, the lines will be laid down in a mold loft and faired if same is necessary. Should any considerable change in lines develop, the architect is to be notified. Substantially accurate molds taken from the lines as laid down will be set up at each station."[14]

The specifications called for a keel "of New England or Maryland white oak, heartwood, sided in accordance with offsets

nd molded as per Laying-Down Plan." The
tem, the gripe piece, the horn timber, the
rames, and the floor timbers were to be con-
tructed of white oak with the transom "to
be of seasoned teak, 1¼ inch thick, finished,
bent to an outside radius of 11 inches."[15]
The planking called for was "flat grain clear
heart-long leaf pine in single length."[16] The
house sides, the coaming, and molding were
to be constructed out of teak.

Fastenings for all main backbone timbers and timbers connecting thereto are
to be securely fashioned together with
suitable, or as specified, galvanized
wrought iron blunt bolts in excess of the
usual number. All such bolts, drifts, etc.,
including iron keel bolts are to be made
of "Burton's Best" wrought iron, as made
by the Burton Iron Works, Troy, N. Y.,
and galvanized by dipping in hot zinc.[17]

Seawitch did not gain great fame beyond the
Chesapeake, but she was immeasurably important to her designer, Philip Rhodes, and to her
builder, Clarence Davis. Their collaboration,
engineered by the will of Donald Sherwood,
blossomed into an association as their work
caught the eyes of other Middle Atlantic
sailors eager to have their new yachts built
nearer to their home ports on the Chesapeake Bay. Rarely do two careers advance
as quickly as Davis's and Rhodes's did as
news of Seawitch reached the public.

Seawitch

Donald Sherwood Collection, Calvert Marine Museum.

*He was working from a full set
of Philip Rhodes's beautiful
drawings—prints so fine they
were almost art—and a set of
detailed specifications.*

67

Sherwood raced *Seawitch* in the late 1920s and the early 1930s in the relaxed racing schedule of the Gibson Island Club where she did fairly well against local competition. He wrote to his friend Rhodes in 1934 that "at Gibson Island in the last five or six years I find that out of fourteen starts I have won six, had two second place finishes, three third place, and finished fourth once."[18] The rig was changed from gaff to Marconi in 1932, and the boat won the Gibson Island to Poplar Island Race the following three years.

Sherwood sold *Seawitch* in 1935. He never had another yacht built by M. M. Davis and Son. He had Philip Rhodes design two other yachts, neither of which was ever built. In 1950, after owning several other boats, Sherwood commissioned a new yacht of a Rhodes design. She was a replica of *Narada*, L. Corrin Strong's cutter, which Davis had built in 1936 and which was lost at sea in 1942.

Sherwood sold *Seawitch* to Albert G. Ober who was lost overboard not long after purchasing the yacht. His heirs sold her to Dr. L. Emmett Holt who owned her for 25 years. Dr. Holt sailed in Maine waters, and every year he made the run down east. Arnold Holt, a son, wrote about the much-loved *Seawitch*:

> She was all you could want in a boat. You could sail her single-handedly or day sail with a party of 12 to 15. My wife and I had our honeymoon on board cruising the Penobscot Bay.[19]

By 1984 *Seawitch* was 58 years of age and it was assumed that the yacht no longer existed. However, Richard Henderson, Gibson Island resident and author of several sailing books including a biography of Philip L. Rhodes, received a letter from *Seawitch*'s owner, Jack Strickland. Strickland reported to Henderson that *Seawitch* was in sound condition and was being used for both his home and livelihood. He and his wife were operating a small charter business for visitors to the Virgin Islands. The Stricklands wrote again in the summer of 1985 with the sad news that *Seawitch* had been damaged during a hurricane:

> One reason that I have not written is the fact that we have been very busy trying to get our lives back together after the events of November 7, 1984. On that day, Hurricane Klaus swept through the Virgin Islands and during the storm a cruise ship, *Nordic Prince*, tried to enter the harbor for no other reason than to keep her schedule. Well, needless to say, she was out of control and hit *Tumbleweed* and *Seawitch*, causing a lot of damage. *Seawitch* was dismasted, the stern above the water line loosened, her bow sprit broken and the stern damaged, but still doesn't leak a drop.[20]

At the end of 1927, Clarence Davis had four yachts in his order book: a motor cruiser and three Rhodes-designed cutters. The motor cruiser, not yet named, was being built for R. L. Ettenger of Washington who had placed his order during the spring of that year. Davis had asked for and received the buyer's approval to delay construction so that the yacht could be delivered in the spring of 1928. Davis selected the naval architect, Alfred Hansen of Washington, to work on the design. Hansen had worked with M. M. Davis and Son on Coast Guard projects in the past. The cruiser's specifications called for a boat 35 feet, 8 inches in length, presumably at the waterline, but during construction her length was increased by 18 inches to accommodate a large engine.

On January 14, 1928, a Saturday, fire broke out at the yard just after the men had left for the weekend. It was caused by open fire containers used by the men for heat in the winter. Clarence Davis prepared the following release for the newspapers in which he described the event:

On Saturday, January 14th, about 2:30 P.M. fire swept the plant of M. M. Davis & Son, Solomons, Md. destroying one large construction shed, mold loft, and joiner shop. At the time of the fire four yachts were under construction, all of which were destroyed including several tenders belonging to yachts now in storage. A quantity of lumber and tools stored in the construction shed were burned.

The rig was changed from gaff to Marconi rig in 1932, and the boat won the Gibson Island to Poplar Island Race the following three years.

Seawitch

Seawitch

"Seawitch was dismasted, the stern above the waterline loosened, her bow sprit broke and the stern damaged, but still doesn't leak a drop."

Fortunately the other buildings in the yard were so arranged that it was possible to keep the fire confined to one section of the yard. The residents of Solomons and vicinity responded very quickly and helped to keep the fire from spreading.

The yard had just completed and delivered the day before a Diesel Ice Breaker and Fire Boat for the U. S. Coast Guard, which happened to be lying at Solomon's Wharf waiting for an engineer before leaving for New York. As soon as the fire was discovered the captain proceeded to the yard and turned a powerful stream of water on the burning buildings, however, the fire was discovered too late to save the three buildings and their contents, so efforts were directed to saving adjoining property.

A new construction shed, joiner shop and mold loft were started yesterday so there will be no delay in the work of the yard, which is very busy building yachts for spring delivery and repair work.[21]

There was insurance to cover the losses, including builder's liability, so financial loss was minimal. Even so, Clarence Davis's composure was exceptional. The same news release to the newspaper about the fire had included a notice of his daughter Dorothy's wedding two days before the fire.

On January 21, one week later, Davis wrote to Ettenger that work was proceeding on his boat and that, "you can rest assure that we will give you just as good a job as we did on the boat that was burned." *Mary Anne* cost Ettenger $5,756. In less than one year she was offered for sale by Ettenger at $4,500. Evidently, Ettenger wanted a larger boat.

The three cutters under construction at the time of the fire were *Saki*, *Windward*, and *West Wind*, all from designs by Philip Rhodes. *Saki* was built for William E. Hill of Brooklyn, New York. The order probably came to Davis through the efforts of her designer, since M. M. Davis and Son was unknown in New York as a yacht builder. *West Wind* and *Windward* were built for members of the Gibson Island Yacht Squadron and were orders Davis and Rhodes received jointly as a result of their collaboration on *Seawitch*.

Saki was 40 feet overall, 12 feet wide, with a draft of 5½ feet. A promotional piece described her in language atypical of Davis:

> Here lies the *Saki* at dock, but can't you just imagine the gay days and nights aboard when her sheets are full, and salt sea air flows over her decks. You could have a lot of fun with a craft like this at a surprisingly low cost. The *Saki* is 40 feet long, designed by P. L. Rhodes, New York, built for Mr. William Hill of New York, and is powered by a Scripps engine.[22]

The cutter *Windward* was built for Gibson Island Yacht Squadron member Aubrey E. King, whose family owned a Baltimore eyeglass company. She remained in the squadron until 1985 with John Lee Chapman, Jr., her owner since 1958. Philip Rhodes summarized *Windward*'s characteristics in a letter to an early owner:

> She was built in the very best manner, and one of the unusual things about her is the fact that they [M. M. Davis and Son] were able to get beautiful yellow pine for the planking in single length, so that when she was built there was not a butt end in her from bow to stern.[23]

71

West Wind and Windward

The three cutters under construction at the time of the fire were Saki, Windward, and West Wind, all from designs by Philip Rhodes.

Chapman, describing *Windward*'s condition, started with her iron fastenings which, he stated, showed signs of corrosion. In 1960 a rotten stern was replaced from the waterline up. He said:

> Teak decks were a never ending problem to keep tight. Some deck carlins began to decay as a result of the leaks. They were sistered in the midship section, then in 1983 the decks were fiberglassed using epoxy resin. I have used her strictly for cruising the bay. She is fairly stiff, requiring approximately twenty knots of breeze under working sails to put the rail awash.[24]

The yacht was donated to the Calvert Marine Museum in the summer of 1987. She was moved to Solomons where preliminary inspections of her condition indicate that she is basically sound. *Windward* will make an important contribution to the museum's collection because of her associations with the Davis yard and with designer Philip Rhodes.

The third cutter under construction in 1927, *West Wind*, had been ordered by Don Sherwood's friend Edward Palmer. Palmer had accompanied Sherwood on the trips to New York, resulting in the original appointment of Rhodes as designer of *Seawitch*. *West Wind* and *Windward* were built side by side, as depicted on photographs taken inside the shed by the original owner of *Windward*, Aubrey King.

On February 6, 1928, Clarence Davis responded to an inquiry about *West Wind*:

> This boat is now under construction, so we have not had an opportunity to get any information as to performance and trials, but there is no doubt that these will prove entirely satisfactory. We figure the cost complete, exclusive of engine, will be in the vicinity of $5000.[25]

Because no invoices remain the final price to Mr. Palmer is unknown. Listed below, however, are Davis's estimates completed in November 1927 prior to construction.

Materials, Supplies and Lumber	$2,187.47
Labor (estimated)	2,200.00
Insurance	135.00
Profit and Overhead @ 22%	1,000.00
Total	$5,522.47[26]

A story retold many times by Donald Sherwood puts Clarence Davis practically in a panic when he boarded *West Wind* following her launching. Being accustomed to the stability of commercial craft, the yacht's tenderness is supposed to have shocked a frightened Davis into telephoning Philip Rhodes to report the situation as he was afraid to step her mast for fear of capsizing her. While the retelling of this tale has heightened its drama, it is not difficult to understand Clarence Davis's apprehension as he was only beginning to learn the intricacies of yacht design and construction.

In November 1930, three years later, Davis estimated costs to duplicate *West Wind* at:

Materials, Supplies and Lumber	$1,731.00
Labor	1,500.00
Insurance	85.00
Profit and Overhead @ 20%	623.00
Total	$3,959.00[27]

The sizable difference of $1,428.13 between 1927 and 1930 can be attributed to a lower labor estimate, lower lumber costs, and lower percentage for overhead and profit. Although

73

Saki

it is possible that lower costs resulted from the market crash, it is more likely that the lower labor estimate actually resulted from greater experience in yacht construction. The substantially reduced lumber cost is attributable to several factors, most important of which is increased experience in buying the more exotic types.

Price quotations given by M. M. Davis and Son to several potential buyers after photographs and designs of *West Wind* appeared in *Yachting* and other periodicals have given rise to a perplexing question.[28] Quotations in the Davis files range from $6,000 to $6,500 in 1928 and 1929, and drop to $5,500 in 1930. All these figures are, in turn, substantially higher than Clarence Davis's original estimate. It is possible that Davis was still very nervous about fixed prices as

Saki was 40 feet overall, 12 feet wide, with a draft of 5½ feet.

he preferred to quote on a time and material basis. On December 27, 1927, he wrote to another prospective buyer:

Our proposition is submitted on a time and material basis in order that the owner may get the benefit of any deduction in cost below the upset figure. We realize the trust and confidence between owner and builder necessary in an arrangement of this character, and all we can say is that you can depend on us to do our utmost to keep the cost down. As I remember, I told you that this was the manner in which we built Mr. Sherwood's boat and are now building Mr. Palmer's and Mr. King's. It is needless to say that we hope you will decide to give us the order.[29]

The yard was not awarded this order.

West Wind's short life ended in 1938 when she was swamped and sunk in the Atlantic Ocean.

The sudden increase in yacht contracts was recalled by Barnes Lusby, the yard's foreman, in an oral history recorded before his death in 1974:

Workmen were compelled to learn new trades such as hollow spar building, casting lead keels and wire rope rigging. They were picked from those present in the plant who seemed to have a "turn" for the particular jobs required.

Proper tools were a necessity and at this early date had to be made by the workmen in the plant as there was nothing on the market made to do the work.

For hollow spars a regular adz (flat) and regular flat planes were out when an egg-shaped hollow was required on the inside of the spar. So a regular old country blacksmith heated a wood working flat adz in a coal hand-operated forge and shaped it to suit the hollow shape of the inside of the spar and then retempered the adz to hold a sharp edge. The planes had to be made of wood so that the bottoms could be rounded as per the adz above and the steel bits ground to suit, for smoothing this hollow shaped wood. Then the spars were hand sanded.[30]

To Lusby's comments, Charlie Elliott, another key man at the yard, added "after we thought the spars were sanded to perfection, Clarence Davis would come along and inspect the work." In Elliott's words, this is what would happen:

He was a man, I'm telling you that he had such sensitive hands. I've seen him with a pair of kid gloves work down a mast with just his hands—working from one end to the other. Then he would walk back saying, "There is a high spot, there is a low spot."[31]

M. M. Davis and Son built more yachts in 1928 than in the previous three years. The pace would continue to accelerate into 1932 when the transformation to yacht building was complete. Commercial activities remained flat until the build-up for World War II.

Windward, 1987   Photographer: Paul L. Berry, Calvert Marine Museum Collection.

Looking back at the Solomons scene in the 1920s and early 1930s as described in Chapter 1, it is interesting to consider the rapid changes that were taking place at the shipyard. Clarence Davis's ability to get into yacht construction so completely in a very short period of time was amazing. This is to be credited to the quality of work performed by the Davis work force, combined with the traditional conservatism of the pricing. No profits were generated from the construction of bay oyster craft. In most instances the buyer was charged for time and materials at cost, with profit represented by a higher wage for the sponsoring ship carpenter. Davis, in building his early yachts, separated overhead and profit, and material costs and wages which had remained fairly stable at Solomons between 1890 and 1930 (except during World War I), resulted in a price that rather accurately reflected the cost of the local operation.

The Alden Connnection

Clarence E. Davis was slightly under average height, about 5 feet, 6 inches; his shape was rotund. He had the look of a man whose passion was for sugary things. One of his daily habits was to boat across Solomons harbor for his midday meal, and before returning to the yard he would stop at his mother's house for a generous piece of pie. After her death, he continued the routine, although the pie was then baked by Mrs. Rekar who ran the hotel next to Cook Webster's store.

On top of Clarence's chubby body was a head as hard and good as the best white oak he used in his work. He was adventuresome, too, as shown in his speculative move into stock cruisers. He was honest and forthright with his clients, his men, and in the goals of his company. He was also tough. He knew exactly how to build high quality vessels, commercial and pleasure, and he was unflappable and unyielding to a client or an architect who would try to compromise his work. For example, he once wrote about a potential order:

> With further reference to the 55 ft. House Boat that you worked up for Mr. Ford. Have gone over this very carefully, and it looks to me as though a round bilge boat will cost approximately $17,000. We could probably scrimp on some of the items and reduce the price, but honestly I would rather not have the order, unless we get enough to do a first class job.[1]

He was opportunistic and resilient.

> Your telegram received. Note that Ford is going after lower figure. He ought not to have any kick on our price of $11,000 on a 48 ft. boat, don't believe he will beat it from any of the first class builders. He may get a lower

figure from some one like Casey, but you know the class of work he does. However, keep me posted and if there is anyway we can get together will try to do it.[2]

He was confident with his decisions.

> Am sorry that we lost out on Mr. Ford's ketch, but you know we could not build it for anything like $9,000 complete. I have seen several of the Casey boats, and, in my opinion, they have certainly been very poor jobs. But even with his poor workmanship I don't see how he can build it and exist for this figure. One thing I would be willing to gamble on is that he will not build a second boat for Mr. Ford. You probably remember he built the *Kissyput* for a Mr. Keidel of Baltimore. Well he sold her last fall and was down to the yard yesterday to see us about building another boat. If he had been satisfied with Casey he would, no doubt, have gone back to him.[3]

While these quotations from his correspondence indicate his direct and clear-headed approach to a policy of good work at a fair price, they also illustrate his vulnerability under the stress of competition and his need to have a knowledgeable friend and confidant such as Philip Rhodes.

In 1930, the year following the great Wall Street crash, there were some delays with new commissions, but Davis wrote that his business was good. It improved in subsequent years, but never does he suggest that success as a yacht builder was bringing him wealth.

When Clarence Davis started building sailing yachts from designer drawings in 1926, John G. Alden of Boston was the most prominent designer in the business. He had won the Bermuda Race in 1923 with *Malabar IV*, and in 1926 he had another win with a new schooner, *Malabar VII*. He was a popular man, in demand for his sailing skills as well as his designs. He lived and supported the New England traditions and images that were found in the many generations of Aldens who preceded him. Riding the crest of success, he was "John O'Boston."

In 1930 the Boston designer finally agreed—or perhaps was forced by client preferences—to come to M. M. Davis and Son, a long distance from his previously favored yards in Maine. This was not their first contact as Davis had written him in 1927 about Alden's preference for Maine builders:

> Mr. Galloway showed me your letter to him, which was written very much in detail. You were somewhat off in your estimate of today's cost on the "Alice," which you said would be $25,000, our price to him was about $16,000 exclusive of engine.
>
> I note with regret the emphasis you place on the advisability of placing order in Maine yards, due, as you say, to better workmanship and construction. It is perfectly natural for us all (due to association and better acquaintances) to have our preference, you to Northern yards and our friends and their friends to us, who have kept my predecessors and myself busy for the past fifty years building boats of every type. I hope some day to be successful in getting some of your business and believe, after better acquaintance, you will have a more favorable opinion of some of the Chesapeake builders.[4]

Davis never built the yacht mentioned in the letter and he did not work with Alden until 1930.

In 1928 there was competition between designers Rhodes and Alden and between builder Davis and his northern competitors for several yachts for Gibson Islanders. This was Clarence Davis's territory now, having built *Seawitch*, *Windward*, and *West Wind* for members of the Gibson Island Club, which is located on the Magothy River and the Chesapeake Bay a few miles below Baltimore Harbor. He now operated a repair facility in the harbor on the backside of Gibson Island to better serve and hold his grip on the expanding fleet. This small facility was run by two brothers of Barnes Lusby, Clarence Davis's right-hand man at Solomons.

Gibson Island was unique during this period in Maryland. Though it was not started as a planned community, it had many qualities of one, especially its close corporate structure and comprehensive regulations for the community which extended beyond the usual rules of a yacht club. Its fine protected harbor became almost the exclusive enclave for its members. Local yachtsmen from other Chesapeake Bay clubs were not generally welcome in the island's harbor, although a member's friend could usually make the necessary arrangements for a mooring or overnight layover.

For Clarence Davis, Gibson Island represented the largest pool of potential customers in the bay area. These were the times when yacht racing and cruising on the Chesapeake were still the pleasure of a precious few. The fleet activities of the Gibson Island Yacht Squadron were the most written about and respected locally and were well known in New York circles.

The Gibson Island Yacht Squadron gave Clarence Davis a testimonial dinner to express their appreciation for his work. Roland King, who married Constance, Davis's older daughter, was present the night that the rich and great in yachting on the bay gathered at the club to honor Davis. According to King, who does not recall the year, yachtsman after yachtsman rose to laud the skills of the yard and the quality of work provided by Davis and his craftsmen. As the intensity of the praise increased, there was a pause as the crowd waited to hear from the man they were honoring. It was only then that it was noticed that his chair was empty. The evening came to a startling and abrupt close when the audience became aware that Clarence Davis, a very shy man, had gone. He had left unnoticed through an open window and gone to his car, ordering his chauffeur to drive him home to Solomons Island.

Back in 1928, however, there was nothing shy about Clarence as he fought to win for himself and Philip Rhodes a second wave of Gibson Islanders who were planning to buy new boats. The most prestigious sailor in the Gibson Island Yacht Squadron at the time was J. Rulon Miller, a blue ocean sailor known far beyond the bar of the club. He owned and raced the Alden schooner *Tradition*, and Davis was convinced that he would attempt to direct prospective yacht buyers to John Alden in Boston. Of course, in the past this had always meant that construction would then go to Alden's favorite New England builders. Davis wrote:

> On the influence of Mr. Rulon Miller, Henderson and Fisher will no doubt buy Alden's boats regardless of what the others do. Dr. Houston, Primrose and Ellicott, I think, are very favorable to their boats being built in this section, therefore, it may mean a split in the design if the Alden [design] does not meet with the approval of Mr. Ellicott after he has seen one of the boats. He intimated to me that some of the parties would probably

want some changes, but, he said yesterday, that Alden did not want to make these and was insisting on one design, as he said he wanted to turn them out like Ford cars.[5]

Davis had figured right: Judge William L. Henderson, D. K. Este Fisher, and C. Ellis Ellicott all signed contracts with Alden for his Design No. 385, to be built in the yard of N. Blaisdell and Sons at Woolwich, Maine. Judge Henderson's son, Richard Henderson, in his book, *John G. Alden and his Yacht Designs*, confirms his father's preference for Alden's work. He wrote:

> In the summer of 1928, my father, William L. Henderson, went to John Alden for a medium-size cruiser that he could race occasionally and use as a summer home at Gibson Island, Maryland. Alden suggested a stock yawl, design number 385, the first of which was then being built, and he offered one of these boats to Dad for an attractive price, provided two other buyers could be found. Dad persuaded two members of the Gibson Island Yacht Squadron, C. Ellis Ellicott and D. K. Este Fisher, to join him in ordering one of the yawls, so three sister boats were built at the yard of N. Blaisdell and Sons at Woolwich, Maine, during the following fall and winter.[6]

Davis had estimated his costs in his letter to Rhodes:

> I have made estimate of the cost of the Alden 34-foot ketch according to the plans and specifications that Mr. Ellicott gave me, and we can build such a boat for around $5,000.00 and make a small profit, providing that they are built two or three at a time. I want to say, in the way of quality of material as specified for these boats, all the corners have certainly been cut using only the cheapest wood and very, very little Mahogany, therefore, should you be successful in getting the orders for the design I would like to go over the kind of material that you will specify.

> There is one point I would like to impress, which is that we can build boats at Solomons to cost no more than Maine builders. It may be that some of those fellows are willing to work for no profit and simply giving the boats to Alden at bare cost. As you say they are getting $3,800.00 and Alden furnished engine, stove and toilet. These I figure will cost around $500.00. This being the case, the cost of the boats to Alden would be approximately $4,300.00. Now, you can bet your sweet life that no builder is growing rich at these figures.[7]

One of the reasons that John Alden had worked so closely with Maine builders was their reasonable prices compared with those of the leading yards of New York and Boston. That cost advantage was disappearing as more and more skillful builders, such as M. M. Davis and Son, entered the pleasure boat market. Davis's reputation spread through the yachting community, and he was overcoming the principal obstacle to his growth. Greater acceptance of his fair prices and high quality work was helping the yard reach its full development.

Experienced yachtsmen such as J. Rulon Miller now had other reasons to bypass the previously favored Maine builders. One was the inconvenience of their location to clients on the Chesapeake Bay. Another reason, of far greater importance, was the trend to build yachts of lighter materials. The Alden "Malabars" were of heavy construction and shallow draft. Younger designers were stressing lighter hulls on sharp, deep keels. These lighter displacement yachts were far more efficient to windward. Maine builders traditionally built boats with heavy sawn frames, while M. M. Davis and Son could now provide steambent frames on a less beamy boat with a great deal of sail area. The time had arrived for an Alden-Davis collaboration.

It is not clear which had come first, the contract to build the Alden-designed tug *Luna* or the orders for two large schooner yachts. All were started in 1930. *Luna* probably was started first, then *Lord Jim*, and finally *High Tide*. In the case of the tug *Luna*, M. M. Davis and Son most likely received the contract from the Mystic Steamship Company of Boston because of the yard's long record in the construction of that type of vessel. The yacht *High Tide*, J. Rulon Miller's Alden-designed schooner, was awarded to Davis by its owner and not because John G. Alden had switched yard preference from Maine to Maryland. Likewise, surviving records suggest that Clarence Davis negotiated directly with Paul Nevin of New York for the contract to build *Lord Jim* from Alden Design No. 476. So while it must have been satisfying to Davis to bring Alden to his "backyard," his satisfaction was no doubt tempered by the realization that he had not really won Alden over. Yet it is fairly obvious these contracts were awarded by owners who were aware of Davis's impeccable reputation.

The building of *Luna* was started early in 1930, and the big, powerful tug was ready to be launched on July 19 of that year. The Mystic Steamship Company contracted for her and a sister tug, *Venus*, constructed by the Abbott Shipbuilding Company of Milford, Delaware. These were the first diesel-electric tugs built anywhere. Though their engines were the newest type, the company decided to stay with wooden hulls rather than use steel because of the resiliency of wood in the face of hard impacts.

In the specifications prepared by John Alden, the opening paragraph reads:

> The hull and joiner work to be of rugged wood construction to suit the following dimensions and as specified below:
>
> | | |
> |---|---|
> | Length Overall | 96' |
> | Breadth molded | 24' |
> | Depth molded | 13' 6"[8] |

Rugged she was, for she served her owners 41 years. *Luna* was constructed of white oak stem, frames, and planking; long leaf yellow pine decks; cypress bulwarks; and No.1 locust treenails throughout. When launched, she was hailed as a "Super Tug." "Super" she proved to be. In 1983, 53 years later, she led the Tall Ship Celebration at the Boston Harborfest. A permanent place of honor is reserved for her at a maritime museum in Boston Harbor.

A launching is a joyful occasion, capped by the traditional bottle of champagne broken across the bow as the vessel starts to slide down the ways toward the sea for the first time. *Luna*'s launching was indeed joyful, even though the bottle across her bow contained mineral water. The ceremonies of the day were described in the Mystic Steamship Company's newsletter:

> Solomons, where the tug *Luna* was launched on July 29th, 1930, is located on the northern shores of the Chesapeake Bay, off the Coast of Maryland.
>
> M. M. Davis & Son, the shipbuilders who constructed the Mystic Steamship's tug *Luna*, have specialized in the building of fine wooden ships for several generations.

Luna

These were the first diesel-electric tugs built anywhere.

Steel ships have gradually superseded the wooden ones for commercial uses, yet there are many cases where the wooden ship has the advantage because of its resiliency in the face of hard impacts. For instance, we know that Commander Byrd's timber ship successfully resisted terrific blows of floating icebergs; and a tugboat encounters the same violent shocks when it noses against the gigantic flanks of ocean liners like the **Leviathan**.

When the launching party arrived here on the morning of the 29th, an inspection of the tug was made, as it stood propped up ready to launch. She is a sturdy, oak-beamed tug, and like her sister ship **Venus**, will be electrically equipped throughout, and these will represent the two largest and most powerful in the Mystic Steamship Company's tug fleet, as well as in Boston Harbor.

After a most satisfying lunch at which about twenty people sat down to enjoy southern chicken and ham and plenty other good things (and which was prepared and served under the guidance of Mrs. Davis, the wife of one of the shipbuilders), it was on the program to proceed with the launching.

The actual christening was scheduled for 2 o'clock, when everybody assembled at the shore about fifty yards from the boatsheds.

On signal, the workmen sawed the staging which held the *Luna* suspended over greased runways, and she slid down surely and swiftly for a deep nose-dive after Miss Howard had broken the bottle on her stern. The lady ran true to feminine form and missed on the first swing but came back with a hearty blow the second time. Several daring spirits got aboard and were launched with the tug, but strangely enough, none of the ladies were that adventurous.[9]

To those who knew Mrs. Davis ("Miss Edna" to everyone), it is easy to conjure a vision of her that day fussing and clucking and chattering as she placed her succulent dishes before her sophisticated guests from Boston. The occasion was dry, as prohibition was the law of the land. Of course, it would not have been unusual had the celebration been fueled with champagne and Maryland rye anyway, except that Clarence Davis and Miss Edna were lifelong teetotalers.

John Alden's career was similar to that of many successful men who know what their life's work will be at an early age and forego a formal education. He worked briefly for Edward Burgess, but his real apprenticeship came from his time with B. B. Crowninshield who owned and designed Gloucester schooners both for yachtsmen and as commercial vessels. Alden's actual experiences aboard these sailing vessels formed his design ideas to which he remained faithful until the twilight of his long career when the demand of yachtsmen for greater speed brought changes in design. Bill Robinson, in his book on yacht designers, described John Alden as the designer who brought yachtsmen and offshore commercial workers together. Robinson also commented that "his influence was profound too on the gentler art of coastal cruising which grew by tremendous leaps during these decades."[10]

The Gloucester fishing schooners were unlike most commercial vessels in that they passed through a series of design and construction changes through the years, rather than making these schooners more efficient or giving them greater capacity, the changes attempted to increase their speed.

The early Gloucester fishing schooners developed from the design work of Andrew Story of Essex, Massachusetts. To develop a fast fishing vessel Story had started with the Chesapeake pilot schooner or pungy design. Howard I. Chapelle, the historian who started his career as a designer with John Alden, wrote that Story's "schooner had the low freeboard, deep drag to the keel, raking ends, straight sheer and marked deadrise of the Baltimore flyers, combined with harder bilges and longer body, to give cargo capacity."[11]

Extremes in the design of the market schooners resulted in the death of thousands of New England fishermen.[12] Alden used the later Gloucester fishing schooner as a model for his yachts.

Lord Jim   Mystic Seaport Museum, Inc., Collection.

*Alden later used the
Gloucester fishing schooner
as a model for his yachts.*

The schooners *Lord Jim* and *High Tide* are typical Alden designs, though they differ in details. *Lord Jim* is clearly a cruising yacht while the finer, slimmer *High Tide* was buil for speed. Both have similarly shaped hulls short overhangs, the familiar spoon bows long keels, large rudders, and the genera look of the Gloucester fishing schooner.

Paul Nevin, for whom *Lord Jim* was built was a yacht broker who had spent his life time climbing over yachts. When he decided to commission his own yacht, naturally he went to John G. Alden for his plans. To build *Lord Jim*, he selected M. M. Davis and Son Clarence Davis wrote Alden on February 18 1930, about his quotation:

> Have just quoted Mr. Nevin a price o $15,500 with Fir Decks and $1,000 addi tional for Teak Decks and Plank Sheers on the 62 ft. Schooner, similar to the preliminary plan and specifications tha you sent us. Delivery around Septembe 1st, 1930, if order is placed not than April 1st, 1930.
>
> I don't know how this price will jibe up with the Maine Yards, but have certainly tried to keep my figure as low as pos sible. We have in mind a first class job ir every particular and no plank on the side above water will exceed 3¾" in width.[13]

The Davis price did not reflect the full price

of a yacht of this size as Nevin expected to purchase and deliver to the yard the rigging, sails, much of the equipment, furniture and fixtures to outfit the yacht, as well as its engine and generator. Following the delivery of *Lord Jim* on September 15, 1930, Davis informed Alden that the cost to duplicate this yacht would be $23,000, a figure on which the designer probably based his commission.

Lord Jim's specifications have been lost, but the yacht was built strong with sawed frames, heavy scantlings, and galvanized forged knees. Her measurements are 62'8" overall, 46' at the waterline, 15' beam, and a draft of 8'7". Soon after taking delivery, Paul Nevin sailed her to the Caribbean Sea. According to Richard Henderson's book on the designs of John G. Alden, she weathered a severe November storm en route, the first of several unusual experiences that would be encountered by *Lord Jim* over the years.

Nevin cruised primarily Down East on her and sold *Lord Jim* in 1938. She was owned by several New Englanders over the next dozen years, and in 1951 was purchased by E. Ross Anderson, a prominent member of the Boston Yacht Club. *Lord Jim* was a familiar sight around Marblehead for the next few years, and by the end of the decade, during Anderson's two years as commodore, she was queen of the fleet. In 1959, while escorting the yacht *Bowdoin* from Boston to Mystic, Connecticut, in company with a Coast Guard cutter, *Lord Jim* was run up on Catumb Rock off Rhode Island in fog. She sank in 20 minutes. Melvin C. Briggs had her refloated, kept her for several years, but never completed repairs.

Lord Jim was then purchased by Dr. Frederic B. Breed of Gloucester, an ophthalmologist. Dr. Breed's hobby is fishing, especially for swordfish—an obsession which provided

the income to pay for his college and medical school. He goes to sea in mid-June and returns to his medical practice in September. Dr. Breed purchased *Lord Jim* to replace a thirty-eight-foot power boat he had been using on his expeditions. He rebuilt the yacht, making some radical changes so that the vessel would be an efficient sea-going fishing schooner. He renamed her *Jaguar*.

Jaguar was a familiar sight in Gloucester for several years. She had sails and large diesel engines so that he could remain at sea for several days until her hold was filled with swordfish. Dr. Breed attached a fishing pulpit to the bowspit for harpooning. He added extensive electronics, including two radar systems, three radios, two fathometers, temperature recorders, and Loran navigational equipment. The main cabin was transformed into a fiberglass refrigerated compartment large enough to hold thirty swordfish. Dr. Breed's voyages usually lasted about ten days, with fishing around the clock. During the day he positioned himself in the pulpit with harpoon in hand waiting for the scarce swordfish. At night, lines of five to eight miles long carrying more than 500 hooks were put out. The lines were suspended from orange plastic buoys and marked by strobe lights as they were often cut by passing ships. In early morning the lines were hauled aboard—with fish, it was hoped.

In this way Dr. Breed kept *Jaguar* occupied for nine years. The schooner was subjected to harsh treatment and heavy work. While her hull and spars remained unchanged, substantial changes were incorporated below and above deck. Amazingly, after these alterations, *Jaguar*, ex-*Lord Jim*, had yet another life to live. Breed sold her to the University of Massachusetts's Marine Science Department which used her for several years. Then the schooner passed through a quick series of sales and owners, ending in Gaston, Oregon,

Jaguar, ex-Lord Jim

Photographer: Frederic Breed, Calvert Marine Museum Collection.

in 1974. A sailor named Roger J. Quigg brought her back to the East Coast, and completely restored her to yacht condition and renamed her *Yankee*.

Yankee became a corporation in 1981 with her hailing port Newport, Rhode Island. In 1985, she was sold to an Englishman, W. F. Cadogan, who transferred the schooner to the Canadian flag. After fifty-eight hard sailing years, the Alden schooner built by Clarence Davis in 1930, sunk in 1959, converted to a workboat in the 1960s, sailed in the Caribbean Sea, the Atlantic and Pacific Oceans in the 1970s and 1980s, is currently under sail in Canadian waters. There is no better measure of a yacht's original construction than her record of long service.

J. Rulon Miller had asked John G. Alden to design *High Tide* in 1929. Rulon was the most experienced and influential yachtsman on the Chesapeake Bay in the 1920s. He gained ocean racing experience over many years, on his schooner *Blue Water* and then on *Tradition*, both Alden-designed yachts.

Jaguar *was a familiar sight in Gloucester for several years.*

Miller had been the guiding hand in the formation of the Gibson Island Yacht Squadron. Through his work this yacht club quickly became an important organization in yachting circles, sponsoring many memorable long-distance ocean and bay racing series.

While Miller was deeply involved with ocean racing, his interests extended to all areas of sailing, particularly small racing boats. He was influential in establishing club-sponsored racing fleet—first, a class of small sloops, then in 1925, a fleet of "Star"-class boats, eight of which were built by M. M. Davis and Son.

Clarence Davis was very pleased and proud when J. Rulon Miller approached him about building his new Alden schooner. The yard had not yet built a yacht for an ocean racing sailor. Because Miller had started sailing as a boy in New England and had raced first as a youngster in Winter Harbor, Maine, it was natural for him to ask Alden to design his yachts. On February 28, 1930, Davis wrote Alden:

> Was in Baltimore yesterday and had quite a long talk with Mr. Rulon Miller and we have come to an arrangement whereby he has now decided to build his boat and start at once for April 1, 1931 delivery. I know this will be good news to you and you will no doubt hear from him in the next day or two.[14]

America had been shocked by the Wall Street crash of 1929, and businessmen like Miller were nervous. He had **High Tide** designed in 1929, but delayed the laying of her keel for a year. The agreement to proceed with construction was in part due to Davis's offer of a lower price if Miller would allow **High Tide**'s construction to be spaced out over a longer period. The yacht was launched in February 1931 while Clarence Davis was in the hospital being treated for hypertension. She was delivered on schedule in April, fitting-out having required roughly two months.

Miller received a beautiful 70-foot 8-inch overall, staysail-rigged schooner with an extremely large mainsail, bugeye-rigged on a tall mainmast. She had steam-bent frames and a double planked bottom. Earlier yachts built by Davis had hollow masts made at the yard, but **High Tide**'s masts were of such size that they were built by one of several specialized New England firms. Alden chose the Pigeon Hollow Spar Company of East Boston. While Davis was responsible for the cost of the spars ($1,600 to come out of the total contract price), Alden was required to inspect and accept or reject their work. The order included:

FOREMAST: 67'1" overall; diameter at deck 9.5"; diameter at shoulder 6.75"; at trunk 3"

MAINMAST: 86'7" overall; diameter at deck 11.5"; at shoulder 6.5"; at trunk 4"

MAINBOOM: 37'4" overall length; the diameter at both ends was 5.5", and 8" in its midsection.

FOREBOOM: 16'4" overall length, about 5" at ends, and 6" in its midsection.

CLUB: 17'0" overall

SPINNAKER POLE: 27'6" overall

High Tide's beam was 14 feet 3 inches. Like other newer Alden-designed schooners, she was narrower; and with her modern sail plan, she was designed to contend with the leaders on the ocean racing circuit. Fully rigged she carried almost 3,000 square feet of sail. With a graceful sheer and balanced overhangs, she was an extremely good-looking yacht, constructed from the finest materials, and equipped with state-of-the-art gear and machinery. She was, at that point, the finest yacht built by M. M. Davis and Son.

On April 11, 1931, Davis wrote about Miller's initial sail:

He came down yesterday and went out for a sail. Had quite a breeze and he seemed very much pleased in every respect, so they have gone out for another trip today and will be back probably tomorrow. Next week we will give her the final painting and varnishing so that he can take her up to Gibson Island next weekend.[15]

On June 26, Davis wrote to Alden:

Have just talked to Mr. Miller and he is very much pleased indeed with the speed and performance of his boat in general. The exhaust line seems to be giving him some trouble with water getting in the engine. So far we have been unable to locate the cause. He came here just before the race and we only had five days to have the boat and paint and varnish it from keel to deck, take out the engine and get a new one from Detroit and install, so we didn't have much time for experimenting. The boat arrived in the yard Monday morning and was completed the following Thursday night, but Mr. Miller just telephoned that it is on its way here now and we don't anticipate any trouble in overcoming the water in the engine.[16]

The race Davis refers to was the New London to Cape May Race on June 20, 1931. The race drew a large number of entries, and *High Tide* was the first to finish—69:32:45 hours elapsed time. But *High Tide* was placed fourth on corrected time, since the yachts *Teregram*, *Malabar X*, and *Poseidon* all had enough time saved to beat out *High Tide*, the scratch yacht.

J. Rulon Miller's untimely death occurred July 18, 1931. This tragedy cost the yacht her full allotment of victories as she was not raced again until 1933. Her new owner, Eugene Eleuthere du Pont, lacked Miller's experience and racing skills.

The New London to Gibson Island Race of 1933 was the first race for *High Tide* and her new owner. It was also the first time the J. Rulon Miller Memorial Trophy, created by the Gibson Island Club in honor of Miller's work to promote yacht racing on the Chesapeake, was to be awarded to the yacht with the best corrected time.

Du Pont picked an able crew for the race. There were nine amateurs in the crew including himself. They were led by John S. Lawrence of Boston who had been managing owner of *Yankee* in the America's Cup defense of 1930. Lawrence was designated master for the race, though the yacht had her regular captain, B. Moberg, on board, plus two professional sailors and two mess stewards.

Fifty yachts were entered in the race which started at Sara's Ledge Buoy. The course took *High Tide* and the other yachts out and around Long Island, across New York Bay, down the Atlantic Ocean to the Chesapeake Lightship (a distance of 300 miles of open ocean), and approximately 170 miles up the Chesapeake Bay to Baltimore Light. The finish line was about a mile from the Magothy River and Gibson Island. Captain Lawrence described *High Tide* as "a staunch, rather narrow, heavily rigged little ship of about seventy feet overall and was scratch boat in this race, allowing all others from two to eighteen hours' time."[17]

Photographer: Edwin Levick, The Mariners' Museum Collection.

High Tide

Like other newer Alden-
designed schooners, she was
narrower; and with her
modern sail plan, she was
designed to contend with the
leaders on the ocean racing
circuit.

There were fifteen Class A yachts in the race in addition to *High Tide*. After a sloppy start, a fresh southerly breeze brought *High Tide* to Montauk Point in three hours. Lawrence wrote:

We all tacked after rounding the point, and carrying a light southerly breeze all afternoon and evening, the five leading boats zigzagged back and forth.

At night we were too far apart to see each other's lights, but at sunrise Sunday [June 25, 1933], we thought we saw a competitor to leeward, one to windward of our wake, and a schooner a mile or so astern. Then the fog shut down thick.

All day Monday was the loveliest of days and the loveliest of sails. The balloon staysail was drawing nicely. This sail never before properly set, was primarily responsible for an extra knot in light air to windward. Genoa jib tugging away and the lee rail just awash.

Once around [Chesapeake Light] we had a fine beam wind and for three hours logged nine miles per hour, fairly jumping from wave to wave and the water roaring about our lee rail.[18]

Tuesday they were becalmed, and Wednesday a light easterly brought *High Tide* within 30 miles of the finish line at Baltimore Light. She crossed first, 87 hours, 20 minutes, and 47 seconds after the start. *High Tide*'s average speed was 5.4 mph—certainly less than spectacular—but she crossed the line 4 hours, 26 minutes, and 40 seconds ahead of the next yacht, *Mandoo*. Since *High Tide* was the scratch boat, requiring her to give time to all other yachts in the race, not

until the following day did her crew know that she was also the winner on corrected time. She beat *Vixen II*, her closest competitor, by 23 minutes, 57 seconds. She was awarded the J. Rulon Miller Memorial Trophy. It was a happy and fitting moment for yacht racing: Miller's own yacht had won.

For the first time a Davis-built yacht won an important blue water race. The publicity and prestige of a winning boat is worth thousands in profits to designers and builders. For M. M. Davis and Son, *High Tide*'s victory had particular importance as it helped remove the stigma in the yachting public's mind that Davis produced heavier crusing yachts. Building *Seawitch* had been important in launching Davis into yacht building, but the victory of *High Tide* on June 28, 1933, put M. M. Davis and Son on an equal standing with the other great wooden yacht builders of the period.

High Tide, with du Pont as skipper, finished third in the Bermuda Race of 1934, and was well down the list of Class A yachts on corrected time, penalized heavily because of her size (seventy feet overall) and extensive sail area. In 1934, du Pont considered changes in her rig and asked John Alden to re-examine her design in the hope of improving her speed and performance, or, perhaps, cutting down her racing measurements. Alden's recommendations were:

If the main boom is shortened three feet, and if the gooseneck on the mast is raised a foot, as well as the gooseneck on the lower staysail on the foremast, it will cut down the racing measurement about sixteenth of one foot, which would mean about twenty minutes difference in the Bermuda Race. It would, of course, make the boat a little easier to handle as the main boom would be farther inboard, and I do not think it would affect her

Photographer: Edwin Levick, The Mariners' Museum Collection.

High Tide

The New London to Gibson Island Race of 1933 was the first race for High Tide and her new owner.

High Tide

speed in light weather to any extent. She would be somewhat stiffer and more comfortable sailing in a breeze, and I think unquestionably the boat would be a little faster as well as a better all-around boat.

However, in a race the difference would not amount to very much. Of course, the boat would be further improved if her present inside ballast were added to the bottom of her keel. I do not think it could be put in the deadwood as it would be too far aft, but it would not be a very expensive job to add a piece to the bottom when the boat is hauled out in the fall.

Of course, the mainmast could be reduced in height which would further reduce the racing measurement, and the boat would be faster in a breeze, but in light weather I think she would suffer considerably. If this were done I would not advise taking more than say three feet off the

She beat Vixen II, her closest competitor, by 23 minutes, 57 seconds. She was awarded the J. Rulon Miller Memorial Trophy.

head as well as the other changes which I suggested. I shall be glad to draw up these changes if you think advisable, and could run down to Chesapeake Bay and take a sail in the boat if desired. I do not know as this would be necessary, however, although of course it will do no harm.[19]

Du Pont decided that Alden's recommendations would not significantly improve *High Tide*'s performance or reduce her handicaps. This continued to bother him in subsequent races and might very well have been a factor in his withdrawal from competition in 1936, though there is no mention of it in his personal papers.

In the 100-mile Gibson Island to Cedar Point Race in 1934, *High Tide* finished in just under twelve hours—a course record. Based on corrected time, however, *Water Gypsy* was declared the winner by almost three hours. This evoked a protest from *High Tide*'s owner. "Our rule is far from perfect," the race committee acknowledged.[20] There were no further comments from du Pont on the subject. He returned in 1935 for the same race, winning Class A by approximately two minutes on corrected time. The Gibson Island Racing Committee probably had made revisions in the method of handicapping the larger boats for the race.

Du Pont put *High Tide* up for sale in 1940 for $25,000, but almost two years later she was still unsold and the price had dropped to $19,000. America's entrance into World War II was only weeks away. In a letter to John G. Alden dated September 9, 1941, du Pont wrote:

Last fall I went over her and spent considerable money in placing her in first class condition. As you know, she is equipped with racing sails, practically new and the boat could be put into commission in a very short time.[21]

For reasons that are unclear, perhaps because of a new interest in motorboating, Mr. du Pont no longer sailed *High Tide*. In 1942 he delivered *High Tide* to the Coast Guard for service in the offshore Picket Patrol where she served with other Davis-built yachts.

The racing performances of *High Tide* had important long-term effects at M. M. Davis and Son. She was a Davis yacht, designed by the country's best known designer, fitted with Ratsey sails and Regatta paint, and publicized in many boating journals, in the New York *Times*, and in dozens of other publications around the country. Many of the firms involved, including Davis, ran advertisements featuring photographs of the yacht and her record. Before *High Tide*, M. M. Davis and Son was practically unknown in yachting circles beyond the Chesapeake Bay. A yard can build the finest cruising boats in the world, made of the best materials, and constructed by craftsmen of incomparable skills, but the yacht will remain unknown if the owner fails to win a race. The industry is primed around the winning of races—often not a happy situation as the winning yachts are generally designed to beat the rules rather than for comfort and safety. *High Tide*, as with many other Alden boats, was more a cruising yacht than a racer. Although her life in the headlines was short, it was long enough to place M. M. Davis and Son on the map. After *High Tide*, yachtsmen beat a course to Solomons.

High Tide's record while in the Coast Guard Picket Patrol is believed lost. After the war she was returned to Eugene du Pont who sold her in 1946 to Victor Till of New York. Till was her owner for three years, selling the yacht in March

Golden Eagle, ex-High Tide

High Tide *got a new name,*
Golden Eagle, *and the famous*
schooner became the center-
piece of the Seven Seas
Sailing Club...

1949 to Sybelen Frank Nydam of Chicago. Nydam, a member of the Chicago Yacht Club, cruised her on the Great Lakes for eight years. After that the yacht returned to the East Coast and was sailed by various owners, finally becoming the property of Theodore C. Cohen, known professionally as Ted Charles. Charles, a jazz musician put out of work by the rock and roll era, had turned to the sea to make a living. Under his ownership, *High Tide* got a new name, *Golden Eagle*, and the famous schooner became the centerpiece of the Seven Seas Sailing Club which he operated. Cathy Stanton, a member, recalls *Golden Eagle*:

> It was on the front page of the sports section of the *New York Times* one bright autumn morning some years ago, maybe 1965. There was a magnificent sailing boat—a 70-foot schooner. No private yacht, this belonged to a sailing club on City Island, located north of Manhattan on the East River.

> I discovered the Seven Seas Sailing Club, with not just one schooner but two. In addition, there were five other boats, all belonging to club members. Trips were offered from one day to two weeks throughout the sailing season.

> The prize [*Golden Eagle*] was in disgraceful condition when towed to City Island from Connecticut, but with lots of tender loving care she was restored to a reasonably magnificent condition by Ted and the club members.[22]

In 1973 *Golden Eagle* was purchased by Phineas Sprague, Jr., who changed her name to *Mariah*. She was again in poor condition, so Sprague began a program of rehabilitation and restoration. The 24-year old Sprague was planning to circumnavigate the globe with *Mariah*, ex-*Golden Eagle*,

ex-*High Tide*. In December 1973, on an ocean trial sail prior to departure, *Mariah* survived a rough North Atlantic storm. Damage to several frames and to some planking was not detected until the yacht was hauled in Florida some weeks later.

Sprague and three crew members proceeded on a world cruise which lasted four years, including six leisurely months in Tahiti. Sprague kept the schooner's wheel, memento of a storm in the Mediterranean Sea. He sold *Mariah* in 1979 in order to "assume the more practical position of raising a family."[23]

Mariah sank in a North Atlantic storm the following year. Speaking of the loss Sprague said sadly: "She was still a fine boat, it should not have happened." She went down somewhere east of the Delaware Bay. Her owner at the time of her last cruise was Edward C. Clark, also from Maine. *High Tide* foundered almost exactly 50 years after Davis laid her keel in September 1930.

A half-model of *High Tide* is displayed in the taproom of the New York Yacht Club. The model is in three-eighths of an inch scale and is numbered 759. Her photograph appeared on the cover of *Rudder* for March 1933.

Clarence Davis built only one other Alden-designed yacht, *Puffin*, a small motor sailer built in 1936 for Walter S. Galloway of Baltimore. Davis may have also built an earlier yacht for Galloway as they had been corresponding since 1929. Philip Rhodes designed a yacht for Galloway in 1933, but no records confirm that a boat was constructed. Since several yachts were built by Davis between 1927 and 1936 for which no specific information has survived, one of these could have been for Galloway.

Puffin

Photographer: Morris Rosenfeld, ©Rosenfeld Collection, Mystic Seaport Museum, Inc.

Galloway's *Puffin* was from John G. Alden's Design No. 601 for *Parthenia*, typical of the designs for small yachts that he did in later years. *Puffin*'s specifications called for oak frames, steam bent, and planking of Philippine mahogany to be fastened to frames, keel, floor timbers, stern, and stern timbers and butt blocks with galvanized nails. Her house was built of Philippine mahogany and her main deck was of white pine with covering boards and king plank mahogany with long hook scarfs, covered with canvas.[24] *Puffin* was about 32.5 feet overall. She had an iron keel of about 4,500 pounds and a Buda gasoline engine. By 1940 she was owned by Theodore C. Briggs of Sodus Bay, New York. The cutter was never Coast Guard-documented, making it impossible to trace her.

In 1941, M. M. Davis and Son, then owned by George Townsend, built an Alden-designed sailing yacht, the ketch *Mike*, for George Marshall Jones, Jr., of South River. She is written about in Chapter 10.

The John Alden-designed yachts *Lord Jim* and *High Tide* were extremely influential in the development of the reputation of the Solomons yard.

Galloway's Puffin *was from John G. Alden's Design No. 601 for* Parthenia, *typical of the designs for small yachts that he did in later years.*

A Scholarly Rhodes

7

With the entrance of M. M. Davis and Son into the select world of fine yacht builders, inquiries came to Solomons from all over the country. Many were from men who had no real intention of buying a yacht but were coaxed by their dreams and by what they read in the yachting magazines. Clarence Davis adopted what became almost a form answer, listing the current yachts that he had built and giving a generalized cost figure for a specific design if the writer requested prices. Most of his letters were similar to this one written May 28, 1930:

We have just received your card asking for our catalog. We are very sorry, but we do not issue a catalog. We are, however, enclosing a pamphlet of our 45-ft Stock Cruisers. Should these interest you we could make very prompt delivery on one of these, (providing, of course, it is not sold in the mean time) as we have one that is practically completed and still unsold.

Our principal business is to build the finest type of yachts from designs of well-known architects. If you have in mind what you want along with a general idea of the interior arrangement we will be very glad to have prepared preliminary sketches covering your requirements and at the same time give you an approximate cost of the completed boat. This, of course, without any obligation to you.

We are listing below some of the yachts we have built in the last few years and the name of owner for whom built.

Ballantrae – 60 ft.
   Robert C. Roebling, Washington, D. C.
Bonhomie – 98 ft.
   Robert C. Roebling, Washington, D. C.
Windward – 40 ft.
   Aubrey King, Baltimore, Md.
West Wind – 28 ft.
   Edward L. Palmer, Baltimore, Md.
Seawitch – 34 ft.
   Donald H. Sherwood, Baltimore, Md.
Saki – 40 ft.
   William E. Hill, Brooklyn, N. Y.
Mary Anne – 36 ft.
   R. L. Ettenger, Washington, D. C.
Carcassonne – 40 ft.
   Dr. Chas. D. Lucas, Boston, Mass.
Loretta – 55 ft.
   Frank H. Reagan, Baltimore, Md.
Orithia – 57 ft.
   Haliburton Fales, New York, N. Y.

We have at present under construction two sailing yachts, one 70 ft. for Mr. J. Rulon Miller, Jr. of Baltimore, Md. and the other for Mr. Paul Nevin, of New York City, which is 62 ft. long, both of these designed by John G. Alden of Boston, Mass.[1]

The last paragraph refers to the Alden-designed yachts *High Tide* and *Lord Jim*, built in 1930 and described in the previous chapter. *Seawitch*, *West Wind*, *Windward*, *Loretta*, *Orithia*, and *Sak*i were the result of the early collaboration between Philip L. Rhodes and Clarence E. Davis. In this same period Rhodes and Davis worked hard on plans for a 55-foot houseboat, to be named *Mother Goose*, for Hobart Ford, vice-commodore of the Cruising Club of America. In spite of a period of intense negotiations, she was never built. Hobart Ford's final choice was a baycraft designed and built in 1931 by Price and Company of Ruark, Virginia.[2]

January 15, 1931, was the 36th birthday of Philip Leonard Rhodes. His career at this point had not caused great excitement in yachting circles and his designs were not noticeably spectacular. Born in Ohio far from the shores of Long Island or the back bays of Boston, he had little opportunity to show the world his talent. Unlike John G. Alden, the famous Boston designer, who was at this time the revered and distinguished designer and sailor of the century, Rhodes was not from a sailing family nor did he grow up in a sailing community. From the day he left the Massachusetts Institute of Technology in 1918, his progress toward acceptance in the world of yachting was slow. His career contrasted greatly with that of young Olin Stephens who, having just created Design No. 1 in 1929, arrived on the yachting scene on the crest of a wave of success.

Both Alden and the Stephens brothers, Olin and Rod, Jr.,

were born with tillers in their hands; and they grew up to work their wonders among the men who had raised them and trained them. In contrast, Rhodes's early jobs were in Ohio and Baltimore, far from the breezy summer regatta weeks at Marblehead and Larchmont. He had come to New York and opened a small office in 1924 without either a constituency or the advantages that his colleagues enjoyed. His first supporters were the members of the Gibson Island Club who lined up behind Donald Sherwood. *Rudder* and *Yachting* magazines published the designs of these early yachts, and Rhodes's work slowly gained acceptance.

In 1931, Clarence Davis was 48 years old, conservative in character, with a personality and outlook already fixed by time and locality. His natural intelligence helped him to continue to grow and adjust to the needs of the yachting public, usually clannish, well-to-do individuals who were nonetheless respectful of talented men like Davis and Rhodes.

Rhodes's advice and guidance were important ingredients in transforming M. M. Davis and Son from a shipyard to a yacht-yard. Not only did he lead Davis to new clients, he indoctrinated Davis in advertising and public relations. Although an outsider himself, Rhodes was able to show Davis the proper postures and nuances of the yachting world. The emphasis was on sailing yachts, with their special gear and equipment—all of this new to Clarence Davis and his men.

At the same time that the yard was being transformed, "Miss Edna," Clarence's wife, who had a sense of "society," was urging her husband to enter the world of fashion. Clarence began to buy his clothes from the best shops in Baltimore and New York. He fancied expensive cars, and soon had his first Packard—at that time the preferred car of affluent Americans. John Janey, head of the caulker gang, was outfitted with a chauffeur's uniform and was asked to drive Davis and meet all visitors. Davis was quick to learn for he had a natural affinity for quality and good workmanship, hallmarks of the successful boatbuilder.

The relationship between Rhodes and Davis was mutually beneficial. The commissions to build *Seawitch*, *West Wind*, and then *Windward* for members of the Gibson Island Yacht Squadron came because of decisions made on Rhodes's behalf by Donald Sherwood and his friends. Several of the commissions that followed, however, were more the initiative of Davis than of Rhodes. *Loretta* and *Orithia* were both Chesapeake Bay native designs built from Rhodes's drawings, though the jobs had originated with Davis. In 1929, when Davis decided to speculate on the two stock "Davis-45" cabin cruisers, he went to Rhodes for assistance. Drawings were paid for by Davis. The amounts seem insignificant now, but they were important contributions to their relationship.

One of the cruisers became the Davis family's yacht after it remained unsold for two years. Clarence named her *Condorth II*, continuing a name used in 1911 for the Davis family's first yacht. The second Davis-45 was sold in 1931 to George Vang, but it is doubtful that she was ever delivered as she was resold to D. C. Elphinstone of Baltimore that same year. Elphinstone named her *Madeira*.

Clarence Davis paid Rhodes $100 to design the Davis-45. Davis planned to create a well-built stock cruiser at a price below that of others already on the market. He asked Rhodes to accept this low fee since the yachts were being built "to keep his crew busy." The speculative venture was unsuccessful as Davis of Solomons was unknown in a market where trade names had a special importance. Davis described his project to a prospective buyer:

We have spent a lot of time in having this boat developed and designed by a well known architect and we feel that we have accomplished a design way ahead of any boats of this size now being built as a standard proposition.

We haven't as yet completed our figures as to just what these boats will be advertised for, but it looks as though we are going to be able to make the price a little less than $14,000.00 for complete boat, based as stated above on 150 H. P. Kermath Engine. This figure is about two thousand dollars less than what the Elco and Dawn Corporations are getting for their boats, and it is my honest opinion that we have a much better boat than they are offering.[3]

The price was $12,000 in a brochure that Davis had prepared, but in an advertisement in *Yachting* in January 1931, the price was given as $14,000. It is not known what price Vang paid for *Madeira*. She was renamed *Aland* in 1947. *Aland* went out of documentation in 1974 and *Condorth II* in 1980.

Clarence Davis and Philip Rhodes maintained close alliance during the early 1930s, although they worked together less as each developed a separate clientele.

With the success of the Alden-designed *High Tide* the reputation of M. M. Davis and Son, which before 1930 had extended only to the northern limits of the Chesapeake Bay, was now known from Maine to Florida. The hurdles were overcome as yachtsmen became convinced that the Davis yard could work successfully with the designs of their naval architects using the materials and equipment that had been developed for fine yachts—materials and hardware that were constantly changed and improved.

Condorth II

Calvert Marine Museum Collection.

Clarence Davis paid Rhodes $100 to design the Davis-45.

Clarence Davis made frequent trips to Boston and New York to the boat shows, and even participated in an occasional race which he said was boring. His strength lay in his confidence in his employees. He was absolutely convinced that his men produced work equal to the best. In letters to potential clients he seldom failed to mention that his yard's work equaled that of Henry B. Nevins, Inc., or George Lawley and Son.

His genius was his ability to manage the broadening interests of his firm with one hand, while with the other he adjusted, trained, and molded his craftsmen into a manufacturing unit that produced a first-rate product. He controlled overhead accurately. The yard's machinery was relatively limited, and building procedures were adaptations of traditional methods of boatbuilding which took advantage of the special skills of the men while relegating modern tools and expensive machinery to specific uses. This ancient system would shortly die as boats built by hand were replaced by plastic molds and assembly lines.

M. M. Davis and Son built the ketch **Dog Star** during the summer of 1931. She was a slightly smaller version of Philip Rhodes's **Tidal Wave**, a double-ender designed for Samuel Wetherill. Wetherill was an editor for *Yachting* magazine, who wrote extensively on the boat and her design, giving it wide publicity and acceptance. **Dog Star** was built for William Edgar Baker of Greenwich, Connecticut, and was delivered in September 1931. Rhodes described her as "a bit smaller than *Tidal Wave*, with the same characteristics except a bit less fore foot and slightly more rake to the rudder post."[4] This change was designed to reduce the boat's weather helm. According to *Yachting*, the owner reported that she sailed well under all conditions.[5]

Philip Rhodes made the following observations about *Tidal Wave*'s plan:

> I know perfectly well that there is nothing new in boats, and that all boats are more or less the same thing. Yet, there are minor differences, enough to classify them into types. With her speed, stability, sea-ability, easiness, dryness, easy-handling, short draft, accommodations and good looks (to most), it is my opinion that weighing good and bad points together, the *Tidal Wave* type has more desirable features than any other type of small cruiser.[6]

Dog Star measured 30'8" by 27'1" by 10'2" by 5'0" and carried 545 square feet of sails. The yacht was never documented with the Coast Guard. *Lloyd's Register of American Yachts* in 1938 lists her as *Dog Star*, formerly *Tide-Rip*. This information is incorrect, unless the yacht which was originally named *Dog Star* was renamed *Tide-Rip* then changed

Sawmill in Shipyard

Calvert Marine Museum Collection.

The yard's machinery was relatively limited, and building procedures were adaptations of traditional methods of boatbuilding...

Dog Star   Photographer: Morris Rosenfeld, ©Rosenfeld Collection, Mystic Seaport Museum, Inc.

"I know perfectly well that there is nothing new in boats, and that all boats are more or less the same thing. Yet, there are minor differences, enough to classify them into types."

back to *Dog Star* by the owner who listed her in the 1938 registry. *Dog Star*'s design made her a character boat, different from the trend in yachts. Her general appearance was somewhat similar to Hanna's *Tahiti* design and to a series of yachts built by the Herreshoff Manufacturing Co.

Philip Rhodes's sailing exploits were more cerebral than physical. Though he sailed frequently on yachts of his design, he was never, unlike Alden or the Stephens brothers, at the helm in an ocean race. Before 1932 he had not owned a boat larger than a dinghy, so some mystery remains about the building of the sloop *Nixie*. Perhaps *Nixie* was designed by Rhodes for his family which included two young sons. That is normal enough. It is also logical that he would ask M. M. Davis and Son to build his boat, as Davis built well-constructed boats, reasonably priced. But two additional facts fog the issue: first, Rhodes did not pay Clarence Davis for *Nixie*; secondly, in the only letter from Rhodes to Davis that survives, Rhodes wrote of a *Nixie* class:

> I now have the construction plan quite complete and will send prints tomorrow. The sail plan too is about done and will detail the spars as soon as I can. You may object to the work I've done to make Constu Plan complete but I did this for sales literature in the hope we can land a class of them this winter.[7]

Could the *Nixie* project have been a joint venture between the two men? As it developed, *Nixie* stayed in the Rhodes family until 1946; and while there was never a *Nixie* class, variations of the design were constructed at other yards over the ensuing years. The project may have resulted in bad feelings between the two men, for when Philip Rhodes came to Solomons in 1936 for the launching of *Narada*, he refused to mount the reviewing stand to take part in the ceremonies. Admittedly, this is conjecture. However, there was a trace of bitterness as the executors of Clarence Davis's estate collected for *Nixie* after his death in November of 1936.

The reason to believe that *Nixie* was created primarily as a class boat is the fact that Philip Rhodes wrote a long, detailed article about her in *Yachting* in January 1933. The article was an obvious attempt to establish interest in a class of small family cruising boats, especially since 1933 was the year that the American economy hit bottom. In the article, Rhodes wrote generously, "*Nixie* was built by M. M. Davis and Son of Solomons, Md., who did a characteristically fine job, true to line, sound in construction and correct in detail."[8]

Nixie was built 25'4" overall, 22'0" on the water, with a molded beam of 7'6", and a draft of 4'0", with a sail area of 277 square feet. Philip L. Rhodes, Jr., who sailed in *Nixie* with his father, believes that the little cruiser may still exist. After the family sold her, she had many names and several owners. The last known was Dudley Butler of Essex, Connecticut, who named her *Silent*.

M. M. Davis and Son, now heavily involved with yacht work, both new construction and repairs, continued to receive commercial contracts. In 1930 the tug *Luna* was delivered, and in 1931 *James S. Whiteley*, a powerful steam tug, was built for the Baker-Whiteley Towing Company of Baltimore. Keel

for a new tow boat for the Smoot Sand and Gravel Company was laid February 1, 1931. This company was an old customer of Davis, having previously contracted for many sand and gravel barges, and at least two dredges, as well as other tow boats. The firm was acquired by the Arundel Corporation about the same time that the new tug was delivered. She was named *Columbia*, and a model of her created by LeRoy "Pepper" Langley is now in the collection of the Calvert Marine Museum.

Langley was working at the Davis yard in 1937 when its last wooden tow boat was built. This was *Virginia*, also built for the Smoot Sand and Gravel Company. Orders for vessels for the menhaden fishing fleet and for tugs and tow boats were important reasons that the yard was able to sustain its profitability into the 20th century.

On September 9, 1931, the keel was laid on still another commercial ship. This was *State Pilot*, one of the larger self-propelled ships constructed by M. M. Davis and Son. Her length overall was 150 feet, and she measured 328 gross tons. Ordered by a Wilmington transportation company, the ship hauled freight between that city and points along the inland waterway for many years. In the early 1930s the M. M. Davis and Son operation appeared to be quite strong. Clarence Davis wrote to his brother Raymond and to his clients that the yard in 1930, 1931, and 1932 had never been busier with its unique combination of commercial and yacht construction plus a booming business in the marine railway division. He did not mention the ominous cloud that hung over him.

In January 1931, Davis was hospitalized for hypertension. A letter of February 26, 1931, probably written by Clara Brooks to a prospective customer, confirms Davis's illness: "We wish to thank you for your inquiry on a 50-foot Bugeye and to

Nixie

Photographer: Edwin Levick, The Mariners' Museum Collection.

Perhaps Nixie *was designed by Rhodes for his family which included two young sons.*

apologize for the delay in sending you price for this, which has been due to the illness of Mr. Clarence Davis."[9]

Clara Brooks was bookkeeper, secretary, and the complete office staff of M. M. Davis and Son through the years. She reported Clarence's condition to his brother Raymond in her letter of March 3, 1931:

> I was up to Hopkins to see Mr. Davis last night and he is getting along fine, but he asked me to write you as it seems that letter writing is rather a task for him right now. The doctor has said he thought Mr. Davis could come home this Saturday and I hope he does, not only for the sake of the business but for his own sake, he didn't seem quite anxious enough to get home to suit me. I don't think it is well for anyone after they get as well as Mr. Davis is to be too well satisfied in a hospital. I told him last night that if he didn't get home soon he would be so lazy we wouldn't be able to get any work out of him.[10]

Davis stayed at Johns Hopkins Hospital for five weeks, and when he returned to Solomons he was on a medical program and diet for the rest of his life, although there were occasional lapses. Dora Lusby Joy, who is now more than 80 years old, has lived in the house next to the yard for most of her life and has many connections with the Davis yard.

She was married to Sybert Joy, one of the many members of the Joy family of Olivet who worked there, and sister of the Lusby brothers, another family that formed the backbone of the yard's crew from the time it moved to Rousby just before World War I. Mrs. Joy related how Clarence often stayed on at the yard after hours to inspect the day's work. Seeing her standing on the high bank that looked down on the yard's ways, he would shout a greeting and with a wink ask her for a piece of her chicken pie. In this way he was able to supplement the prescribed meal Miss Edna would have prepared for him across the creek.

A very large project of the yard in 1931–32 was the construction of the yacht *Manana*. She was a whale of a schooner, 92 feet overall and the largest sailboat built by M. M. Davis and Son. The yacht was built with beautiful woods of the highest quality and expensive bronze fastenings. Judged by her record, however, she was not very successful.

There is no final criterion for measuring a successful yacht except that it fulfill the purpose for which it was designed and built. If the yacht is a racer, it should win races. A cruising yacht would be a failure if her design or size made her unmanageable for a crew under usual sailing conditions. It is not clear what Roger Young wanted when he asked Charles D. Mower to design the schooner *Manana*, although he had owned yachts as early as 1917 and was an experienced bluewater sailor. Young had owned the Lawley-designed and -built schooner *Caroline* which he raced in the New London to Bermuda Race in June 1923. She did not do very well, then went on to win the New Rochelle to Halifax Race in 1924 against light competition. Young on *Caroline II* finished sixth in the New London to Gibson Island Race of 1927.

Charles Mower was 56 at the time he designed *Manana*. His career in yacht design spanned the first third of the 20th century. He was trained on the job by Arthur Binney and B. B. Crowninshield, and was for several years design editor of *Rudder* magazine. His designs were consistently satisfactory to his clients. Among his more famous yachts were *Windjammer*, *Duckling*, and the beautiful *Wanderer IV*. He was a popular designer of the 50–50 motor sailer concept and had designed George Townsend's *Cheerio* back in 1923. By 1931, however, he was somewhat out of the limelight.

Manana was handsome, but she was probably too large at 92 feet. Since her size precluded sailing her as a family boat, she would have required a paid crew. By 1931, however, it was no longer possible to keep poorly paid immigrant crews aboard pleasure boats that the wealthy had had access to before World War I.

To understand the problem of handling *Manana*, look no further than the size of her spars. Her main mast's height was 112 feet, with a diameter at the deck of 16 inches. The length of the main boom was 45 feet. Her foremast was 92 feet. These giant dimensions create much work during a normal sail, and in any kind of blow, several skilled hands would be needed on deck to handle a schooner of this size.

When Roger Young, through an aide, questioned the high cost of the yacht, Clarence Davis responded:

> Mr. Mower has planned a very fine boat, but he hasn't given much consideration to cost, which is all right if the owner doesn't care, but when it is a question of dollars and cents with him, there is always a happy medium which can be reached, and be satisfactory in every way. You know architects are rather peculiar and I want to keep on the good side of all of them, so please don't let it get to

Manana   Photographer: Morris Rosenfeld, ©Rosenfeld Collection, Mystic Seaport Museum, Inc.

Her main mast's height was 112 feet, with a diameter at the deck of 16 inches.

him that I am criticizing his specifications, as it would be much better for Mr. Young to approach him on the question of modification rather than us.[11]

In spite of the changes agreed to in reaching a lower contract price, no consideration was given to reducing the yacht's overall size. Between the time that Davis gave his original cost estimates and the arrival of the designer's plans, the overall length of the schooner was actually extended five feet.

Mower designed a gorgeous boat. Her frames were to be built of sawn white oak, and specifications called for double-planking the topsides with fir on the inside and mahogany outside. Her decks were teak, as were her skylights and hatches. Specifications called for Everdur fastenings throughout, but this was changed to galvanized bolts for the clamps, bilge stringers, and deck beams. While there is no record of her final cost with engine and furnishings, it was probably in the area of $75,000.00.

The contract between M. M. Davis and Son and Roger Young required Davis to have the schooner ready by May 1, 1932. The contract was signed on September 24, 1931, which meant that construction would take place during seven months of fall and winter weather, requiring Davis to maintain a full work force during the winter of 1932.

Manana's specifications called for an outside lead keel of about 65,000 lbs., to be cast in new lead as per design and bolted to keel with 1½ inch diameter Everdur bronze bolts, set up with bronze nut and washer on top of floor frames. Keel bolts to be located as shown on plans. Heads of bolts to be countersunk and covered with cement.[12]

Ruby Dixon worked on *Manana*'s keel along with Charles Elliott. Both described their work on this yacht. Dixon, when interviewed on January 21, 1975, recalled:

I feel everyone working in the yard was involved that day. What happens—they made a mold and put it outside the boat house. They piled dirt up on the side to keep the lead from burning through and running all over. They painted the inside with asbestos and plaster of Paris. They had a great big tank up on a thing [a support] they built to hold the tank with lead in it. There were hundred pound great chunks of lead and they

*Mower designed
a gorgeous boat.*

Photographer: Morris Rosenfeld, ©Rosenfeld Collection, Mystic Seaport Museum, Inc.

Manana

put them in the tank cold, a few at a time. They melted and they had a valve on the tank and a big piece of angle iron, six inch, and ran it from the tank to the form.

It was firewood that heated the tank.

When the valve letting off the molten lead was opened and the lead flowed into the mold, Dixon explained what happened:

That iron should have been preheated. For to run that lead in as it was, it curled the other end [of the angle iron] up and we had to cut the lead off. Well, there was a man there on a tugboat that was tied up during depression time and he said I got a big kerosene heater board there. I'll preheat that iron at the next time you try to run it. With his help of heating the angle iron and men holding the end down with them iron rods, pipes or whatever, we were able to run that hot lead in there. There were inch and a half bolts that had to go through there and things called dowels were made and placed in the right position in that form. What happens, that lead shrinks and moves your pegs. So you had to use a shrink rule to estimate how much shrinkage would be in between each space. Two through each floor. There were 30 some of them.[13]

Charles Elliott said that he had no specialty because when he went to work in the shipyard everybody did the same thing: "I clipped lead with an adz." After pouring the lead and letting it cool, the lead keel was slid out of the mold and jacked up under the wooden keel. Elliott relates: "It's all rough. Then you set down there on your haunches with an adz— smooth it out. We just peck what you could. Get it off a little bit at a time. You never sandpaper that much lead."[14] More information on casting the lead keels was provided by Barnes Lusby who added that the wood fires burned day and night;

finally a brick furnace was constructed to hold the tank several feet above the ground level, and large kerosene torches were placed under the tank until the lead was pink hot.[15]

The complete M. M. Davis and Son estimate for the *Manana*, dated September 22, 1931, was:

Lumber.	$6,876.30
Materials & Equipment.	25,887.27
Subtotal	32,763.57
Labor.	15,000.00
Subtotal	47,763.57
10% overhead	4,776.26
Subtotal	52,539.83
10% profit	5,253.99
	57,793.82
Workmans Comp	450.00
Subtotal	$58,243.82
Misc. items	300.00
Total	$58,543.82[16]

In 1932, Davis's labor rate for his top men was about 65 cents an hour, while others made significantly less. Using 50 cents as an average rate per hour, M. M. Davis and Son probably projected 30,000 labor hours to reach the $15,000 total labor charge for construction of *Manana*. Davis based his overhead and profit at approximately 20 percent, a very low figure in a business producing a luxury product. Since material and equipment were standard costs, Davis tried to make his yard competitive by training individuals to move freely from one job to the next as construction of a yacht proceeded. There were plenty of skilled men and no competition for their time other than the oyster season. Management was benevolent, and labor cooperated by accepting local rates of pay rather than those of competitive yards. Another factor in Davis's low costs was the basic efficiency of management, its own functions as well as in its control over production. There seemed to be little need to modernize.

The specified price for *Manana* was the same as the estimated figures prepared by Clarence Davis. However, during construction many changes had occurred which raised the final price approximately 40 percent. Davis received Young's first payment on October 3, 1931, by which time the yacht was about 70 percent laid down in the loft. His acknowledgment stated that actual construction was scheduled to start in a very few days.

In the January 1932 issue of *Yachting*, the designer's lines and other pertinent information on the new yacht appeared. The yacht's measurements were given (92'2" by 68' by 20' by 12') with a general description of her expected sailing qualities.[17] The yacht was delivered on schedule in May 1932. However, Coast Guard records show she was not documented until 1934, which has resulted in some confusion about the actual year of completion.

One of the legends of the yard is that *Manana* was built to be the prop for a Hollywood film, but there is no evidence to support this. In 1934 the schooner was on the market for charter. According to Charles Elliott, Roger Young sailed *Manana* to the West Coast in 1935. Once there, Young decided she was too much boat, so he offered her for sale. Her purchaser was a well-known West Coast yachtsman, Stanley H. Barrows, who had won many races in his previous yacht, the 6'7" Ford and Payne-designed ketch *Dragoon*. Since *Manana* was not an ocean racer, Barrows must have bought her for cruising. After six months *Manana* returned to the East Coast. Barrows sold her to Morgan J. Callahan, Jr., who was the last owner to maintain her as a yacht. In 1941 she was classified as a commercial vessel, and on August 17, 1946, she went aground and was lost while bound for Curacao from Barbados.

Gibson Island in the 1930s was a summer colony, although there were some year-round residents. Because boating activities of the yacht squadron were an integral part of the island's community life, small boat racing classes were held for the children of the residents. In 1935 the Gibson Island Yacht Squadron added a junior fleet of pram-type sailing boats measuring 11 feet, 6 inches overall. They had a single Marconi sail and were named after birds. The boat was designed by C. Loundes Johnson of the Miles River who had been active in Star class boat racing and had also designed the first "Comet." Over 40 were built, the first 17 at Solomons by M. M. Davis and Son. After Clarence Davis's death many of the later ones were built by the Lusby brothers who now owned the marine facilities at Gibson Island.

In 1932 Davis built a small but lovely sloop, *Mimi II*, of Rhodes design for Dr. Roger P. Batchelor of Gibson Island. Davis wrote Batchelor in December 1931 as negotiations bogged down:

Don't you think that you are taking the so called depression a little too serious? As I see it nothing drastic has happened in the last few weeks. I notice, which is all to the good, a great many of the banks that closed in the early fall are now beginning to open up, and it does seem that the bottom has about been reached. Of

L. J.

Gibson Island Historical Association Collection.

The boat was designed by C. Loundes Johnson of the Miles River who had been active in Star class boat racing and had also designed the first "Comet."

course, every one knows their own business best and I wouldn't attempt to advise you either way. But what I think will happen that things will brighten up in the spring and you will be sorry that you did not start your boat.[18]

While Davis's economic forecast may have been unreliable, the yacht he delivered to Dr. Batchelor was not—Batchelor sailed her out of Gibson Island for the next 25 years. When a man keeps the same boat for such a long time he pays his craft a special compliment. This is particularly true in yachting where so many men spend fortunes for new boats, then cast them off quickly when the yachts fail to perform to expectations. While speed at any cost is the passion of the most competitive sailors, often it is their own poor seamanship that limits a yacht's performance. When an owner reaches a level of experience comparable to his boat's performance, a truly happy and lasting relationship is formed. Such was the case with Batchelor's *Mimi II.*

She was 24 feet overall, 18 feet at the waterline, with a beam of 7 feet, and draft of 4 feet. She carried 284 square feet of sail. Too small for a cruising boat, she was used for day sailing, mostly single-handed, until the day Batchelor gave up sailing.

There is no record that M. M. Davis and Son built any yachts from Philip Rhodes's designs

etween *Mimi II* in 1932 and *Trivet* in 1935.
Trivet was a small sloop. Her length overall
was an inch over 30 feet, and 21 feet, 8 inches
on the waterline. She had a long cabin,
making her easy to identify—a classic Rhodes
profile. Describing her in *Yachting*, Rhodes
wrote: "I tried to produce a wholesome little
cruiser with lots of room for two and a boat
that would be a smart day sailer."[19] The owner,
C. W. Moore of New York, sailed her for four
years. In 1942 she was owned in Washington,
D. C., by Captain A. S. Haffley. After World War
she no longer appeared in *Lloyd's Register of
American Yachts*.

M. M. Davis and Son built the Rhodes-
designed centerboard ketch *Lady Patty* for
Edward E. Bishop in 1935. The design traced
its lineage back to one of Philip Rhodes's
earliest yachts, *Tidal Wave*, which had
received an unusual amount of publicity and
attention over the years. *Lady Patty* was ac-
ually designed in 1931 for Robert B. Noyes
who never had her built. (The fact that her
lines appeared in *Yachting* in 1932 under the
name *Saona* has caused some confusion.)
Below deck, *Lady Patty* had one great cabin
similar to *Tidal Wave*, but quarters for a paid
hand were laid out in the forecastle. Her
dimensions were 39' by 32'1 by 11'6" by
4'4". *Lady Patty* was yet another undoc-
umented yacht. Lack of documentation became more common as yachting grew in
popularity. In the years between 1939 and
1973, *Lloyd's* listed *Lady Patty* as jointly

Mimi II

Calvert Marine Museum Collection.

*When an owner reaches a
level of experience comparable to his boat's performance, a truly happy and
lasting relationship is formed.*

Trivet

owned by Edward E. and Lillian Bishop and James W. Crawford, Jr., all of Tampa, Florida. Coincidentally, in 1953 Edward and Lillian Bishop bought the bugeye yacht *Ko-Asa*, also built by M. M. Davis and Son.

Crawford raced *Lady Patty* in the Southern Ocean Racing Circuit, entering her in the Havana Race on at least two occasions, and winning in 1951. After the 1948 race, *Lady Patty* was knocked down in a heavy blow and Crawford nearly lost her when a port hole was inadvertently left ajar. Crawford raced her in the Transpac Race to Hawaii in 1953.[20]

Lady Patty was another centerboarder that proved herself able, fast enough to handle long ocean voyages and blue-water races. When Philip Rhodes wrote about his design in 1932, he stated that his careful calculations would prove her to be decidedly stiff, her stability increasing with the angle of keel.[2]

She had a long cabin, making her easy to identify—a classic Rhodes profile.

Crawford wrote that *Lady Patty* was an exceptionally able boat.

Philip L. Rhodes's work was true, functional, elegant, with ageless beauty. He brought these characteristics together successfully in the design of the cutter *Narada*, launched at M. M. Davis and Son in June 1936. Rhodes designed *Narada* about the same time that he designed *Kirawan*. The latter yacht, built by Jakobson and Peterson in Brooklyn, was an immediate success, winning the Bermuda Race of 1936. The race was sailed in rugged, heavy weather, the prevailing wind on *Kirawan*'s nose at levels as high as 45 miles per hour. In spite of the fact that she was given time by 27 of the 44 starting yachts, she was the third boat to finish. Among the beaten yachts was *Stormy Weather*, the famous Sparkman and Stephens yawl that later raced *Narada* on the Chesapeake Bay.

Lady Patty *was another centerboarder that proved herself able, fast enough to handle long ocean voyages and blue-water races.*

Lady Patty   Photographer: Morris Rosenfeld, ©Rosenfeld Collection, Mystic Seaport Museum, Inc.

Narada

Kirawan *and* Narada *were similar in many ways, though* Narada *was the smaller at 34 feet on the waterline…*

Kirawan and *Narada* were similar in many ways, though *Narada* was smaller at 34 feet on the waterline, compared with *Kirawan's* near 39 feet. *Narada* got off to a fine start by winning the Virginia Cruising Cup and a first in Class B in the Hampton Race of 1936. These back-to-back victories of his cruising yachts came at a propitious time for Rhodes, now partner in the well-known naval architectural design firm of Cox and Stevens.

With *Narada*, everything seemed to come together for Rhodes. This yacht was something special. His carefully worked out hull design had been tank tested and her cutter rig complemented her proportional lines. Her owner, L. Corrin Strong of the Gibson Island Yacht Squadron, had agreed to have her built of the best materials and equipment. Her builder, M. M. Davis and Son, with a fine-honed crew of artisans, was at its peak of performance. On the hot day in June 1936 when she slid down the waxed ways, a special feeling of satisfaction lifted everyone associated with her creation.

Strong had asked for an able craft—fast, yet comfortable and roomy, as he intended her for cruising as well as for sailing the important races of the Chesapeake Bay. The yacht was double-planked with cedar and Honduras mahogany. Her decks, house, trim, and sole were of Burma teak. Everdur fastenings were used throughout. Her spars were made of Sitka spruce, hollowed out by the carpenters at the yard. Her rigging was stainless steel.[22]

One of the most interesting aspects of *Narada*'s participation in the racing schedules of 1939 and 1940 was her competition with two fine Sparkman and Stephens-designed yachts: *White Cloud*, built by M. M. Davis and Son in 1937, and the famous yawl *Stormy Weather*, then owned and raced by a Marylander, William H. Labrot. *Stormy Weather* had been designed by Olin Stephens as an improved version of *Dorade*, the yacht that brought the Stephens brothers fame and fortune when they sailed her to victory in the Trans-Atlantic Race of 1931. Francis S. Kinney, biographer of Olin and Rod Stephens, wrote:

> *Stormy Weather* did soon turn out to be a better boat than *Dorade* in many ways, because of her proportionately greater beam. She could perform better under sail on every point of sailing, in almost every sea condition and strength of wind.[23]

Narada measured 45'10" by 34'0" by 11'3" by 6'6". After 1939 she carried a masthead rig. The two yachts differed substantially in their rating, resulting in *Stormy Weather* being raced in Class A (her measurements were 53'11 by 39'9" by 12'6" by 7'11"), and *Narada* usually in Class B. The two yachts' racing performances can only be compared on a corrected time basis.

In the Love Point to Swan Point Race of May 28, 1939, the two yachts squared off against each other: and *Stormy Weather* won, beating *Narada* by forty seconds. On July 30, 1939, in the Poplar Island Race, *Narada* beat *Stormy Weather* over the finish line, a decisive rout of the larger yawl on

corrected time. Neither yacht was a winner in their respective class, as *White Cloud* won Class A over *Vamarie* and *Stormy Weather*. *Narada* was beaten in Class B by *Egret*. The Cedar Point Race of 1939 produced *Narada*'s greatest victory. *White Cloud*, first across the finish line, placed second to *Stormy Weather* in Class A on corrected time; but both were solidly beaten by *Narada*. Raced by Strong, *Narada* was first in the fleet on corrected time.[24]

After *Narada*'s victory in the 1940 Love Point to Swan Point Race, the Baltimore *Sun* wrote:

> The squadron's own flagship, Commodore L. Corrin Strong's white cutter, *Narada*, outsailed everything in sight, including the Naval Academy's big *Vamarie* and William H. Labrot's *Stormy Weather*, both among the finest in the ocean-racing game.
>
> *Narada*'s performance was probably as fine a one as bay racing has seen in many a day. It was by no means her kind of weather. No racing freak, but a substantial, able-cruising boat that could take her afterguard across the Atlantic in perfect safety.[25]

In the 1940 Rhode River to Gibson Island Race, *Narada* beat *Stormy Weather* on corrected time by 56 seconds. At the Poplar Island Race that year, *Stormy Weather* beat *Narada* by one minute and 31 seconds.

The Cedar Point Race on September 1, 1940, which takes the yachts to the mouth of the Patuxent River just a mile or so from the Davis yard, brought joy to the hearts of the men of M. M. Davis and Son. In this race *White Cloud* was the winner in Class A and *Narada* was the winner in Class B. While *White*

Narada

Photographer: Howe Lagarde, Calvert Marine Museum Collection.

Cloud won the Whiting Trophy as the first yacht to finish the race, *Narada* won the Chesapeake Bay Cruising Cup for the best corrected time in the cruising division, beating **White Cloud** by 22 minutes and 56 seconds. In *Narada* Philip L. Rhodes designed a yacht able to compete with the best.

World War II affected the yachting community in 1942 when the Navy Department put out a call for yachts, sailing as well as motor, to serve as picket boats in the antisubmarine service on the North Atlantic Ocean. Thousands of yachtsmen responded, and the best were inducted into the Coast Guard Reserve.

"Narada's performance was probably as fine a one as bay racing has seen in many a day."

t first the unit was only quasi-military since the Navy, under hich the Coast Guard then operated, was not convinced of he value of its contribution to anti-submarine warfare. The en who volunteered for the service were enlisted initially or short tours of duty. Eventually the service became a more ermanent part of the Coast Guard and the men who served n the yachts were enlisted into the Guard for the war's uration.

his was not easy duty. Once the yachts ventured beyond he sight of land, the glamour and excitement of playing war aded. If a day passed uneventfully, the small crew of a half ozen men or so handled their tasks as a unit. The absence f stress masked any deficiencies in training or capabilities. he limited space aboard was no problem, as the different atches rotated in a friendly game of apportioning bunks nd food. But when clouds covered the sun, or during the lack night of the stormy North Atlantic with chilling temperature drops, the game became serious.

ach tour of duty was seven days at sea, just long enough to ake the patrol worthwhile, but too long if conditions were ad. A week at sea on a sailboat of 45 to 60 feet can become an eternity when the wind buffets the small craft connually and green water crashes down on the watch huddled an open cockpit. The patrols covered the shipping lanes, ach yacht being responsible for a small square on a grid. he winter months were the most dangerous for the patrols: he North Atlantic is usually at its most turbulent and the crew ould have had no way to prepare themselves for the terror nd danger of the sea in nights so black that everything xcept oneself is invisible. Sickness and the bone-chilling cold ould be relieved only by such intense activity as reefing a ail or retrieving some piece of gear which had worked itself ee under the difficult conditions.

In the history of World War II, the story of these valiant men who volunteered for this silent and dark service is mostly unrecorded. The information about their experiences appears in the wartime issues of *Yachting*. The idea for the Corsair Service, as it was officially titled, is credited to Alfred Stanford, Commodore of the Cruising Club of America. He had presented a plan for a yacht patrol to the Navy prior to Pearl Harbor, but the plan was rejected. Not until May 4, 1942, did Admiral Ernest King order the Coast Guard to organize a volunteer patrol.

A picket patrol station was normally about 24 hours offshore where the yachts located their assigned areas by dead reckoning and sun sights. Much of the time on patrol was spent drifting downwind off of the grid, then the sails would be hoisted and the craft would tack back to what the patrol thought was its designated position. The watches were usually six hours on and six off to midnight, then, four on, four off until noon. There were two watches. Lookouts were posted forward and aft and were doubled at night. Should someone sight an object or vessel, one of the crew climbed the ratlines to the masthead or spreaders for a better look in the pitching and rolling sea. These maneuvers were repeated endlessly.

A member of the service described one of his patrols in *Yachting*:

Midway in the cruise, which lasted seven days, we were ordered to another grid which took us a considerable distance offshore. During most of that time there prevailed a hard easterly blow which piped up to 50 miles per hour in the squalls, so that the crew had its hands full, especially at night, sailing the boat under jib and reefed mizzen. Tremendous seas would roar down on us as if to

117

engulf the whole craft, but we rode over them easily, and it was rare freak waves that came aboard.[26]

The Coast Guard chose sailing yachts for the Corsair Service as they were better designed to handle the sea and because, under sail, their movements could not be detected by submarines. Several M. M. Davis and Son yachts were loaned by their owners to this service. They performed well and most were returned to their yacht clubs at the war's end. The Davis-built yachts known to have entered Coast Guard picket patrol were *High Tide*, *Kiboko*, *Diana* [described in Chapter 8], *Ko-Asa*, Strong's handsome *Narada*, and *North State*, a bugeye converted for yachting (she was built by M. M. Davis in 1883). Evidently, the Service, which began in September 1942, did not maintain records of individual cruises or craft. Ironically, there was little to write about. By 1942, German submarines had deserted the north-south sea lanes and were concentrating on the North Atlantic convoys en route to the United Kingdom.

When *Narada* entered the service in 1942, her gleaming white topsides were repainted navy gray and the identification code "CGR2012" was painted on each side at the hull. She was equipped with a ship-to-shore telephone and a radio set. It is not known whether she had submarine detection devices.

Narada was a casualty of her war service. On January 27, 1943, Colonel Strong received a wartime notice:

> I notify you with regret that your vessel, *Narada*, CGR 2012, was lost at sea on the morning of 20 December 1942. She sank immediately, as the result of a collision. Fortunately, all hands were saved.[27]

Strong's efforts to find and salvage her off Old Point Comfort after the end of the war were unsuccessful.

Narada was the last Rhodes-designed yacht built by Clarence Davis. In 1939 two small Rhodes-designed sloops of the "Little Sister" class were built by M. M. Davis and Son, Inc., then owned by George Townsend. These are described in Chapter 10.

The Crown Prince of Design

Clarence Davis carried M. M. Davis and Son on his shoulders during the yacht-building decade between 1926 and 1936. He culled through the labor force, shifting and molding his craftsmen. He spread himself over all phases of the company's operation, assisted by old-timers like Barnes Lusby who had learned how to read specifications and blueprints, as well as how to schedule work. With one clerical assistant, Davis handled the purchasing and all correspondence, quotations, and estimates. He inspected all completed work, and on the road he handled sales, advertising, and public relations.

Yacht work was complicated—the owners demanding, the designers precise in their plans. The strain was immense. The ongoing problem in the yard was low profits generated from yacht work.

Davis's standard 10-percent markup on labor and materials to cover overhead was too low; and his 10-percent profit margin was too small to cover contingencies, overruns, risks, delays, management costs, and all the other miscellaneous items not included in the 10-percent overhead. This is illustrated by the specific cost and profit figures for the cutter *Narada*. M. M. Davis and Son contracted with L. Corrin Strong to build *Narada* for $13,000.

The actual costs were:

Material	$6,680.78
Labor	5,835.94
Insurance	175.08
Total	$12,691.80[1]

The difference between the costs of building this yacht and the amount paid under the contract was only $308.20.

Barnes Lusby summarized the situation in a letter to George Townsend:

> I can only say that I feel sure that on small yachts we are not going to be able to meet prices of Maine yards or smaller yards anywhere. We have never been able to do so, even years ago when we counted our boats by figuring our material exactly as we do now and estimated our labor as we do now. We found our field was in the higher

class and larger jobs that seemed to steer clear of small yards and were able to beat Nevins [Henry B. Nevins, Inc.] and the old Lawley [George Lawley and Son] yards occasionally. Please allow me to say again that we have never been able to clear up any money on building yachts. But I thought perhaps our contracts were poor and that the prices given were too low, but it seems that if a price is given where we can make money that the jobs go elsewhere.[2]

Lusby's letter was written in January 1939, when the company was on the verge of bankruptcy. Clarence Davis had died a little over two years before when the yard was at its busiest. Lusby's letter to Townsend is one of the rare documents to have survived concerning the pricing problems and profitability of the yard under Clarence Davis.

In 1932 M. M. Davis and Son delivered *Manana*, *Nixie*, and *Mimi II*. By 1933 new orders for yachts were at a low ebb. The yard built one motor cruiser, *Shirley Ann*, and evidently nothing else. *Shirley Ann* was ordered by Maxwell Anderson of Baltimore.

Many economists believe that 1933 marked the low point of the depression. It was a grim year for Solomons. The local bank failed. In August a great hurricane hit the Patuxent River. Homes and the local fleet of work and charter boats were damaged significantly. A bugeye loaded with watermelons entered Solomons Harbor during the storm. Much to everyone's surprise her anchor held firm throughout the storm while almost every other boat in the harbor was beached. When the storm ended and the sun broke through the clouds the next morning, the lone man on the bugeye was seen chopping away a crab house that had become impaled on the bowsprit. The great hurricane cut away 40 feet from the river bank along the front of the island.[3]

In 1934 the fortunes of M. M. Davis and Son completely reversed. The year brought the first collaboration between Clarence Davis and Olin J. Stephens, of the firm of Sparkman and Stephens. Lawrence Bailliere commissioned Sparkman and Stephens to design a cutter, later named *Aweigh*. He decided that she would be built by M. M. Davis and Son.

Stephens was then 26 years old, half the age of Clarence Davis but already America's best-known designer. Fame came quickly with his design of the yawl *Dorade*. She finished second in her class in the Bermuda Race of 1930. In 1931 she won the ocean race between Newport, Rhode Island, and Plymouth, England, and went on to win the Fastnet Race in Britain. Stephens and his crew, including his brother Rod Stephens, Jr., returned to New York and were treated to a ticker-tape parade down Broadway, assuring the young designer/sailor recognition never afforded any designer before or since. By 1934, the year *Aweigh* was built, his fine reputation was firmly supported by a series of successful yachts. Other than *Dorade*, Stephens's best-known early design was the schooner *Brilliant*, now at Mystic Seaport where she is used as a training vessel for children.

Aweigh was a great success, and Bailliere sailed her for 30 years. She was a good sailing yacht, fast enough in her early years to win her share of important ocean races, then comfortable enough for cruising by a contented owner who kept her active on the Chesapeake Bay and other waters years after he dropped out of racing competition. To Olin Stephens, this was the desired ideal, as there is in every sailor a zest for competition, yet she was built with the comforts of a weekend cruising yacht.

Yacht racing had become a multi-million dollar business. As in fashion, there have always been basics and fads, but nothing really new. To produce successful racing machines, one must challenge the current set of basics—in the case of yachting, the rules for measurement and handicapping. Winners are those vessels that successfully test and survive the rules fixed by both tradition and fashion. In the case of Olin Stephens, early success came without a great deal of formal education and after a short period of technical preparation. His success was based on his solid understanding of the direction that design must go. Stephens recommended that the best materials and state-of-the-art equipment go into the construction of his yachts. These advantages, along with good seamanship and Stephens's own striving for perfection produced winning yachts.

Aweigh was just over 47 feet in length overall; her beam was 11 feet, 9 inches; and her keel carried 11,200 pounds of lead, bringing her down into the water just 6 feet, ideal for sailing out of her owner's home port of Gibson Island. She was Lawrence Bailliere's first yacht from Davis, although he had been corresponding with the firm since 1928. Before owning *Aweigh*, Bailliere raced and cruised the Alden schooner *Harpoon*.

Stephens was probably pleasantly surprised when Bailliere took *Aweigh* south in the winter of 1935 and won the Nassau Trophy on best overall corrected time in the Miami to Nassau Race, a 186-mile course across the

Aweigh

Calvert Marine Museum Collection.

Aweigh *was just over 47 feet in length overall...*

Caribbean Sea. Winning the race was no fluke, as *Aweigh* beat the famous ketch, *Vamarie*, on corrected time, and she also crossed the finish line about an hour earlier than the scratch yacht, *Azara*. *Rudder* wrote:

> *Aweigh*'s performance is noteworthy in view of *Vamarie*'s demonstrated ability to eat up the miles and the fact that she is 70 feet on deck and can carry plenty of light canvas.[4]

The reporter for *Yachting* wrote:

> The little cutter with her handy rig and in smooth water outsailed the larger yachts in beautiful fashion.[5]

Eager for another triumph, Rod Stephens, Jr., now a partner with his brother in Sparkman and Stephens, signed on as skipper in the sixth annual St. Petersburg to Havana Race scheduled for noon, March 30, 1935. Although *Aweigh* followed *Vamarie* over the finish line behind by eight hours, she was more than 13 hours ahead of the next finisher. It was an extremely impressive performance. *Vamarie*, the scratch boat, held on to her victory as *Aweigh* had less than four hours handicap in this 284-mile race. *Aweigh* won second place on corrected time; and as icing on the cake, she won the race back to Key West from Havana.

When Bailliere raced on the Chesapeake Bay, he won the 1936 Gibson Island to Poplar Island Race. After that win he practically gave up serious competition, racing *Aweigh* occasionally in later years, but never as a serious contender. Contented with cruising, he satisfied an occasional urge for competition aboard other men's yachts. Richard Henderson, a writer and Bailliere's neighbor, wrote warmly of him:

Although Bailliere had more than a few talents and a great deal of charm he was a restless man who seldom stuck to anything for very long. But one constant element in his life was his beloved *Aweigh*. He kept her for about thirty years, until his death, I believe, and that is certainly the best testimonial for any boat.[6]

Bailliere and *Aweigh* were frequent visitors to Solomons over the years. Solomons' principal attraction for yachtsmen, other than its location and the Davis repair facilities, was the bar at Bowen's Inn, still open today and little changed from earlier days. Captain Mortimer Bowen presided over the establishment, entertaining sailors, politicians, celebrities, and an occasional local. Saturday nights the place was a bright spot in the otherwise quiet village. Drinks were stronger than the law allowed, and the tinkling sound of silver coins falling into and out of his one-armed bandits was accompanied by music pounded out by a black man at the ancient piano. Following Captain Bowen's death, his seat at the end of the bar was occupied by his daughter Althea. She has remarked that of all of the people who have stood at her bar, the sailor she remembers best was the gentleman known as "Bally."

A half-model of Lawrence Bailliere's *Aweigh* is displayed in the taproom of the Annapolis Yacht Club.

Clarence Davis built two Stephens-designed motor sailers: the first, *Kiboko*, in 1934, and the second, *Diana*, in 1936. Similar in size, both were built for prominent New Yorkers, men who had been racing for years and were slowing down, ready to trade excitement for comfort. *Kiboko* was built for Clarence Sterling Postley and *Diana* for Langhorne Gibson, both members of the New York Yacht Club. The selection of M. M. Davis and Son to build the motor sailers for such important clients indicated the designer's confidence in Davis's work. Also, it confirmed that the yard had not lost its reputation for constructing heavy, strong boats.

The order for *Kiboko* signaled a revival in business, although there were some constraints on expense. For example, Sparkman and Stephens specified fir planking and decks; fastenings of galvanized iron were authorized as another economy measure.

Clarence Davis had long been an advocate of iron fastenings because they had been used in local craft successfully for generations. He often mentioned the danger of electrolysis when bronze screws and fastenings,

Stephens was probably pleasantly surprised when Bailliere took Aweigh *south in the winter of 1935 and won the Nassau Trophy...*

Aweigh

Photographer: Morris Rosenfeld, ©Rosenfeld Collection, Mystic Seaport Museum, Inc.

Kiboko

popular with the yachting industry, were called for in specifications. Davis was correct, as many yachts with galvanized fastenings have outlasted similar boats fastened with bronze. Other early Davis-built yachts, such as *Seawitch*, *Windward*, and *Orithia*, were built with iron fastenings, and they survive today, as does *Kiboko*.

Kiboko was built with crew quarters forward, galley and a stateroom amidship, and the owner's double-stateroom aft. A large wardrobe and a complete bathroom were included. Originally, she was gaff-rigged with a total sail area of 1,223 square feet. Her engine was a 75 horsepower, three-cylinder, Fairbanks-Morse diesel. *Kiboko*'s length overall is 59 feet ½ inches. Her ballast is 6,500 pounds outside, and 2,000 pounds in her bilge.

Other early Davis-built yachts, such as Seawitch, Windward, and Orithia, were built with iron fastenings, and they survive today, as does Kiboko.

Postley owned *Kiboko* for three years. Edwin Athearn, an authority on motor sailers, remembers the first time he encountered her. The owner had her in Miami and Athearn was nearby the day her young Dutch skipper headed her toward her berth. As the skipper shifted her into reverse, the gear failed and her forward motion drove her under a covered boat shed, clipping off her two spars.

After Postley, *Kiboko* was owned by several New Yorkers. In 1942 she was taken into the United States Coast Guard, probably used as a picket boat and given some wartime changes and equipment. Following the war, she was put up for sale. Sparkman and Stephens were the brokers and their ad stated that she "has been in Coast Guard Service, but is offered at a price at which reconditioning costs have been taken into consideration." There were no takers in the postwar yachting world, so *Kiboko* was sold into commercial service.

Her new owners, Isle of Shoals Steamship Company of Portsmouth, New Hampshire, used her in an island passenger service for several years, as did her next owner, Moura Navigation Co. She passed through several owners in Maine, and then was brought to Boston. Newly named *Virginia C*, she was operated as a sightseeing boat until she sank in Boston Harbor in 1978.

Virginia C had just been raised when Milton "Buzz" Hamilton found her. At age 44 she was very old and tired from hard service as a passenger and freight boat. She had seen no yachting since before World War II.

Hamilton, a restorer of well-built wooden yachts, had arrived in the East from Chicago a few years before purchasing *Virginia C*. He had worked on old yachts in New England

and Fort Lauderdale before establishing his own restoring business. He and his wife Diane, who had also operated a yacht-restoring service in Fort Lauderdale, told their story of the motor sailer they renamed *Arthur C. Nielsen*:

When we first saw the boat she had just been raised off the bottom of Boston Harbor and towed to the Boston fish pier. She looked cosmetically horrible. Paint was peeling everywhere, the engine room was covered in oil. Hatches were all adrift, the rails were rotten, the deck house top was falling in, and the deck leaked everywhere. She looked very sad.

On the other hand, she had a beautiful sheer and all her lines had remained fair through the years. She was for a yacht, ruggedly built, with 4" x 4" double sawn frames on 15" centers. She has 1⅞" straight grain fir planking, most of which is still original, hard pine main deck beams, and beautiful hackamatack hanging knees.

It took some imagination to see her as a motor sailer at that time. She had been a working passenger carrying vessel for just over 30 years. She had a cyclone fence railing all about. A pilot house was built on top of her after cabin trunk, where her original outside steering had been. Her deck house served as a passenger salon, and the aft cabin housed two heads. There were bright red benches built of 2 x 4's all about the deck. Her original oak steering wheel was painted red.

After the vessel had been purchased she spent the winter at the Fairhaven boat yard at Fairhaven, Massachusetts. She had a sheet steel patch covering the 10" hole in the engine room.

Arthur C. Nielsen, ex-Kiboko

*"The fact that she exists today at all,
52 years after she was launched, is
a tribute to the Davis yard."*

126

She was hauled in April 1979, and her bottom was painted and the planking was properly repaired. We installed some temporary wiring, and necessary gear to make the trip to south Florida.

As soon as she arrived in Ft. Lauderdale, the refurbishing started. It is most important to properly assess the problems, what caused them, and what the priorities will be before commencing repair work. This boat suffered from poor maintenance. The fact that she exists today at all, 52 years after she was launched, is a tribute to the Davis yard. The joiner work everywhere is excellent, and they used the right materials in the right places.

The first project was to get the deck sealed up, and rebuild the hatches. Also, ventilation below deck was very poor, all of her port lights had been removed, possibly when she was in Coast Guard service. We replaced all of her ports and added a few. Another project was to add a small cabin trunk, and a new hatch on the forward deck. The new trunk has ten opening ports to improve air flow. Next the deck house top was completely replaced. We built a new outside steering station, and installed inside steering, using the original wheel in the deck house. The existing dry exhaust system was a

Kiboko's Knees

Photographer: Milton Hamilton, Calvert Marine Museum Collection.

"The joiner work everywhere is excellent, and they used the right materials in the right places."

127

ridiculous affair, and was completely replaced with all stainless steel piping and a new stainless funnel. The boat was completely wooded inside and out and a new teak cap rail installed. The decks had been covered with ⅜" plywood and fiberglassed. This had to be completely redone.

The below deck areas of the boat had been changed around and messed with to the point where it had to be stripped out and completely rebuilt. We used 1" x 3" oak staving, grooved and splined for all bulkheads. The cabin sole is planked with maple in the same manner. The cabinetry, furniture and trim are mostly Honduras mahogany. The engine room equipment and electrical systems are basically all new, with the exception of the main engine and 3–1 Twin Disk manual gear. Fuel tankage is 860 gallons in four stainless steel tanks. She is equipped with a power and manual hydraulic steering system, coupled with a Wood-Freeman auto pilot. Electronics include: Decca radar, Sitex Loran, and Sailor VHF radio. She also has central heat and air throughout.

We have tried to keep everything we have done in keeping with the style of the boat. The aft cabin has a Shipmate wood-burning stove, and an 1880's type copper bathtub, with oak rails. There is still a lot to do to finish the boat, plenty of detail work and the spars and rigging. It has been a lot of fun, along with loads of work. We have learned quite a bit from the Davis yard, just working on this boat. They definitely were masters at their trade. A fifty-two-year-old boat that still looks good is proof of that.[7]

Diane and Buzz Hamilton moved to Alva, Florida, in 1982 where they operate a marina and continue their restoration

work. In the spring of 1986 they sailed *Arthur C. Nielsen* back to Solomons for a visit.

Tejeria, built for Theodore J. Hoster in 1936, was the next yacht built by M. M. Davis and Son from Sparkman and Stephens designs. Like *Aweigh* she was a cutter, but about three feet shorter. While she did not become as well known, she was lovingly sailed by Hoster for many years, mostly on the Chesapeake Bay. Her home port was Gibson Island. *Tejeria* was Olin Stephens's Design No. 102, and the specifications were for a sturdy cutter to be built of the best woods and fastenings. Her dimensions were:

L.O.A.	44 ft. - 10½ in.
L.W.L.	33 ft. - 6 in.
Beam	11 ft. - 4 in.
Draft	5 ft. - 0 in.

Frames of 1⅞" square, white oak, steam-bent, spaced 10" center to center, fair with the inside of planking. Frames aft of station 10 should be overbent on floor and put in cold. The planking used was Philippine mahogany, dressed to 1⅛" butts spaced throughout the yacht. Two 2 ¼" #16 Everdur wood screws in each frame and at the butts at least 3¼" Everdur head screw bolts through 1½" white oak butt blocks from which inside corner has been cut off to prevent water standing above.[8]

Hoster entered *Tejeria* in the 1937 ocean race from New London to Gibson Island. Other Davis boats in this race were

Narada and the large cutter *White Cloud*. *Tejeria*'s performance was not good: she finished ninth in the Class B division, about 28 hours behind the class winner, *Golden Eye*, a yawl three feet shorter. She had done better in local waters in 1936, finishing second to *Aweigh* in the Gibson Island to Poplar Island Race in Class B. Hoster won the Rhode River to Gibson Island Race the same year.

Ted Hoster sold *Tejeria* in 1949 to C. W. Crouse of Oxford, Maryland. Crouse changed her name to *Taneek*. He sailed her for several years as did two later owners, Dr. Kenneth B. Brown of Huntington, New York, and Philip A. Lund of St. Thomas, Virgin Islands. In 1974 she was sold to Robert Hawkins of Gloucester, Massachusetts. After that her fate is unknown. A half-model of *Tejeria* is on display at the Annapolis Yacht Club, and Mrs. Hoster owns a full model of the cutter.

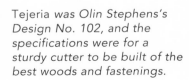

Tejeria *was Olin Stephens's Design No. 102, and the specifications were for a sturdy cutter to be built of the best woods and fastenings.*

Tejeria

Photographer: Morris Rosenfeld, ©Rosenfeld Collection, Mystic Seaport Museum, Inc.

129

Motor Sailer *Diana*   Photographer: Morris Rosenfeld, ©Rosenfeld Collection, Mystic Seaport Museum, Inc.

In 1936 M. M. Davis and Son was a very busy yard. Launched at almost the same time as *Tejeria* was a second Sparkman and Stephens designed motor sailer, *Diana*. Measuring 60' 6" on the load waterline, by 16' 8" across the beam, with 6' 3" draft, the sturdy yacht was designed to carry 1,090 square feet of sail with a loose-footed mainsail. She was originally powered by a six-cylinder Buda diesel engine on a vibrationless bed installed in a sound-proof engine room. The yacht was built with a deckhouse and two double staterooms adjoining. The galley was in the raised house abaft the deckhouse.

Langhorne Gibson owned *Diana* for little more than a year. Subsequently she had several owners and as many names. At the start of World War II she was called *Piquino* and was owned by H. R. Kamhardt, Jr., of Greenwich, Connecticut. She was requisitioned by the United States Coast Guard on August 14, 1942, and released from the service to Kamhardt in 1945. In 1972, then called *Varina*, she was sold to a Canadian and sailed to the British Virgin Islands.

...the sturdy yacht was designed to carry 1,090 square feet of sail with a loose-footed mainsail.

York started on the cutter *White Cloud* in May 1936. Clarence Davis, by then an accomplished publicist for the company, kept the yachting world abreast of her progress by releasing periodic reports to the press. In June he announced the signing of the contract for the yacht.[9] In September he announced that "the yard had completed laying down the lines of George Whiting's *White Cloud* in the mold loft," and that "she would be just over 60 feet overall, with rather long overhangs, fore and aft."[10] *Yachting* stated that the cutter was designed for speed and that her single spar would tower ninety feet over the deck. The November 1936 issue of *Yachting* included the announcement that the keel of the cutter had been laid and she would be launched in the spring of 1937.[11] That issue was on the newsstands when the news of Clarence Davis's death on November 15 spread through the yachting world.

An untimely death is often felt with great intensity by those very close to the deceased; the shock then spreads from the center like ripples from a stone tossed on the surface of a smooth sea. Thus was felt the sudden and premature death of Clarence Davis. The yachting community lost a great builder, a man who had in just a few years raised his company to a level where there were few peers. The designers who had come to know his work felt the loss keenly. The owners for whom Clarence Davis had built yachts lost a fine craftsman. All had admired his correctness, his exactness, and his integrity.

M. Davis and Son was a business operated by one man, Clarence Davis. His son was still a child in 1936. Of the many fine artisans at the yard, no one knew about operating a business. When Mrs. Davis found a buyer within weeks after her husband's death, everybody was relieved. The new owner was George H. Townsend of New York. He was a successful businessman and an experienced sailor, although he had never built boats before. Townsend did not move to Solomons. Edward Johns, another New Yorker, became general manager of the yard. J. Barnes Lusby, continuing as superintendent, rallied the men and work quickly resumed.

White Cloud was launched in May 1937. George Whiting was hopeful as he prepared his new cutter for the New London to Gibson Island Race which was scheduled to start on June 27, 1937. Her designers, Sparkman and Stephens, wrote that *White Cloud*'s lines were "worked out in conjunction with model tests and certain refinements have been made over earlier designs which, it is hoped, will result in an exceptionally good performance."[12] Her models were tank-tested in the laboratory of the Stephens Institute of Technology at Hoboken, N. J., her sails were by Ratsey, and her rigging was state of the art. *White Cloud* is 60'6" in length overall, 42'9" on the waterline, 13'1" beam, and 8'6" draft. Materials used in construction were oak keel and frames, Philippine mahogany planking, and cedar decks. Fastenings were Everdur, and her keel was lead.

Superstition plays a major role with ships and the sea. Was it a bad omen that *White Cloud*'s builder died before she was completed? It was said that Davis, accompanied by Whiting and Rod Stephens, found rot in the oak keel, and that Davis's death occurred just following this discovery.

The New London to Gibson Island Race of 1937 was to cover the same 475-mile course that *High Tide* had sailed in 1934. Alfred Loomis of *Yachting* wrote that it was the most

White Cloud

Photographer: Morris Rosenfeld, ©Rosenfeld Collection, Mystic Seaport Museum, Inc.

important race of the year in American wa ters.[13] Seventeen large yachts started in Clas A and seventeen sailed the course in Clas B. As it developed, strong winds and severa squalls served to the advantage of the large boats. *Narada* and *Tejeria*, Davis-built boats finished out of the money in Class B. Al though Philip Rhodes's and John Alden' yachts were entered, the greatest numbe of new yachts were designed by Olin Ste phens. This portended his future dominance in racing, which he maintained into the 1970s. In Class A, Sparkman and Stephen were represented by four new yachts including *White Cloud*.

In Maryland, interest in the race was high The newspapers referred to the "mysterious" *White Cloud*. Peter Chambliss, yachting reporter for the Baltimore *Sun*, wrote abou her on the day of the race:

> The performance of this last craft will be watched with the closest attention o

...Sparkman and Stephens wrote that White Cloud's *lines were "worked out in conjunction with model tests and certain refinements have been made over earlier designs which, it is hoped, will result in an exceptionally good performance."*

designers, skippers and deep-water sailing yachtsmen, for it is the embodiment of the last word in yacht design. Built especially for this race, this sixty-foot craft of remarkably beautiful lines was started at a Solomons Island shipyard only after exhaustive experiments on models in testing tanks. Though yet almost untried, this graceful yacht, with her towering mast and clouds of snowy canvas, has shown speed as well as great beauty.[14]

White Cloud finished eighth in Class A, more than eleven hours (corrected time) behind the winner Avanti, a new Sparkman and Stephens yawl. George Whiting must have been disappointed by the showing of his new yacht. Yet the relatively poor performance of White Cloud may have been due in large part to poor seamanship even with the famous Sherman Hoyt was at the helm. The Stephens brothers, perfectionists always, knowing the importance of the initial performance of a new yacht, had asked Hoyt to skipper White Cloud's first race. Hoyt was the best. Rainbow, in the America's Cup Races of 1934, a slower boat than Endeavor, had been expertly sailed to victory by him. He was also at the helm of Nina when she won the Fastnet Race in 1926. In his memoirs, Hoyt wrote about White Cloud's performance in her initial blue-water race. He felt that the primary problem was that the crew, including himself, was inexperienced with her characteristics and gear. Hoyt wrote that "the designers had gone rather radical in rig details, probably led astray by 'J' boat practices hardly applicable in many instances to smaller craft."[15] The real cause of her eighth-place finish is candidly revealed in a later paragraph:

We got too much to the westward before reaching the Chesapeake and had a dead beat against a stiff breeze

and head tide before reaching the [Chesapeake] lightship, where in confusion, darkness and excitement, hooking on the forestay went wrong and we were lucky not to lose the mast.[16]

White Cloud had bad luck in her first big race, but her long life, which continues as this book is written, belies any notion that she was an unlucky boat.

George Whiting did not race White Cloud often. Henry Strong, whose father owned Narada, recalled that as a boy growing up on Gibson Island, he and his young friends observed the graceful White Cloud riding her anchor as the rest of the squadron got under way on race weekends. They dreamed of boarding her and sailing her to the starting line. When George Whiting did race, White Cloud performed well. Ted Hoster, owner of Tejeria and Chesapeake correspondent for Yachting, reported in the November 1938 issue:

The Bay classic of the season, the 100-mile race from Gibson Island down to Cedar Point and return, over Labor Day, saw twenty-seven entries in the cruising and racing divisions. Vamarie led the fleet covering the distance in 14:36:03. George Whiting's White Cloud, which made one of her rare appearances in the yachting scene this summer, won on corrected time.[17]

White Cloud beat Vamarie over the finish line by one second in the Poplar Island Race of 1939. Olin Stephens's famous Stormy Weather was third across the finish line, approximately 28 minutes later. The order of finish was the same for corrected time. White Cloud continued her winning ways in the 1939 Cedar Point Race, and she won that race again in 1940.

Rod & Olin Stephens with *White Cloud's* Owner George Whiting   Photographer: Morris Rosenfeld, ©Rosenfeld Collection, Mystic Seaport Museum, Inc.

In the autumn of 1941, as the U.S. prepared for World War II, George Whiting sold *White Cloud* to Charles E. Sorensen of the Detroit Yacht Club. Sorensen, like most every other blue-water sailor on Lake Michigan, wanted the Mackinac Trophy.

The Mackinac Race, first run in 1898, is the oldest annual long-distance race in America. 1904, however, is considered the official date of its origin, when the Chicago Yacht Club sanctioned it and published a list of rules covering the entries. The 1942 race started on July 18. *White Cloud's* winning time, 38:14:05, was the fourth best time over 35 races. The fastest race was won by *Amorita* (31:14:30) in 1911.

A tale about *White Cloud* was told so many times around Solomons that it finally became information on the historical marker at the site of the original Marcellus Mitchell Davis boatyard. The story was that *White Cloud* defeated the Davis-built yawl *Manitou* (described in Chapter 9), the perennial victor of the Chicago to Mackinac Race. Records show, however, that the yachts never raced against each other for the cup. Kenneth

Was it a bad omen that White Cloud's *builder died before she was completed?*

134

roehler, owner of *Manitou* after the war, confirmed that his *Manitou* and *White Cloud* were never matched in the Chicago to Mackinac Race. He recalled, "My first year of racing on Lake Michigan was in 1946. George Sollitt still had *White Cloud* for part of that season. We raced against her a few times when she didn't do too well. *White Cloud* was sold that year to a West Coast yachtsman before the Mackinac Race."[18]

The 1942 Mackinac Race was a wide-open affair as *Manitou* was in moth balls, and *Bangalore* was not entered. The number of competitors dropped to 30 from 52 in 1941. Samuel M. Clarke, the Chicago Yacht Club librarian, reported that the prevailing breeze was fair.[19] Fred Beam, writing in *Yachting*, described the race:

> *White Cloud*, sailing her first season under the ownership of Charles Sorensen of the Detroit Yacht Club, "stole the show" as has no other entry since the inaugural of the race in 1898, finishing first, winning the Mackinac Cup, and even beating the racing division which started two hours ahead of her.[20]

> *White Cloud* used her 3000-foot parachute for the first 200 miles of the race, then about seventy-five miles from the finish the wind veered around to the northwest. With rising seas and the wind blowing forty miles in puffs, a big genoa jib sent her flying into the Straits of Mackinac, and she finished her tremendous 330-mile demonstration at fourteen minutes past five o'clock, Monday morning, taking just over thirty-eight hours to cover the distance.[21]

The shorter Port Huron to Mackinac Race was run on July 11, 1942, and *White Cloud* was the scratch boat. She finished a poor second in Class A, approximately six hours behind *Hostess II*. The race was described in *Rudder* as "the kind of ride you could take your best girl along."[22]

White Cloud was acquired from Charles Sorensen by George Sollitt and Philip Hill of Chicago in 1943, and after the 1943 racing season she was owned by Sollitt. In the 1943 Mackinac Race, which was run at the height of World War II, there were only 20 boats entered and just four, including *White Cloud*, in Class A. The only memorable event of this race was the remarkably similar performances of the competitors in Class A. The four entries stayed close to one another throughout the race, the elapsed time variance between the first (*Trident*) over the line and the last (*Hostess II*) was only eight minutes and 39 seconds in the 330-mile race. *White Cloud*, again scratch boat, was last on corrected time.

For the remaining war years, *White Cloud* was under charter to the United States Navy for one dollar a year. The Navy, which was operating an officer training school at the Chicago campus of Northwestern University, used several of the Chicago Yacht Club yachts for familiarization cruises for the ninety-day midshipmen, most from the midwest and never before aboard anything floating.

White Cloud's racing record on Lake Michigan was short and mixed. While some historians minimize the importance of her 1942 victory to Mackinac Island, one cannot overlook that her time was the fourth best ever. The 1943 Hamilton Club Trophy, awarded to the winner of the Tri-State Race (Van Buren Street in Chicago to St. Joseph; St. Joseph to Michigan City; and Michigan City back to Chicago's Jackson Park), was another of *White Cloud*'s accomplishments. In the three-race set, Sollitt and Hill were able to finish with a first, fourth and third, the best in the fleet.

The 37th and 38th editions of the Mackinac Race were both "drifters," and the winners in the cruising divisions in both years were Class B and C yachts. In 1944 *White Cloud* lost to *Hostess II*, a fifty-two footer. In 1945 she was badly beaten in her division by *Blitzen*, a fifty-six footer, designed by Sparkman and Stephens. The outstanding yacht in both years was *Bangalore Too*, also designed by Olin Stephens.

The year 1987 marked *White Cloud*'s 50th anniversary. While she has raced on the Atlantic Coast and on the Great Lakes, forty of her 50 years have been on the West Coast. Several of her owners have raced her along that coast and in two of the Transpac Races. While her distinctive profile, with its single tall spar, made sailors' eyes glisten, she was never a consistent winner. Over her long career, which had started badly when Sherman Hoyt navigated her in her first ocean race, she might be considered to be a hard-luck vessel; at the very least, a poorly sailed one. The fact that her single most important victory was a wartime Mackinac Race in 1942 adds to the mystery of her true strength. Most racing performances are a combination of factors, and there is little doubt that Rod Stephens's rig made her difficult to sail.

Frank Kent, *White Cloud*'s first West Coast owner, entered her in her tenth season in the 1947 Transpac Race where she finished fourth in the fleet and won third place in her class. Frank Bilek was aboard as navigator and recalls that, "Had we been a hundred miles further south with the boats that beat us, we might have won."[23] Bilek said that *White Cloud* was not raced often by Kent, and when she did race, she was constantly plagued by sail and gear failure. "However, she was not noticeably tender, but tacking in [our usual] strong winds called for a large frantically busy crew."[24]

In 1965, *White Cloud*'s owner was David O'Brian Barclay. She

finished eleventh in her class in the Transpac Race that year. Barclay had bought the cutter just before the race and had redocumented her, as her previous owners had taken her out of documentation between the years 1949 and 1965. It is thought that during that period she had various home ports in Southern California. After Barclay, there were several owners. In 1976, Dr. Jerry Wolohan bought the aging yacht and renamed her *Shamrock*. He brought her back to the San Francisco Bay area where he used her for cruising until 1984.

A boat's life can be extended almost indefinitely if its owner has the will and skill to replace bad wood and start a maintenance program that never allows needed work to go unattended. Considerable time, skill, and money—money to live on and money to buy time and materials—are required. Stephen F. David is one of these fortunate people. Since 1984 he has lavished time, money, and craftsmanship on the old Davis cutter, once again named *White Cloud*. In 1986 his restoration program was completed. He began to think about sailing *White Cloud* around the world.

When asked about the quality of the work of the original construction, David responded matter-of-factly that he considered himself a fine craftsman, but he could not begin to match his work with the perfection of the original construction.

> In the boat, construction is unbelievably good. No matter what ceiling joist you examine, the angles are perfect. Everything that was installed was cut and fitted within $1/32$ of an inch. I am not able to master the quality of the work that originally went into this boat. The fit was flawless.[25]

His restoration started from the bottom up. In every step he endeavored to rebuild her as she was originally. Because of new equipment, modern hardware, and fittings, *White Cloud*

136

stronger today than she was originally.
ays David:

> I will probably own the boat the rest of
> my life. I am the type of person who
> does not like to give up his possessions.
> I have cars and other things that I ac-
> quired when I started. I am sure that
> after the amount of work, always a labor
> of love, I will never be able to sell *White
> Cloud*. Because of her design, and the
> interest in her by other sailors, I know I
> must keep her forever.[26]

A six-cylinder diesel engine now powers
White Cloud smoothly at speeds in excess
of eight knots. Radar, Loran, and other
modern electronic devices were installed by
David as necessary for global circumnaviga-
tion. He says of these changes:

> I had much to learn about my boat. I
> had to make it easier to sail. I did not
> want to change her much, but changes,
> particularly to the size of the mainsail,
> were necessary; a shorter boom by about
> twelve feet, smaller main and better sails.[27]

When interviewed in 1986, David had already
skippered *White Cloud* to victory in seven
consecutive Golden Gate Challenge races on
San Francisco Bay. She is now berthed at the
St. Francis Yacht Club, where her mast towers
above those of the other yachts at the club.
There is a half-model of her in the clubhouse.

White Cloud

Stephen F. David Collection, Calvert Marine Museum.

*Stephen F. David is one of
these fortunate people. Since
1984 he has lavished time,
money, and craftsmanship on
the old Davis cutter, once
again named* White Cloud.

Bilek summarized *White Cloud* best when he said,

> *White Cloud*, unlike so many modern boats, was always under total control and easily sailed with her tiller. Remember, she was a sixty-one foot boat. This speaks well for her hull and sail plans.[28]

Work continued at the Davis yard after *White Cloud* was completed. Clarence Davis had died November 15, 1936, and George H. Townsend had his new management in place by February 1, 1937. J. Barnes Lusby, who had started at the yard in 1915, was general superintendent, and his first major responsibility was construction of the yawl *Manitou*. The laying down had begun in the mold loft during the last quarter of 1936. She was built in the large shed alongside *White Cloud*.

Rod Stephens, Jr., summing up his collaboration with Clarence Davis and the yard, has written:

> We had a most satisfactory relationship with the yard and with Clarence E. Davis and his excellent foreman [J. Barnes Lusby] who did contribute a great deal to the success of that operation.[29]

> On a typical visit for inspection or maybe a trial, I recall that we went across to the yard by boat. Mr. Davis was very cooperative and easy to work with and they did their very best to accomplish just what we recommended.[30]

The boss was gone and it was up to the old hands to rally around Lusby to bring the beautiful *Manitou* to life. John Elliott, Ruby Dixon, the Joy brothers, and others—shipwrights and ship carpenters, natives of Dowell, Olivet, and Solomons—organized themselves into productive teams. They shifted from job to job as the finishing work on *White Cloud* increased and then ebbed. Then they moved on to *Manitou*, first five men, then more and more until the whole yard was working toward her completion under the watchful eye of Robert Henry, Sparkman and Stephens's supervising architect.

9

A Sweet Boat

The physical features of the land, creeks, and coves adjacent to M. M. Davis and Son form the landscape into a storybook setting with deep, small bays and a harbor with a single, narrow entrance at which Solomons Island is situated. This creates a perfect haven for small craft. Before Isaac Solomon arrived, families had been living for generations on these bluffs and coves along the shores of Mill, St. John, and Back creeks, generally isolated by land but connected to the rest of the world by the water at their feet. Members of these communities lived out their lives largely cut off from the changing fortunes of the outside world. Each family was an economic unit, self-contained yet connected to their neighbors by positive and negative circumstances of survival.

Where houses were grouped, villages such as Olivet and Dowell developed. In some cases, families lived miles apart by land but were separated from each other by only a few strokes of an oar. Money for items they could not make themselves came from the catch of the waters of their creeks and the Patuxent River, rich in the wealth of oysters sought by outside markets. The men caught these oysters from September to May in log canoes and larger brogans which they built during the summer using skills passed along by fathers to their sons.

For a long while after Solomons Island became an important oyster shipping point and boatbuilding center, this way of life was little affected by change. The market for oysters grew as improved transportation made them more accessible, increasing the prosperity of these isolated watermen.

Olivet and Dowell remained essentially inaccessible by land to the rest of Maryland, and even to Solomons, long after Solomons was connected to Annapolis by a state highway. Residents of these villages formed the backbone of the group of craftsmen who brought M. M. Davis and Son from a small family-owned yard into the mainstream of American

Davis Craftsmen Arriving at Work

The physical features of the land, creeks, and coves adjacent to M. M. Davis and Son form the landscape into a storybook setting with deep, small bays...

yacht building. These same artisans would continue on without a Davis to lead them.

Family and the Methodist Church controlled the Olivet and Dowell communities. For the most part schooling was lean. In one-room schools the children learned to read, write, and, above all, to calculate measurements for their boats. Circumstances of location and strict parental discipline, supported by the uncompromising laws of a stern church, shaped their lives, molding the men into marvelous wood carvers and craftsmen.

Economic and political separation of these communities usually isolated them from the most important national events. Wars were seen as particular interferences into community life as it was only during these times that the federal government took an interest in them. Their reaction was to ignore such a crisis or to use it for their benefit.

When World War I arrived on Mill Creek in the form of the military draft and large contracts for the Davis yard, the young men of Olivet and Dowell drifted into the new Davis facility across from Solomons to build wooden ships and barges for the war effort. There was probably little patriotism involved, as their choices seemed to them to be either to work at the yard at home or go to war in France. The extensive wartime growth at M. M. Davis and Son provided a pool of skilled men to meet the requirements of the yacht-building years after the close of World War I.

J. Barnes Lusby was born and reared in Olivet. At least five of his brothers worked at one time or another for M. M. Davis and Son. Lusby seldom moved very far from his house, his work, or the surrounding creeks. He attended the little schoolhouse of the village and sat on Sundays in the church built by James T. Marsh, a shipbuilder of earlier times. A quiet man with gentle ways, Lusby acted with conviction in his trade. His leadership asserted itself in his work rather than in words. One of his contemporaries at the yard described him as not the best ship carpenter, not the greatest painter; certainly he was good in the mold loft, and generally he was a good craftsman, but he was not the best craftsman in the yard. His leadership qualities were so special, however, that co-workers spoke of him with a certain reverence. Men of the yachting world who met him remember his many contributions to M. M. Davis and Son. Lusby, the craftsman, never really replaced Davis, the boatbuilder. Time and circumstances had made Davis an entrepreneur. Passing time had molded Barnes Lusby into an artisan.

With Barnes Lusby setting the pace, the men of Olivet, Dowell, and Solomons built *Manitou*. Recalling those times, Rod Stephens, Jr.,

J. Barnes Lusby

Time and circumstances had made Davis an entrepreneur. Passing time had molded Barnes Lusby into an artisan.

141

writing specifically about the contributions of Barnes Lusby, said, "If by chance he is still around, I would love to communicate with him. His contributions were manifold in the same period and I felt a great personal friendship for him."[1]

Chosen by his peers, Lusby was project leader during that long winter of 1937 when Clarence Davis was so sorely missed. *Manitou*'s keel had been laid in the late fall of 1936 after the great bugeye ketch *Ko-Asa* was moved to the finishing dock. Walter Joy, who worked on all three yachts, recalls that the main construction shed accommodated four smaller yachts or two larger ones. Work on *White Cloud* and *Manitou* proceeded slowly as the sure hands and eyes of Lusby and his crew worked their magic under the scrutiny of a nervous designer and two worried owners.

Rod Stephens called *Manitou* a lovely, ocean-racing yawl. She was built for James R. Lowe of Grand Rapids, Michigan. The goal he had set for his new yacht was to win the Mackinac Race, the world's longest fresh-water contest.

Today, at the end of the long wharf at the Harry Lundeberg School of Seamanship at Piney Point, Maryland, sits *Manitou*, easily recognizable as a composite of the unique characteristics of an Olin Stephens-designed yacht. The overriding impression is perfection. The sheer is perfect as it relates to the typical Stephens snub full bow; the hull tapers in a lovely curve to the stern which balances perfectly with the rest of the yacht. One sees something of *Dorade*, *Stormy Weather*, *Avanti*, and the other high-performing yawls of the 1930s that placed the firm of Sparkman and Stephens beyond its competition. For many years, men who wanted to win races felt they needed a boat designed by Olin Stephens and rigged by his brother, Rod Stephens, Jr.

During the winter of 1937, while most of the yard's men worked on completing *White Cloud*, a small crew worked on *Manitou*'s hull. After finishing work in the mold loft, two men were assigned to laying and building her wooden keel and her bow and stern timbers. The slow, exacting work to steam bend her ribs or frames followed. Under the leadership of Olin Joy, oak pieces were placed in the long, wooden box into which live steam was forced. This procedure required placing the box under low pressure so that the wood frame was slowly softened. The time allowed was normally one hour per inch of thickness. After softening, frames were bent into proper shape.

The outside surface of bent frame was then fitted to the inside surface of the fore and aft ribbands, and the heel of the frame was fastened to the floor which had previously been shaped and fastened to the keel. The joisting of the keel to the floor and the floor to the frames provided the means for attaching the keel to the boat. This also provided basic strength to the completed hull, thus preventing wringing when the yacht was driven hard under sail. All of this was done by a small crew of two to six men, depending on the phase of the work. At the same time, another crew was building a mold for the lead keel and pouring the molten lead. With the aid of pulleys and derricks, the lead keel was jacked up into position and bolted to the wooden keel already in place.

The first planks attached to the frames were the top strake and the garboard next to the keel. These are tapered and laid with the run of the boat. *Manitou* has carvel planks, fastened flush at the seams and beveled slightly for proper caulking. According to LeRoy "Pepper" Langley, who started working at the yard in 1937, four men performed this work.

Manitou

The sheer is perfect as it relates to the typical Stephens snub full bow; the hull tapers in a lovely curve to the stern which balances perfectly with the rest of the yacht.

Next, the yacht was caulked, adding strength to the hull and keeping it watertight. At M. M. Davis and Son, the caulking gang were blacks from Olivet, led by John Janey.

After the last plank, called the shutter, was fastened to the frames, longitudinal members were bolted in place and the deck beams, partitions, and built-in furniture made fast. At this point in construction, fuel and water tanks and the engine were put in place before the hull unit was closed in its teak decking. The final phases of construction included joiner work in the cabins, outfitting, stepping the masts, and rigging the boat. These operations were performed by the full crew of the yard.

The completed *Manitou* had six berths and two heads, one for each cabin. She was a beauty inside and out. Below deck she was finished in rare woods. Her cockpit was made of teak. Her main mast towered 81 feet above the water. While her working sails totaled 1,780 square feet, a total of 5,000 feet of sails could be carried on her spars. Her owner registered *Manitou* on August 9, 1937. The carpenter's certificate was signed by J. Barnes Lusby.

Manitou was delivered too late in the racing season for James Lowe to reach Lake Michigan for the big race. Lowe, a member of the New York Yacht Club, sailed north after leaving Solomons and kept *Manitou* on the East Coast for the remainder of the year. A half-model of *Manitou* hangs in the taproom of the New York Yacht Club, which indicates that she was entered in a club-sanctioned race in 1937.[2]

Manitou's debut in Lake Michigan was the Columbia Yacht Club's 47th annual race to Michigan City.[3] No doubt there were other races for *Manitou* before the July 23 start of the Chicago to Mackinac Race in 1938. For Jim Lowe, the excitement was intense, as he prepared for the race for which *Manitou* had been designed and built.

Forty-six yachts were at the starting line for the 31st edition of the Mackinac Race. In 1938 there were three divisions for the 333-nautical-mile run down Lake Michigan to the Mackinac Straits. This race is a supreme test of seamanship and sailing skill. It has been the most important reason for the development of yacht-racing of all classes on Lake Michigan, the leading event attracting fine yachtsmen and fast boats to the Midwest. After a good start, Lowe sailed *Manitou* up the west shore. The breeze was out of the northeast. About ten miles out, *Manitou* picked up a good wind and made "money."[4] On Sunday, July 24, the winds held, but that night she lost her spinnaker in a squall. A writer on board reported that the steering wheel, which had considerable play at the start, worsened as the race progressed. "But *Manitou* kept on driving, going places. Using the strongest of the winds and most of her sails."[5] Finally, the wheel became unmanageable and the metal emergency tiller was broken out and used in tandem with the wheel.

The Coast Guard patrol boat *Rush*, stationed at North Manitou Island, reported the yachts as they were sighted. At this point in the race, about 100 miles from the finish, the North and South Manitou Islands are separated from the Michigan mainland by the Manitou Passage. The *Rush* reported that the first yacht into the passage was *Manitou*. It was one of those classic moments in sports and a moment of high excitement for Jim Lowe and his crew as the yacht entered the waters of her name. *Manitou* followed her script to the word and finished her first Mackinac Race almost six hours ahead of the second yacht, *Maruffa*. Her elapsed time was 45:05:49;

er corrected time was 44:18:34, still best by over three hours. Entered in the cruising division, *Manitou* was awarded the 1938 Chicago to Mackinac Trophy. The Mackinac Cup, awarded in alternating years to the racing and cruising divisions, went to the winner of the racing division in 1938.

In the 1939 Chicago to Mackinac Race, *Manitou* lost the lead to the 71-foot *Windigo* by four minutes. Both lost on corrected time to *Bangalore*. *Windigo* was another big yawl from drawings by Sparkman and Stephens, Inc. While almost ten feet longer overall than *Manitou*, she lacked her speed. James Lowe and *Manitou* were first across the finish line in the Chicago to Mackinac Races of 1940 and 1941, but in both years other yachts were rated winners on the basis of their longer time handicaps.

At this point in the race, about 100 miles from the finish, the North and South Manitou Islands are separated from the Michigan mainland by the Manitou Passage. The Rush *reported that the first yacht into the passage was Manitou.*

Manitou

Photographer: Edwin Levick, The Mariners' Museum Collection.

145

Although his particular goal had been the coveted Chicago to Mackinac Race, Lowe, a Michigan native, must have gained particular pleasure from his victories in the annual Port Huron to Mackinac Island Race in 1939 and 1940. At the time, the all-Michigan race was sailed on a 204-nautical-mile course the length of Lake Huron, and was seventy miles shorter than the Chicago to Mackinac Race. The course along Michigan's shoreline made the race a popular spectator event, with families gathering along the beaches to picnic and to view its progress. It was first sailed on July 15, 1925. *Manitou*, with Lowe at the helm, won the 1939 race with a corrected time of 48:41:08 for the course. However in 1940 the beautiful yawl really kicked up her heels and led the fleet with an astounding winning time of 32:45:21, the best ever for the race, and a record that stood until 1946. In the 1941 race *Manitou* was second in Class A behind *Kitty Hawk* on corrected time, although *Manitou* was first to cross the finish line.

When World War II began, Lowe stopped racing *Manitou*. After the war, *Manitou*'s new owner Ken Kroehler entered her in the Mackinac Race for the next 10 years. Heavily handicapped and outperformed by newer yachts, she never won again. Ken Kroehler claims, however, that her best Chicago to Mackinac Race was in 1953:

It was a light, directly downwind race. *Manitou* is a rather heavy, narrow, deep-keel boat, built to go to windward. She had a ⅞" fore triangle which means a small spinnaker, so I decided we had no chance trying to run straight downwind. We started tacking, and I guess we got lucky on our angles, as we and *Escapade* slowly pulled ahead of the fleet. *Escapade* is a seventy-two foot centerboard yawl, and with her bowsprit and masthead rig, she carried a huge spinnaker. She was running dead downwind and each time we crossed the line, we were anywhere from one-hundred yards to a half-mile astern. Entering Gray's Reef Passage the morning of the last day, we were less than one-hundred feet behind. About two or three miles from the finish, we could see a heavy squall approaching from the south. *Escapade* dropped her light sails but we decided to hang our chute on the hope it would last long enough to beat her in. It lasted fifteen seconds and *Escapade* was first over though we beat her on corrected time. But, as often happens in yacht races, the rest of the fleet, far behind, had picked up the heavy wind hours before it hit us and *Manitou* was not able to hold her time and win the race.

Manitou was surprisingly fast in smooth water and a light breeze. With a sloppy sea and a light breeze, she wouldn't go very well. With more, she was good on wind and reaching. She was a little tender in a heavy breeze and probably would have been stiffer and faster with a modern metal spar. Her mainmast was very strong and quite heavy. The rig was tall and the weight helped to make her somewhat tender.

Her hull was extraordinarily tight and dry. Actually the bilge was usually "dusty" and we used an ordinary vacuum cleaner on it many times. About the only times we had had extra pumping was from deck leakage before I recaulked the deck with the newer type of rubber seam compound.[6]

Ken Kroehler raced *Manitou* in almost all of the races on Lake Michigan from 1946 until he delivered her to the Coast Guard in 1956. No complete record was kept of her victories and misses. She won the George Owens Clinch Trophy

vice—once for Lowe in 1938, and again in
1948 when skippered by Ken Kroehler. She
won the Shelton Clark Trophy in 1946 and
again in 1953. In 1948 Kroehler sailed *Manitou*
to victory in the annual Tri-State Labor Day
Race and was awarded the Hamilton Club
Trophy. Then, in 1953, she won the James
Offield Perpetual Trophy.

Like several other Olin Stephens yachts of
the 1930s, *Manitou* was not a single-purpose
racing machine. Of solid, rather heavy construction, her beauty and functional design
combined with a sailing ability that made
her a comfortable cruiser and an efficient
racer. Below, she was much more than just
gear lockers and pipe berths. The luxurious
interior woodwork of butternut in *Manitou*'s
main cabin was in the grand tradition of rich
living on the water. Says Kenneth Kroehler,
"The finish looked ¼" thick and not a dust
mark anywhere. Best of all was the way it
lasted. All we did was keep it clean."[7] The
owner's double cabin was aft of the com-
panionway ladder and very private. Forward
was a large galley with all necessary equipment. In the bow section are the gear lockers and crew's quarters with their own washing
and toilet facilities.

*"Manitou was surprisingly fast
in smooth water and a light
breeze."*

Manitou

Photographer: Morris Rosenfeld, ©Rosenfeld Collection, Mystic Seaport Museum, Inc.

147

By 1956, when Kroehler gave *Manitou* to the United States Coast Guard Academy at New London, she had established a fine record in her long career on the Great Lakes. Yet there would be more good races and even an occasional victory.

An older sailing-racing machine, built to the design requirements of the racing rules and of an ambitious owner, can become an over-aged embarrassment. This was not true of *Manitou*. The functional qualities of comfort in cruising or casual sailing on Sunday afternoons gave her a certain ageless class and beauty. Her distinctive lines and wooden spars, carrying 2,000 or more square feet of sail, produced an eye-pleasing sight much as does a fine piece of architecture. Through the years she gained respect and admiration. This senior lady of sailing took her place easily among the academy fleet and became the leading racing representative of the cadets of the Coast Guard school.

Manitou arrived east and was passed as fit for the 1956 Newport to Bermuda Race. Her former owner, Ken Kroehler, was along for the ride and described *Manitou*'s performance:

> After a start with almost no wind, it quickly started to build and by evening we had about all the wind we wanted. It turned out to be about the fastest race they had had, at least up to that time. The wind was a steady 30-35 knots with apparent wind forward of the beam. I am quite certain the wind hit 50 or more at times. It was a rough, wet ride going over one Gulf Stream sea and through the next with a couple of feet of green water coming down the deck. It was the kind of sailing that would be great for a few hours, but when it goes on steadily for 70 hours it becomes a little bit tiring. We broke the old elapsed time record and *Bolero*, a 73 footer,

set a new one. In spite of a delay at the start and a tactical mistake in navigation near the finish, we did quite well in the race.[8]

On corrected time, *Manitou* finished seventh in Class A approximately two hours behind the Class A winner, *Nina*. She beat a number of younger yachts and finished five hours before the other big Coast Guard Academy yawl, *Petrel*. Overshadowing all the other fine performances that year, however, was Carlton Mitchell's first of three Bermuda victories in *Finisterre*.

Gifts of large sailboats to the service academies have brought important benefits to both the yachts and the schools. Maintenance costs of wooden yachts rise with their years, making them prohibitively expensive for private individuals. Yachts donated to the academies in the 1950s received what amounted to a second life. Midshipmen trained on refurbished yachts benefited by becoming an active part of the racing world, participating in a fine, competitive tradition. Furthermore, the academies gained by receiving positive publicity by participating in the great races, win or lose, most frequently the latter. Their entries were handicapped by time, by new rules, and by the rapidly changing technology of rigging, electronics, and design. Added to these handicaps were budget limitations on upkeep and purchase of new sails, the latter being an expense that the civilian blue-water sailor accepts as an unavoidable requirement of a winning boat.

Manitou had entered the Bermuda Race twenty years after she left her builder's yard and made a good showing among the best, proof that she was well designed by Olin Stephens and beautifully built at M. M. Davis and Son. She was back in ewport in 1958 for the start of the Bermuda Race. Her skipper was Lt. Commander Lawrence A. White of the Coast Guard who described the race to President Kennedy some years later.

Manitou was out ahead a good part of the way as we hit the rhumb line just right. There were alternate periods of calm, after a strong breeze at the start, then sixty miles from the finish at David's Head, a hard knockdown squall hit and blew out the old mains'l that came with the boat in 1955. That ended our chances.[9]

n the 1960 Bermuda Race Manitou did not perform well, nishing well down in the fleet. It was a small boat's race. he winner, third time around, was Finisterre.

While Manitou had been a star on Lake Michigan, by 1962, n eastern waters, she was just another aging warrior in the Coast Guard fleet. But fate turned her career around once gain. She became the first choice of the aides of the President of the United States in a search for a blue-water sailing acht for John F. Kennedy. While the President's aides followed certain guidelines, ultimately Manitou's functional beauty ained her the selection. As summarized by Kennedy, no ovice at sea, "She is a sweet boat."[10]

was partly because of what Manitou was not, however, hat helped her gain the President's acceptance. He did not vant a pretentious yacht requiring a large crew while he sat n the afterdeck viewing her monotonous wake.

ohn F. Kennedy had handled small sailing boats all his life nd had raced as a youngster. At Harvard he was rated mong the best when he won the coveted McMillian Cup.

An honest-to-goodness sailor, his past experiences made him ache for the discomfort of a good sail. Hard work, fear, and disappointments, all prerequisite to a good race or a successful cruise were the real reasons that led to the selection of Manitou, a true blue-water yawl.

Little has been written about John F. Kennedy's days aboard her. The arrangements were elaborate involving the Secret Service, the Navy, and the Coast Guard. There was little press coverage of those days of private relaxation at the helm of the old yawl. To insure security at sea a certain amount of secrecy was necessary. A Coast Guard crew, two Secret Service men, and Kennedy's friends or family sailed aboard Manitou. The only other frequent member of the official party was a White House photographer who took glorious photographs of the photogenic Kennedy. A bond was soon to form between the President and the yawl. A part of John F. Kennedy, like most others who seek freedom and pleasure at the helm of a sailboat, was reserved for the sea. It is a passion that puts a person on a higher level the moment the foot crosses the gap between a stable dock and a floating deck. Under way, a sailor must interpret the wind and will of the sea. To accomplish this, he shifts the focus of his senses to catch the changing notes of nature's songs. Kennedy knew well those tunes.

A competitive man, Kennedy wanted to race Manitou. His security staff, however, advised that racing situations, such as at a crowded starting line or on a course beyond sight of land, made security impossible. While the President was able to schedule a surprising number of days at sea, particularly in 1962, there were long periods of inactivity for Manitou. This allowed her to return to the Coast Guard Academy for an occasional race. In early February 1963, after a complete

John F. Kennedy on *Manitou*   Photographer: Robert Knudsen.

*A bond was soon to form
between the President and
the yawl.*

maintenance overhaul which included removing and replacing
all of *Manitou*'s screws and fastenings, her Coast Guard crew
entered her in the Miami to Nassau Race. She was forced to
withdraw because of a broken head-stay. She did enter and
finish seventh in the short Lipton Cup Race; and she repeated
the same finish in the Governor's Cup Race on February 14, 1963.

The following summer she raced in the Newport to Annapolis Race, and on August 17 she was at the starting line for
the 185-mile Nantucket Lightship Race. Thirteen yachts were
entered in Class A. With winds that varied from light to gale
force, *Manitou* led the fleet around the lightship. Under gale
force conditions, the President's yacht increased her lead with
reefed mainsail, crossing the finish line seven hours before
the second yacht. Once again, *Manitou* demonstrated that
she was endowed with a combination of features that allowed
her to continue to win after 26 years, a period in which
design and technological developments changed boats and
gear more than in all the preceding centuries of the development of the fore-and-aft rig. Following the race, the victo-
rious *Manitou* returned at dawn to Newport, reportedly
observed by Kennedy from the beach of the mansion where
he was staying.

Late summer and fall at the White House in 1963 were no
easy times, and Kennedy was able to sail only infrequently.
Manitou was ferried once more to Florida for the winter.
The shooting at Dallas in November tragically ended Kennedy's
life, and *Manitou* was returned to the Coast Guard Academy
fleet to resume her former role. Here she remained for several
years. She never stopped racing, she never stopped winning.
In 1964 *Manitou* won the Martha's Vineyard Race, and in
1967 she was first in the Corinthian Race. In between, she
was always able to give a good account of herself at Annapolis,
Bermuda, and Block Island.

*ate summer and fall at the
Vhite House in 1963 were not
asy times, and Kennedy was
ble to sail only infrequently.*

President Kennedy

Photographer: Robert Knudsen, Kennedy Library Collection.

151

As her annual maintenance bill rose, the Coast Guard's ability to keep her in racing condition declined. In April 1968 the government sold her at auction. The winning bid was placed by the Seafarers International Union, which wanted to use her for the Harry Lundeberg School at Piney Point, Maryland. Here, at the junction of the Potomac and St. Mary's River, just a few miles from Solomons Island where she was built in 1937 by Barnes Lusby and the other men of M. M. Davis and Son, *Manitou* is berthed at the end of the school's dock.

Manitou was briefly returned to the headlines when Aristotle Onassis, owner of a fleet of tankers, attempted to buy her from the union. Onassis, whose fleet sailed under foreign flags of convenience, was engaged to Jacqueline Kennedy, the widow of the President. She had placed this powerful man in an untenable situation by requesting *Manitou* as a wedding present. Though Onassis offered the seamen's union any price they named, to a union of American seamen he was one of a group who had destroyed the United States Merchant Marine. Selling to him would have been akin to

trading with the enemy in wartime. *Manitou* was not to be Jacqueline Onassis's wedding gift.

Manitou remains one of the school's fleet of historic vessels which include a bugeye, a skipjack, and many other boats, both sail and power. Except for the small craft, most are never put to sea. *Manitou*, pride of the fleet, has been used to drill the school's trainees in seamanship and the traditions of the sea. She is worn, but not neglected. Her teak decks, great spars, and everything below deck are the original wood used by the builder. Her bilges are dry, but her 18 years at Piney Point have turned her butternut cabins dark as time saps her strength gradually, almost unnoticeably, until today she is delicate where once there were strong frames and a sound hull.

The order from James Lowe to build *Manitou* was received at M. M. Davis and Son before Clarence Davis died. His death came just after the laying of her keel. Her construction was the work of his skillful team—their accomplishments a testimonial to his leadership.

The Talk of the Town

As the summer of 1937 arrived and the stately *Manitou* was fitted out, George Townsend realized that along with the death of Clarence Davis had come the demise of custom yacht construction at M. M. Davis and Son, Inc. The yard received only one order for a yacht beyond those already under construction in 1936 at the time Davis died. This was the motor cruiser *Spree*, a twin diesel vessel of 37 feet, built for Edward K. Warren of Greenwich, Connecticut.[1] Townsend, a successful businessman, sensed that delay would bring disaster to the yard which had come under his ownership earlier that year.

George Townsend's principal interest, other than speedboat racing, was the motor sailer, a type of vessel that was becoming increasingly popular. He commissioned Olin Stephens to design a class of these comfortable cruising boats. He also ordered his resident manager, G. Gunther Wallen, to prepare the

ways to build six, even though he had no buyers for any of them at the time the project was initiated. His goal was to avoid a work stoppage and losing his key men—craftsmen who, if lost, were irreplaceable.

Surviving records of M. M. Davis and Son, Inc., indicate that Townsend was a man of great energy with a deep interest in boating and yachting. As time passed, he may have regretted reaching beyond the automotive industry where he had gained some fame and fortune. There is no doubt that owning M. M. Davis and Son, Inc., brought him many agonizing problems, though over the long run he was successful at Solomons. Few other men could have followed Davis and survived. Townsend had retired as president of the Boyce Motometer Company when he acquired M. M. Davis and Son from Mrs. Davis in January 1937. His success had brought him prominence in the business world and had allowed him time to pursue his hobbies on the water—racing high-speed power boats and cruising in his motor sailers, first *Cheerio*, then *Cheerio Too.*

Like most businessmen he was very competitive, and on the water this made him one of the country's leading speedboat drivers. A profile appeared in *Yachting* in November 1927 and the following excerpt summarizes his racing activities:

> When the Gold Cup was brought East in 1924, Townsend entered the list of challengers the next year with *"Miss Motometer."* Dogged by hard luck, he was not able to get into the Gold Cup event that year, as his boat turned over just before the race. Far from being discouraged, he had some changes made in his craft, changed the name to *Greenwich Folly*, and the following year he came through beating a fleet of fourteen starters and winning the Gold Cup. Racing at Washington for the President's Cup, *Folly* bowed to *Cigarette IV*, but this year [1927], faster than ever, she again won the Gold Cup.[2]

In 1934 Townsend was president of the American Power Boat Association. Not until 1935 did he first learn about M. M. Davis and Son. He had acquired his first motor sailer, *Cheerio*, some years after she was built in 1923 from a design by Charles D. Mower. When Townsend decided to replace *Cheerio* with *Cheerio Too*, he went to Mower for his plans and to M. M. Davis and Son in 1935 to have her built.

The motor sailer had become increasingly popular after World War I when engines became more reliable and powerful for their size. Many articles have been written about the type, and much time has been spent defining the real thing. Since these boats are built for comfortable cruising, they are

the personal manifestations of their owners. Comfort is usually the common denominator. From that point the variation depend on owner preference for sail or motor. Townsend' *Cheerio Too* was designed to carry 906 square feet of sail and she was built with a centerboard housed below the floor Obviously, Townsend wanted a motor sailer's comfort, bu he also wanted her to really sail! *Cheerio Too* was rigged a a ketch and measured 48 feet, 6 inches overall, with a beam of only 12 feet, 6 inches. She was reportedly a fine sailer.

Clarence Davis delivered *Cheerio Too* in June 1935. Town send liked the boat and used her for about four years, doing some long-distance cruising. Always the competitor, he raced her on Long Island Sound in the 320-mile Fire Island Race sponsored by the Larchmont Yacht Club. *Rudder* wrote about her performance in September 1936:

> *Cheerio Too* is a motor sailer and hardly the average man's idea of an ocean racer, but she showed a surprising ability under sail until forced to withdraw by illness of one of the crew.[3]

Later, in 1938, many of the characteristics of *Cheerio Too* were designed into the "Crusailer," the Sparkman and Stephens motor sailer that Townsend ordered built on speculation

As the new owner of M. M. Davis and Son, Townsend seldom came to Solomons but used the Davis office on 42nd Street in New York City to direct the affairs of the corporation. He had originally hired William Edgar Johns, a naval architect who had been Clarence Davis's New York representative, as general manager. G. Gunther "Gunny" Wallen, Townsend's son-in-law, was the yard's resident manager. Johns did not stay long, and within a few months the management team consisted of Townsend, Wallen, and Barnes Lusby as general superintendent at the yard. Clara Brooks, Clarence Davis's secretary, became the firm's secretary and treasurer.

The Sparkman and Stephens Crusailer, which Townsend placed into production as the last of the Davis yachts moved out, was a ketch approximately 41 feet overall, and was similar in profile to Mower's *Cheerio Too*. With a waterline length of almost 36 feet, and a beam of eleven feet, four inches, her sail area of 606 square feet made her a real sailer, in keeping with Townsend's philosophy of the design. Under motor, she was a nine miles-per-hour power boat. Her original outside ballast was 7,000 pounds, but this weight was increased after the first trials.

When Townsend decided to replace Cheerio *with* Cheerio Too, *he went to Mower for his plans and to M. M. Davis and Son in 1935 to have her built.*

Cheerio Too

Photographer: Morris Rosenfeld, ©Rosenfeld Collection, Mystic Seaport Museum, Inc.

Townsend placed his hopes and his money on the motor sailer, but nothing went well for the project. During the same period, the Annapolis Yacht Yard commissioned Charles Mower to design a series of motor sailers which were placed on the market in competition with the Crusailer. Additional competition for the local market came from Ralph Wiley's yard in Oxford as he, too, began producing motor sailers. Most of all, the times hurt the boat as Europe moved into World War II; the seas were uninviting to those of the yachting public who may have been interested in having a motor sailer to cruise southward into international waters.

At $12,500 Townsend's motor sailers were difficult to sell. The company was forced into an expensive sales and advertising campaign, one that necessitated having a demonstrator at City Island in New York. It took nearly two years to sell the six yachts, named by their original owners *Gray Ghost*, *Awab*, *Cygnet*, *Tui-Hana*, *Moon Maid*, and *Down Wind*. At least two, *Down Wind* and *Cygnet*, were still sailing in 1988.

The Sparkman and Stephens Crusailer, which Townsend placed into production as the last of the Davis yachts moved out, was a ketch approximately 41 feet overall, and was similar in profile to Mower's Cheerio Too.

Ariadne, ex-Cygnet

Photographer: Edwin Levick, The Mariners' Museum Collection.

Downwind is owned by the Dash family of Annapolis.[4] Tom Dash is a professional sailor who lives on his Crusailer with his family. They bought *Downwind* in 1980 and have worked continually to keep her in fine condition. Jean Dash reports that they replaced the decks, the pilot house frame, and in 1981 spent nine months taking her hull down to the wood. While doing this work, they replaced some butt blocks and gave her a new transom.

Our opinion is that the boat, if properly cared for, will last another forty-eight years. She is quiet and forgiving under sail. Twenty-five knots of wind is perfect for a nice *Downwind* sail.

People stare and smile when Tom tells them she's an older Sparkman & Stephens design. They think all S & S boats were high-tech racers. If you are a "woodie" you can't dislike the butternut interior of this vessel which has all natural knees and meticulous cabinetry. She gives off a very warm comforting feeling.[5]

Cygnet, now named *Antares*, won first place, the Best of Sail, at the Chicago International Wooden Boat Show in 1986. This Crusailer is owned by Margie and Dave Grow who live aboard several months each year. Home is Rensselaer, Indiana, and for the past 12 years they have been sailing her into every port on Lake Michigan. Winter home for *Antares* is New Buffalo, Michigan.

Downwind

Photographer: Jean Dash, Calvert Marine Museum Collection.

"People stare and smile when Tom tells them she's an older Sparkman & Stephens design. They think all S & S boats were high-tech racers."

Townsend's courageous initiative resulted in losses that strained the slim assets of the small company. The only pleasure he could gain from his project was the favorable comments of the industry. A reporter for *Yachting* sailed on a Crusailer and wrote:

> The engine was cut off as we filled away before the wind and she started to slide along at a good clip, a conservative estimate, almost seven knots. We were probably traveling within a knot or a little over of the speed of any sailboat of the same waterline length. We'll grant that the boat should have performed very well under those conditions. The real test, however, came when we flattened her down for a beat back to our starting point. She went to windward beautifully—not slowly, getting there eventually —but stepping right out, holding high to the wind and moving right along as if her designer hadn't given a thought to her power equipment until his lines had been completed.[6]

After construction of the last of the Crusailers, the yard on Mill Creek found itself in serious trouble. As the months passed, the labor force was reduced or had drifted away to other jobs. Orders were received for a couple of fishing trawlers and for one custom yacht. The yacht was for J. B. White, owner of the Columbia Peanut Company of Norfolk, Virginia. William H. Hand, Jr., designed the motor sailer and contracted for her construction with M. M. Davis and Son, Inc. No photographs of this yacht have been located, but there is reference to her in the March 1938 issue of *Rudder*, which lists her as an unnamed motor sailer, 51'8" overall, 48'5" WL, 14'6" beam, and 4'10" draft,

with a sloop rig.[7] As White had her documented under the name *Whitecap*, she can be traced through various owners until 1976, when she was renamed *Sharks Tooth*, and her owner obtained a mortgage to pay for her from the National Bank of St. Petersburg for $63,000. Then, according to Coast Guard records, the yacht and owner were never heard from again.

Another boat built under Townsend was the motor sailer *Cheerio Tree*, originally designed as a larger version of the Crusailer, but, when completed as Townsend's dream yacht, she was another Sparkman and Stephens design success. Olin Stephens stamped his special style on the yawls he designed after *Dorade*, which included the famous Davis-built yacht *Manitou*. Similarly, but with less fanfare, he created a new class of motor sailers. His first efforts, such as *Kiboko* and *Diana*, both built at Solomons, were similar to those that had preceded them in the yachting world. They were heavy-bodied motor boats designed to have their sails used downwind or at least, abaft the beam. The Crusailers, too, were basically motor boats but were designed to be sailed more consistently. By the time *Cheerio Tree* was finished, Stephens had created a new type of motor sailer. The bulky look of the old motor sailers was eliminated. Her high freeboard, deckhouse, and conservative sail plan on a ketch rig made her resemble a motor sailer, but critics at the time wanted to call her an auxiliary because she had a slick, slippery look when she flew her 1,239 feet of canvas.

Like Stephens's yawls, *Cheerio Tree* was a handsome boat with a balanced hull that featured the pronounced sheer of her racing cousins. Her controls, wheel, and binnacle were in the cockpit abaft the mizzen in the traditional auxiliary fashion. Her stand-by controls were in the deckhouse, which in motor sailer fashion was furnished with living room furniture, including a small piano for Mrs. Townsend. The layout included a galley and forecastle in her forward area, followed by the main cabin, then an engine room. In her aft section was a large stateroom with two berths, lockers, and a separate bathroom. George Townsend built her as his own yacht, thus providing the yard with work during the winter of 1939.

The year 1939 was a difficult one, and hard times in the yacht world put M. M. Davis and Son, Inc., in financial jeopardy. War fears ruined the market for new yachts. Yet there were exceptions that kept some of the men working even as the firm lost money. Harry MacDonald, a yacht broker, commissioned Philip Rhodes to design a small sloop which he hoped to sell in quantity to the weekend cruising crowd. Two of these yachts, just over 27 feet in length, were built by Davis in 1939. *Valmer*, the first of the "Little Sister" class, was built at Solomons for Edward L. Valier of Palm Beach, although the order was actually placed by Harry MacDonald. The sloop was a typically neat Rhodes design. To accommodate a couple on a weekend cruise with comfort, Rhodes designed a prominent doghouse with large windows which gave her occupants full head room, an innovation for a small yacht. She was only 22 feet at the waterline and 8 feet, 3 inches at the beam, so having full head room gave her owners considerably more space.

The price for *Valmer* was $3,100 less MacDonald's commission. The yard's actual labor cost was $1,419, almost 50 percent of the purchase price. Townsend figured his loss on *Valmer* at $512.88. Naturally, he was not pleased when he was told that the yard had accepted a second contract at the same price. Work began on the second "Little Sister" in March of 1939. She was built for George Marshall Jones, Jr., of Annapolis who named her *Pinard*. She was to be the first of three yachts he would order from M. M. Davis and Son, Inc.

During the first quarter of 1939 the yard was busy, but George Townsend foresaw trouble ahead. On March 13 he wrote:

> I am delighted to know that the yard is buzzing along merrily, but on the other hand, I feel that a certain amount of it is work on borrowed time, namely my *Cheerio Tree*, my pedal boats, and the work on the Crusailer for Dr. Kelly, which has already been paid for. However, it is nice to know that things are buzzing, and I feel that everybody is getting so much more in the spirit of working fast that we may be able to get somewhere.[8]

"Pedal boats" referred to a contract for a number of pontoon foot-pedal boats for the New York World's Fair. M. M. Davis and Son, Inc., built this order plus several lots for amusement parks.

Business did not improve at the yard even though some money was made on the pedal boats and losses were cut a little on *Pinard*. No new work materialized. As the labor force drifted away from the yard, craftsmen became difficult to find. The younger men, who had been let go in 1938 and 1939, had found other jobs as economic activity picked up, fueled by an increase in military orders. Barnes Lusby wrote Townsend on October 20, 1939, that while work continued slowly on *Cheerio Tree*,

> we do not figure on stopping your boat for anything and we do honestly believe that we can find men when they know there is definite work for a definite period of time. They are discouraged at present because they were expecting plenty of work here in the yard under the present set-up, and this summer and fall many of them had little or none.[9]

In 1939 the wage scale for the most experienced ship carpenters was 60 cents per hour. While this was less than one-half the

Pinard

Harry MacDonald, a yacht broker, commissioned Philip Rhodes to design a small sloop which he hoped to sell in quantity to the week-end cruising crowd.

ate earned during World War I, it was still six times higher than at the start of the century, and there had been no improvement in productivity over the years. The extreme care and perfection that Clarence Davis had demanded in yacht work may have caused a decline in productivity. Townsend complained frequently about this double-edged problem. He felt that the methodical search for an unreachable level of craftsmanship played havoc with the company's profits. Times had changed only slightly at Solomons during the first third of the 20th century, but as World War II approached, the rate of change accelerated. The old ways of working and the rates of pay became increasingly unmanageable.

Yacht building was finished for the duration. The war in Europe, however, provided opportunities for M. M. Davis and Son, Inc., to bid on military contracts. Yet the yard faced another problem—the impracticality of bidding on government work. There were no funds to pay for performance bonds or to advance for the cost of materials for work that would not be paid for until completion. The company was now on the brink of bankruptcy. Resident manager Wallen wrote his father-in-law on October 10, 1939:

> I have given your letter of last week the deepest consideration and I feel that it would be foolish to consider bankruptcy at this time, our creditors are not pushing us to that extent.[10]

One positive event for M. M. Davis and Son, Inc., in 1939 was that the Calvert County Commissioners contracted to have an all-weather road built to the yard. Unbelievably, it came 26 years after Marcellus Mitchell Davis had opened the facility on Mill Creek just before World War I. During this long period direct deliveries by truck were possible only when the rutted road was frozen!

Davis of Solomons survived these lean times. Townsend's dream yacht, *Cheerio Tree*, was outfitted and delivered. Fortunately for the yard, he lavished his money and time on the planning and construction of the yacht. Olin Stephens had designed an extremely attractive motor sailer with fine sailing capabilities. She beat the Stephens-designed cruiser/racing yawl *Avanti* (which had beaten *White Cloud* to win the 1937 New London to Gibson Island Race) on June 10, 1941. *Rudder* reported the event in its August 1941 issue.

> The portly motor sailer, *Cheerio Tree*, caused all the excitement when she roared across the finish line first in her class, crowding-out the slim racing yawl *Avanti* by three minutes in elapsed time. *Cheerio Tree* is 54 feet, 8 inches overall; *Avanti* is a foot longer in a range where every foot makes a difference in speed, and also carried an additional 136 square feet of sail. Yet, in spite of this advantage, *Cheerio Tree*, with her spacious hotel accommodations, piano and all, romped away and reached the finish first.[11]

Why *Cheerio Tree* instead of "Three"? According to John G. Earle, who asked her owner, she got her name because Mrs. Townsend, whose native language was Russian, could not handle the English sound "th."

Cheerio Tree was later owned by Philip Mallory, a fine sailor and member of the shipping family active with the Mystic Seaport Museum in Connecticut. Near the end of her career the handsome ketch was used on treasure hunting expeditions. Like so many other fine yachts, she disappeared leaving no marked grave. There is a fine oil painting of her in the collection at the Mystic Seaport Museum.

The last yacht built by M. M. Davis and Son, Inc., prior to World War II was a ketch, *Mike*, designed by John G. Alden (No. 718).

161

Cheerio Tree

Built for George Marshall Jones, Jr., who had purchased the Rhodes-designed sloop *Pinard* from Davis two years earlier, she was 44' overall, 32'6" at the waterline, 12' beam, and had a draft of 6'3". More than one yacht was built from this Alden design which became known as the "Pussy Willow" class. *Mike* sailed under several owners and with several names: *Kim*, *Vision II*, *Compass Rose*, and *Axia*. This yacht is another example of the good fortune of finding preservation through caring owners. Alfred Stanford renamed her *Vision II* and owned the ketch for several years in the 1950s. Joseph Wadsworth was her owner for about twenty-five years. Then Leslie L. Youngblood of New York City and William G. Winterer of Essex, Connecticut, bought *Compass Rose* in 1975 and restored the Alden-designed yacht. Much of her, from the gammon iron on the bowsprit to the fastenings on her boomkin, has been replaced or rebuilt, though her original planking and decks survive. She was renamed *Axia*, and the yacht and her owners received the Certificate of Excellence for 1989 from the Mystic Seaport Museum. (See frontispiece.)

Olin Stephens had designed an extremely attractive motor sailer with fine sailing capabilities.

162

hortly after *Mike* was completed, the Japanese attacked 'earl Harbor. The effect of the war on Solomons was lescribed by a correspondent in the Baltimore *Sunday Sun* n July 17, 1943:

There could scarcely have been a community anywhere in the country that was worse prepared for the changes brought about by war. War did not come to Solomons Island gradually, but it hit it a sudden and terrific wallop. The Navy let contracts for several big projects in the neighborhood. Outside labor poured in, prices soared, and the old life was torn up by the roots.[12]

Vith big military contracts from the Army Transportation Corps came a new lease on life. M. M. Davis and Son, Inc., vas profitably humming again after three years on the verge of bankruptcy. Labor was no longer a problem. Men were eager o work in an industry so critical to the war effort because nilitary deferments were almost automatic. Once employed by the shipyard, the men, who were often paid less by M. M. Davis and Son, Inc., compared with wages of the new military ontractors in the area, were forbidden to switch companies.

More than fifty 65-foot wooden personnel craft, called T-boats," were built, as were larger wooden freight and assenger craft. For the first time production lines were set p to build the military craft. This change became perma- ent in the postwar era as the assembly line replaced the ge-old craftsman approach of shifting skilled artisans from ob to job as construction of a vessel advanced. M. M. Davis nd Son, Inc., won several "E" awards for its war work.

Custom boatbuilding did not cease completely during the var. America became responsible for feeding much of the

world. New fishing fleets were built to help accomplish the job. Davis-built trawlers for the fishery trade included: in 1943, *Elsie Jane*, *Rowe*, and *Betty and David*; in 1944, *Ann Bryan*, *Judith Fay*, *North Wind*, and *Bessie Ann*; and in 1945, *Choctaw* and *Gannet*. The yard built *McClain's Pride No. 1* and *McClain's Pride No. 2* for William M. McClain of Phila- delphia. The design was by Colley-Maier, Inc., of Boston and both trawlers were completed in February 1945. They were 62 feet overall, diesel powered, and their cargo holds were lined with two inches of cork.

Townsend earned his success during the war years, as no one could have worked harder to keep the yard open. He was able to pay off the company's debts and place the yard in a good position to capitalize on the demands of a postwar public which had been denied consumer goods for several years. Townsend and Gunny Wallen had drawn up plans for a 26-foot family power cruiser in 1939, but the war deferred its construction. In 1946, the first production motor cruiser came off the line, 20 feet long, with the trade name of "Cruis-Along." Gradually, the line was expanded to include the "Vacationer 22," the "Express 26," and an open fishing boat called the "Buccaneer," all designed by Eric J. Steinlein. Steinlein, a Marylander, had a long and distinguished career as a naval architect and writer. He worked for the Smithsonian Institution and in the 1930s directed The Historic American Merchant Marine Survey for the federal government's Works Progress Administration.

With these new boats, George Townsend became known as a pioneer and a brilliant innovator in the pleasure boat world. The new Cruis-Along was a fabulous success. The early models were well-constructed, sound, and safe. They were fairly rea- sonably priced, too, as their planking, decking, and bulkheads

U. S. Army Fireboat

*For the first time production
lines were set up to build the
military craft.*

were made of waterproof plywood. There were no frills, but Barnes Lusby saw to it that they were carefully built and soundly engineered. They were not luxury yachts nor were they speedy; but selling them for $2,000 each, Townsend opened up the world of yachting, water sports, fishing, and fun for the average family and ushered in the start of the mass market for pleasure boats. For the first time, M. M. Davis and Son was a household word in boating. The Cruis-Along put Solomons on the charts nationally as the leader of a new concept in boating.

In 1946 gross sales were almost one-half million dollars, and the figures continued to grow. At the New York boat show in 1947, $1,070,000 in sales for the Cruis-Along were closed, nearly half of the total sales of all of the exhibitors. Cruis-Along was truly the "Talk of the Town" as the *New Yorker* reported:

> Went around to the motor boat show at Grand Central Palace one drizzly afternoon last week, back-tracking the wake of a rumor that some forty-thousand-dollar motor boats on display there were selling like hot cakes. The rumor may be considered scotched, though Lord knows it wasn't far from the truth. The hot cakes turned out to be only two-thousand-dollar hot cakes. Five-hundred of just one model at this price had been sold by the time we arrived.[13]

In 1949 George Townsend retired. He brought in Gates Harpel to take over management of the yard. Harpel had been president and a major stockholder in the Century Boat Company which he had orchestrated into a merger with Great Lakes Freight Corporation. He was not popular with the old hands at the Davis yard. In 1953, for example, a strange decision was made to interrupt the production of the popular Cruis-Along line to accept a contract from the Navy to build two minesweepers. This interruption helped other

Cruis-Alongs

For the first time, M. M. Davis and Son was a household word in boating.

manufacturers gain a foothold in Cruis-Along's market. In 1954 Harpel left and Bernard P. Lankford, a Solomons man, became president. That same year Townsend sold all of the stock of the company to its employees for $100,000. Shortly after this, the employee-owners sold additional stock to several outsiders, including Gates Harpel and Raymond V. Nelson, who replaced Lankford as president in 1957. That year, sales reached $1,518,095.

After the success of the Cruis-Along line, no efforts were made to revive custom yacht construction. In 1946 the yard built the first five hulls of the famous Owens cutter. When the first, named *Den E Von*, won the St. Petersburg to Havana Race that year, the yacht was an immediate success. While M. M. Davis and Son, Inc.'s role was a small one, these first five boats led a long list of sister yachts that won numerous trophies down through the years. *Den E Von* was 40 feet, 6 inches overall, and Norman Owens was probably the designer, although several others have claimed credit. Hinkley produced a fiberglass version of her in later years.

Two years later M. M. Davis and Son, Inc., built what probably was the last custom-built yacht on Mill Creek. Barnes Lusby, now vice-president and an almost legendary figure because of the success of the Cruis-Along boats, designed the motor yacht *Jupiter* for George Marshall Jones, Jr. This was Jones's third Davis-built yacht. *Jupiter* measured 57 feet overall and had a hull designed after the army personnel craft that the yard had built during World War II. She was strongly built of heavy oak frames, fir planked, with a full ceiling.

Jupiter's original appointments were pure luxury and even included a spinet piano. Jones cruised in *Jupiter* until his death in the mid-50s, and then the boat was sold to a Californian. She remained on the West Coast where after several owners and changes of name, she was acquired in 1982 by A. W. Bayer of Marina del Rey.

Al Bayer has been involved with the aircraft and aerospace industry most of his life. He was an army pilot at age 18 in World War II; a test pilot in his twenties; and a test pilot, pilot-chauffeur, vice-president, and then trusted associate of Howard Hughes until Bayer set up his own company in 1961. A power broker, Bayer is a friend of presidents, foreign and cinema royalty, and a booster of military and civilian aviation, yet it is his on-going affair with *Double Eagle*, ex-*Jupiter*, that brings him into this story.

Bayer has a consuming passion for his beamy, full-chested yacht on which he lavishes meticulous attention and care. Nothing is amiss in the perfection of *Double Eagle*, with her beautiful joiner work, and high quality furnishings, which include oriental rugs and a chest of carefully chosen wines. Her engine room is immaculate, her tool chest complete, and her staterooms beautiful and comfortable. Marty Vaden, full-time ship carpenter and part-time captain of *Double Eagle*, praises her still strong hull fastened the old fashioned way with galvanized iron spikes. (Captain Vaden extracted several fastenings and found them to be in excellent condition after forty years.)

When Bayer purchased *Double Eagle*, he had never heard of M. M. Davis and Son. He was searching for a classic Trumpy-built yacht as he had recently cruised in Florida on one owned by a friend. It was some time before he discovered the builder of *Double Eagle* was Davis, and by then he knew that the sturdy hull of *Double Eagle* was more suited for his cruises on the Pacific Ocean. Its heavy diesel engine and great capacities for fuel and water combined to give him a safe comfortable yacht—a classic too, which lacks only the lighter, more stylish profile of a Trumpy.

Another vessel still in existence is *Beryl*, an Army T-Boat conversion built at Solomons during World War II. After the war she was used as a commercial fishing boat, then brought to Southern California and rebuilt as a yacht. Her conversion design was by Blaine Seely. In 1979 she was sold for $75,000 and is now owned in the San Francisco Bay area.

Throughout the 1950s, the Cruis-Along line was expanded and the number sold reached 2,700 by 1957. Employment figures at the Davis yard averaged between 100 and 150 workers; the average hourly pay scale was $1.70. In 1957 Raymond Nelson, then president, dropped the name M. M. Davis and Son, Inc., in favor of Cruis-Along Boats, Inc. But heavy clouds were on the horizon as fiberglass construction was being developed as a replacement for wood.

The story of a yacht yard that was always called "the shipyard" reaches its denouement here. From 1958 until the final closing of the yard in 1974, most of the major decisions concerned mergers, first with the Century Boat Company, and later with Ventnor Boats of New Jersey, and finally, bankruptcy in the 1960s. Fiberglass was closing an era, not just at Solomons, but everywhere. The craftsmen who worked with M. M. Davis and Son, and who were owners of its successor firms, served as the pallbearers, not only for the company, but, also for the wooden boat industry—an industry older than recorded history.

Double Eagle, ex-Jupiter

Photographer: Al Bayer, Calvert Marine Museum Collection.

...yet it is his on-going affair with Double Eagle, ex-Jupiter, *that brings him into this story.*

The yard was reopened in 1972 as a last-ditch effort by the county and some local businessmen. One of the last men to leave the doomed company in 1974 was Barnes Lusby.

As this book was nearing completion, an inquiry was received about a recently located sports-cruiser built by the Davis company in 1972: What did we think of her builder? The response was, while there had been no Davises at the yard for 35 years, this yacht was built by the only Davis-trained craftsman still working at the yard in 1972, J. Barnes Lusby.

167

Chapter 1

1. Hulbert Footner, *Charles' Gift, Salute to a Maryland House of 1650*, (New York: Harper & Brothers, 1939), p. 222. This quotation has been altered slightly to identify correctly the *Kaiser Wilhelm II* as the *Kronprinz Friedrich Wilhelm*.

2. Clarence E. Davis to American Express Company, 5 July 1925, Davis Archives, Calvert Marine Museum (hereafter cited as CMM-Davis).

3. "Governor Bowie's Message to the Legislature Accompanying the Enabling Act for the Baltimore and Drum Point Railroad," in *Prospectus of the Baltimore and Drum Point Railroad*, (Baltimore: 1888), p. 6-7.

4. R. S. Stewart to Frederick Barreda, 10 June 1871, Barreda Papers, Calvert Marine Museum (hereafter cited as CMM-Barreda).

5. Lewen W. Wickes, "Isaac Solomon," unpublished manuscript, Calvert Marine Museum (CMM).

6. James A. McAllister, comp., "Abstracts from the Land Records of Dorchester County, Maryland," (typescript compilation), 75:1 FJH 538, 28 April 1852; 75:1 FJH 541, 28 April 1852; 76:2 FJH 147, 23 October 1852; 76:2 FJH 254, 9 April 1853; 76:2 FJH 316, 17 May 1853; 77:2 FJH 426, 9 April 1853; 77:2 FJH 667, 22 June 1854; 77:2 FJH 668, 22 June 1854; 78:2 FJH 29, 22 June 1854; 79:2 FJH 548, 27 February 1856.

7. Wickes, "Isaac Solomon."

8. Solomon and Son Account Book, CMM.

9. R. S. Stewart to Frederick Barreda, 21 June 1871, CMM-Barreda.

10. Judge D. R. Magruder to Frederick Barreda, 30 June 1871, CMM-Barreda.

11. Solomon and Son Account Book, CMM.

12. "Panic on Wall Street," *Harper's New Monthly Magazine*, 48:127.

13. Mrs. Matilde de Barreda to a friend, December 1875, *Calvert Historian*, 1(no.2):25-26.

14. Solomon & Son and Davis Day Book (Job No. 64:60-121), CMM.

Chapter 2

1. Solomon & Son and Davis Day Book (Job No. 64:60-121), CMM.

2. Charles Solomon Store Book, 406, CMM.

3. John Henry Davis, a successful shipwright for many years, was suddenly hauled into court by his creditors. Dorchester County Chancery Court, Case 955, April 1878. Levi D. Travers was the appointed trustee of his properties. Dorchester County Land Records, 12 FJH 551, Deed in Trust, 9 September 1878.

4. Ships known to be built by John Davis are listed in Appendix A; information supplied by John G. Earle.

5. U. S. Federal Census of 1810, Talbot County, p. 384. According to the records, John Davis had one son under ten years and another between sixteen and twenty-six, plus three daughters, one under ten, and two slaves.

6. Talbot County Newspaper Abstracts, 22-277-RSH, 7-31 July 1810.

7. Levi D. Travers, Account Books and Ledgers, MS. A-22, 29, and 30, Dorchester County Historical Society. (DCHS) No entry for George Davis appears prior to 1819. George and Isaac Davis's accounts were intermingled, indicating a family relationship, probably brothers.

8. Talbot County Land Records, 34:224, 22 May 1810. John Davis sold his furniture, food, tools, oakum, blocks, timber, chain, and two negro slaves.

9. Talbot County Newspaper Abstracts, 2-321-RST, 19 February 1811, 3-2-RST, 5 January 1813.

10. Talbot County Land Records, 38:90-91. John Davis sold his remaining possessions, including a horse, to Nathan Harrington and Wm. Wrightson.

11. Talbot County Newspaper Abstracts, 4-265-RSM. John Davis discharged from imprisonment.

12. Talbot County Land Records, 40:418. According to the Bill of Sale, George Davis bought household furniture from Blaney Davis.

13. Katherine H. Palmer, comp., "Dorchester County Marriage License Records, 1780/1865," MS. No. 101, DCHS.

14. McAllister, 56:10 ER 399, 5 May 1826, George Davis acquired Risdon's Beginnings and Locust Neck; 59:12 ER 699, 28 July 1832, Isaac Davis bought *Pilgrim's Rest*, *Aaron's Folly*, and *Smith Folly*.

15. Carpenter's Certificate, U. S. National Archives.

16. "An Act to Prevent the Destruction of Oysters in this State," *Laws of Maryland*, 1820, chapter 24. This was Maryland's earliest oyster protection law. It prohibited dredging in the state except for the use of "drags on the western shore." Further, it reserved the transportation of oysters to Maryland-owned

vessels, except that "nothing in this section contained shall be construed to extend to the basin and harbour of the city of Baltimore."

17. Ships known to have been built by George Davis and the schooner *Miranda* built by Isaac Davis (Clarence E. Davis's great grandfather, not the Isaac Davis who worked for Isaac Solomon, then at Cambridge in the 1880s) are listed in Appendix A.

18. MS. F-325, DCHS.

19. Nellie M. Marshall, comp., "Tombstone Records, Dorchester County, Md.," Cemetery Records Commission. Isaac Davis, born 14 June 1800, died 17 June 1869; George Davis born 26 May 1790, died 4 March 1842.

20. McAllister, 81:4 FJH 383, 23 February 1859. John Henry Davis was a member of the building committee for the Bethlehem M. E. Church. This church's early records are kept by Mrs. Stapleford Nield, Taylors Island. Davis is mentioned as a reader and trustee. Also MS. F-177, DCHS.

21. Taylors Island Lyceum Minute Book, MS. A-130, DCHS.

22. Nellie M. Marshall, comp., "Bible Records of Dorchester County, Maryland," 612-1969, DCHS.

23. A list of vessels built by John Henry Davis is in Appendix A.

24. Levi D. Travers Freight Book, MS. A-2, DCHS.

25. Clarence E. Davis to John G. Hanna, 12 September 1928, CMM-Davis.

26. Robert H. Burgess to the author, 24 June 1986.

27. Dorchester County Land Records, 12 FJH 553, 13 September 1878.

28. U. S. Federal Census of 1880, Calvert County.

29. M. V. Brewington, *Chesapeake Bay Log Canoes and Bugeyes*, (Cambridge, Md.: Cornell Maritime Press, 1963), p. 105.

30. John G. Earle to Clarence E. Davis, 3 December 1933, CMM-Davis. The letter says in part: "When I had the pleasure of meeting you several weeks ago, you mentioned the fact that your grandfather had built two pungies called *James A. Garfield* and *John Henry Davis*."

Chapter 3

1. Brewington, p. 100.

2. Calvert County Land Records, 7 SS 82-83, Deed of 1 August 1885, from Thomas and Margaret Moore of Baltimore to Marcellus M. Davis for Solomons lot number 6 on the Grover Plat.

3. Vessels built by Hayward and Davis, M. M. Davis, and M. M. Davis and Son are listed in Appendix A. This list, along with the boats of the other Solomons builders, was compiled by members of the staff of the Calvert Marine Museum.

4. Interview with Charles F. Sayle, Sr., 2 November 1985, Nantucket, Massachusetts. Also letters to the author from Mr. Sayle dated 30 October 1985 and 19 January 1986.

5. Calvert County Land Records, 1 TBT 205-208, Articles of Incorporation, 28 October 1892, M. M. Davis Marine Railway Company.

6. Calvert County Land Records, 5 TBT 549-50, Bill of Sale signed 19 June 1899: "Emma R. Davis and Marcellus M. Davis, late of Calvert County but now residing in Baltimore, in consideration of the sum of $800 paid by J. Cooke Webster, sell to Webster the Marine Railway and all fixtures, late, the property of the M. M. Davis Marine Railway Co. which was bought by me [Davis] from the receivers of said company on the 24th day of April,

1899." Also Calvert County Circuit Court Docket, Case 281, 30 August 1898.

7. *First Kiss*, starring Gary Cooper and Fay Wray, directed by Rowland V. Lee. Information from the archives of the Chesapeake Bay Maritime Museum.

8. Charles Harper, former owner of the tug *M. Mitchell Davis*, interview with the author, March 1986.

9. Calvert County Land Records, 4 GWD 553-56, Partnership Agreement, 5 July 1904.

10. Calvert County Land Records, 11 AAH 591-92, Partnership Agreement of 1 January 1921, filed March 1925.

11. Footner, p. 27. The *Gadabout* experience must have been intense since he gives it full treatment in these memoirs.

12. Ibid, p. 30.

13. Contemporary newspaper item, undated, origin unknown, CMM.

14. Contemporary newspaper item, undated, origin unknown, CMM.

15. Leonard S. Tawes, *Coasting Captain* (Newport News: The Mariners' Museum, 1967), p. 432.

Chapter 4

1. *Forest and Stream*, 23 February 1888, p. 96.

2. "Yachting in Baltimore," *Forest and Stream*, 16 June 1881, p. 396.

3. *Forest and Stream*, 3 January 1889, p. 487.

4. "A Capsize at Baltimore," *Forest and Stream*, 19 July 1888, p. 525.

5. Paul L. Berry and Geoffrey M. Footner, "Boatbuilding at Solomons, The Marsh Shipyard," *Bugeye Times*, 10 (Summer 1985):2.

6. "The Steam Yacht Dungeness," *Forest and Stream*, 12 May 1894, p. 411.

7. There exists a myth that John Alden, on a race from New England to Gibson Island or Annapolis, had rounded Chesapeake Lightship and was headed up the bay. It was sunset and he found his schooner abeam a cargo-ladened bugeye, handled by a single sailor. At dawn, as the yachtsman closed in on the finish, Alden is said to have been shocked to find the bugeye still on his beam. This was in the late 1920s, and soon most designers, including Alden dropped gaff rigs and adopted the triangular sails of the bugeye.

8. *Forest and Stream*, 6 August 1885, p. 36. In the late nineteenth century the terms "buckeye" and "bugeye" both appeared in the literature; origin of neither term is known.

9. Ibid., 3 January 1889, p. 487.

10. J. T. Rothrock, *Vacation Cruising on the Chesapeake and Delaware Bays* (Philadelphia: J. B. Lippincott & Co., 1884), p. 33.

11. E. W. Beitzell, *Life on the Potomac River* (Abell, Maryland: The Author, 1968), p. 67.

12. N. T. Kenney, "Off the Deep End," *The Chesapeake Skipper*, June 1948, p. 34.

13. Robert Barrie and George Barrie, Jr., *Cruises, Mainly in the Bay of the Chesapeake* (Philadelphia: The Franklin Press, 1909), p. 69.

14. "The Rudder Stations, Eastern Seaboard, Solomon, Md. (Gasolene) M. M. Davis," *Rudder*, July 1908, Advertising Section, p. 46.

15. Clarence E. Davis to Philip L. Rhodes, 9 February 1929, CMM-Davis.

16. *Rudder*, June 1929, pp. 48-49; also *Yachting*, November 1929, p. 88.

17. Clarence E. Davis to Paul Nevin, Henry J. Gielow, Inc., New York City, 1 July 1931, CMM-Davis.

18. "A Cabin Boy to Yacht Builder to Sailboat Maker, One Life," Baltimore *Sun*, 21 April 1935, page unknown.

19. A. S. Crockett, "Cruising on the Chesapeake," *Forest and Stream*, 1 October 1910, p. 474.

Chapter 5

1. *Log of the Star Class, Silver Jubilee*, (New York: International Star Class Yacht Racing Association, 1936), p. 189.

2. Mrs. John G. Hanna to the author, 4 June 1985. Also Clarence E. Davis to Philip L. Rhodes, 18 February 1927, CMM-Davis. Also, Weston Farmer, "How the Tahiti Got Her Name" *The Skipper*, August, 1970; also John Stephen Doherty, *A Ketch Called Tahiti*, (Camden, Maine: International Maine Publishing Co., 1987).

3. Clarence E. Davis to John G. Hanna, 12 September 1928, CMM-Davis. The schooner referred to here was probably the *Augusta*, built by John Henry Davis and written about extensively in Chapter 2.

4. Oral History of Ruby Dixon, Master Carpenter, M. M. Davis and Son, 21 January 1975, p. 18, CMM.

5. Estimate on Planking and Changing Bilge on Yacht *Bonhomie*, May 31, 1928, CMM-Davis. The cost of materials totaled $1,468. Labor cost was $4,460. This was figured on a ten-hour day at a wage of fifty cents per hour; as Davis charged overhead and profit separately, this was probably fairly near his actual cost of labor. If the average rate paid was in fact fifty cents per hour, the rate remained stable up to World War II.

6. Donald H. Sherwood, *The Fishing Years* (Privately printed, 1971).

7. Donald H. Sherwood, *The Sailing Years* (Privately printed, 1971).

8. Ibid., p. 2.

9. Ibid., p. 71.

10. Donald H. Sherwood's interviews with the author, 1984. In addition to information about the building of *Seawitch*, Mr. Sherwood presented the Calvert Marine Museum with his correspondence, blueprints, and photographs of the *Seawitch*.

11. Donald H. Sherwood to W. S. Galloway, 7 December 1927, CMM.

12. Oral History, Orem Elliott, 1976, 3, CMM.

13. The complete estimate lists of Clarence E. Davis, consisting of twelve pages plus original quotations by marine suppliers, are in CMM-Davis.

14. Philip L. Rhodes, "Specifications of Labor and Materials for 34-foot O.A. Auxiliary Yawl, *Seawitch*,"(1927), 6, CMM.

15. Ibid., p. 8.

16. Ibid., p. 10.

17. Ibid., p. 21.

18. Donald H. Sherwood to P. L. Rhodes, 5 June 1934, CMM.

19. Arnold R. Holt to the author, 23 February 1985, CMM.

20. Jack D. Strickland to the author, 11 July 1985, CMM.

21. A carbon copy of this news release is in CMM-Davis. Presumably it was sent out the following Tuesday, 17 January 1928, as Davis writes, "A new construction shed, joiner shop and mold loft were started yesterday." It is doubtful that any new building was started on a Sunday.

22. In the early 1930s M. M. Davis and Son issued a brochure (although Davis called it a

catalogue). It consisted of photographs of several of the yachts built at that time, and the descriptions of the yachts were obviously the work of an advertising agency. CMM-Davis.

23. John Lee Chapman, Jr., in a letter to the author, 6 May 1985, quotes from a letter written by Philip L. Rhodes in March 1958 to Alex W. Schoenbaum who bought *Windward* in 1957. Chapman owned her from 1958 to 1985. CMM.

24. Ibid.

25. M. M. Davis and Son to Frank P. Erbe, Jr., 6 February 1928, CMM-Davis.

26. The original estimates prepared by Clarence E. Davis, as well as the revised one dated 12 November 1927, are in CMM-Davis.

27. Clarence E. Davis ran out the costs of duplicating *West Wind*, 21 November 1930. CMM-Davis.

28. Philip L. Rhodes's drawings and lines of *Windward* appeared in *Yachting*, March 1928, pp. 98-99. *Rudder* also covered the *Windward*, July 1928, pp. 46-47.

29. Recollections of J. Barnes Lusby of the M. M. Davis and Son Shipyard. Unpublished, CMM.

30. Oral History of Charles Elliott, 10 January 1980, 10. Interviewed by Barbara Wilson and Dave Bohaska, CMM.

31. Ibid.

Chapter 6

1. Clarence E. Davis to Philip L. Rhodes, 3 January 1930, CMM-Davis.

2. Clarence E. Davis to Philip L. Rhodes, 31 January 1930, CMM-Davis.

3. Clarence E. Davis to Philip L. Rhodes, 13 February 1930, CMM-Davis.

4. Clarence E. Davis to John G. Alden, 19 December 1927, CMM-Davis.

5. Clarence E. Davis to Philip L. Rhodes, 21 September 1928, CMM-Davis.

6. Richard Henderson and Robert W. Carrick, *John G. Alden and His Yacht Designs* (Camden, Maine: International Marine Publishing Co., 1983), p. 160.

7. Clarence E. Davis to Philip L. Rhodes, 21 September 1928, CMM-Davis.

8. John G. Alden, "Specifications for the Tug *Luna*," 1930, CMM.

9. "Down to the Sea with the Tugs *Luna* and *Venus*," *Massachusetts Gas Companies Bulletin*, 12(no. 10):3-5.

10. Bill Robinson, *The Great American Yacht Designers* (New York: Alfred A. Knopf, 1974), p. 4.

11. Howard I. Chapelle, *American Sailing Craft* (New York: Bonanza Books, 1936), p. 63.

12. One of the saddest memorials in America is the one dedicated to the 10,000 sailors who lost their lives in the nineteenth and twentieth centuries sailing out of Gloucester on fishing schooners.

13. Clarence E. Davis to John G. Alden, 18 February 1930, CMM-Davis.

14. Clarence E. Davis to John G. Alden, 28 February 1930, CMM-Davis.

15. Clarence E. Davis to Roger Young (owner of *Manana*), 11 April 1931, CMM-Davis.

16. Clarence E. Davis to John G. Alden, 26 June 1931, CMM-Davis.

17. John S. Lawrence, "*High Tide* and the Gibson Island Race," in *Sportsman*, undated clipping, from the private papers of E. E. du Pont,

du Pont Archives, Hagley Museum (hereafter cited as Hagley-du Pont).

18. Ibid.

19. John G. Alden to E. E. du Pont, 10 July 1934, Hagley-du Pont.

20. William L. Henderson of the Gibson Island Yacht Squadron to E. E. du Pont, 10 September 1934, Hagley-du Pont.

21. E. E. du Pont to John G. Alden, 9 September 1941, Hagley-du Pont.

22. Ms. C. E. (Cathy) Stanton to the author, 17 December 1984. Ms. Stanton was a member of the Seven Seas Sailing Club. CMM.

23. Phineas Sprague, Jr., to the author, conversations by telephone, 1984. See also Henderson and Carrick, *John G. Alden*.

24. John G. Alden, "Specifications for Design No. 601," 7 April 1936, CMM.

Chapter 7

1. Clarence E. Davis to Mrs. J. A. Jones, Chicago, 5 May 1930, CMM-Davis.

2. *Lloyd's Register*, (1932), p. 253.

3. Clarence E. Davis to Alexander F. Jenkins, 27 November 1928, CMM-Davis.

4. *Yachting*, February 1932, pp. 82-83.

5. Ibid., p. 83.

6. Philip L. Rhodes, "Tidal Wave, Part IV," *Yachting*, February 1931, p.114.

7. Philip L. Rhodes to Clarence E. Davis, 4 June 1932, CMM-Davis.

8. Philip L. Rhodes, "*Nixie*, A 22 foot Cruiser," *Yachting*, January 1933, p. 51.

9. M. M. Davis and Son [Clara Brooks] to Daniel Combs, 26 February 1931, CMM-Davis.

10. Clara Brooks to Raymond T. Davis, 3 March 1931, CMM-Davis.

11. Clarence E. Davis to G. Dennison, 14 November 1930, CMM-Davis.

12. Charles D. Mower, "Specifications for Auxiliary Cruising Schooner," 24 September 1931, CMM.

13. Ruby Dixon, Oral History, 21 January 1975, CMM.

14. Charles Elliott, Oral History, 10 January 1980 CMM.

15. J. Barnes Lusby, "Recollections of the M. M. Davis and Son Shipyard," unpublished, CMM.

16. Clarence E. Davis's estimates for the schooner *Manana*, 22 September 1931, for Roger Young, CMM.

17. *Yachting*, January 1932, p. 96.

18. Clarence E. Davis to Dr. R. P. Batcheler, 7 December 1931, CMM-Davis.

19. *Yachting*, October 1936, p. 66.

20. James Warren Crawford, "Neptune's Anger," *Yachting*, August 1962, p. 156. This statement is disputed by Thomas G. Skahill who states that Crawford sailed *Dirigo II* in the 1953 Transpac Race.

21. *Yachting*, March, 1932, p. 92.

22. *Narada's* Lines and Specifications from *Rudder*, January 1937, p. 66, and *Yachting*, September 1936, p. 68.

23. Frances S. Kinney, *You Are First: The Story of Olin and Rod Stephens of Sparkman and Stephens* (New York: Dodd, Mead & Co., 1978), pp. 54-55.

24. L. Corrin Strong, *Logs of the Yacht Narada*, CMM.

25. Baltimore *Sun*, 3 June 1940, page number unknown.

26. *Yachting*, December 1948, p. 68.

27. United States Coast Guard to L. C. Strong, 27 January 1943, CMM.

Chapter 8

1. J. Barnes Lusby to George H. Townsend, 4 January 1939, CMM-Davis.

2. J. Barnes Lusby to George H. Townsend and G. Gunther Wallen, 5 January 1939, CMM-Davis.

3. Hugh B. Wallis, "Eye Witness Report," *Bugeye Times*, 5(no.2):2.

4. *Rudder*, March 1935, p. 65.

5. George M. Pynchon, "Miami-Nassau Race," *Yachting*, March 1935, p. 65.

6. Henderson, *Choice Yacht Designs*, p. 23.

7. Milton and Diane Hamilton (owners of *Arthur C. Nielsen*) to the author, 23 March 1986.

8. Sparkman and Stephens, Inc., "Construction of a 33 ft. Waterline Cutter, Specifications"; CMM.

9. *Yachting*, June 1936, p. 104.

10. *Yachting*, September 1936, p. 92.

11. *Yachting*, November, 1936, p. 94.

12. *Rudder*, March 1937, p. 57.

13. Alfred Loomis, "On to Gibson Island," *Yachting*, August 1937, pp. 70-72, 160-62.

14. Peter C. Chambliss, "Anchors Aweigh for the Ocean Race," Baltimore *Sun*, 27 June 1937, page number unknown.

15. C. Sherman Hoyt, *Sherman Hoyt's Memoirs* (New York: D. van Nostrand Co., Inc., 1950), p. 211. Hoyt wrote erroneously that *White Cloud* was built by Dauntless Shipyard of Essex, Connecticut.

16. Ibid.

17. Ted Hoster, "Chesapeake Bay Activities," *Yachting*, November 1938, p.88.

18. Kenneth Kroehler to the author, 3 June 1986, CMM.

19. Samuel M. Clarke, retired librarian and historian of the Chicago Yacht Club, to the author, 4 March 1986, CMM.

20. Field Beam, "Fast Time To Mackinac," *Yachting*, September 1942, p. 29.

21. Ibid., p. 68.

22. George E. Van, "Port Huron-Mackinac Race, July 11-14 [1942]," *Rudder*, August 1942, p. 46.

23. Frank E. Bilek to the author, 25 August 1986, CMM.

24. Ibid.

25. Stephen F. David to Nancy Footner, taped interview, 1 June 1986, CMM.

26. Ibid.

27. Ibid.

28. Frank E. Bilek to the author, 25 August 1986, CMM.

29. Roderick Stephens, Jr., to the author, 24 April 1984, CMM.

30. Roderick Stephens, Jr., to the author, 23 July 1984, CMM.

Chapter 9

1. Roderick Stephens, Jr., to the author, 4 June 1984, CMM.

2. New York Yacht Club racing rules require members to place an exact half-model of their yachts when entered in a New York Yacht Club-sanctioned race. *Manitou*'s model is No. 760, hung on Panel No. 5 in the club's taproom.

3. Chicago *Daily News*, photograph and caption, undated, CMM.

4. Morrow Krum, "Saint Elmo Lights the Way to Mackinac," *Yachting*, September 1938, p. 28.

5. Ibid.

6. Kenneth Kroehler to the author, 7 May 1986, CMM.

7. Ibid.

8. Ibid.

9. J. Julius Fanta, *Sailing with President Kennedy* (New York: Seashore Publishing Co., 1968), p. 32.

10. Tazewell Shepard, Jr., *John F. Kennedy, Man of the Sea* (New York: William Morrow & Co., 1965).

6. *Yachting*, May 1938, pp. 79-80.

7. *Rudder*, March 1938, p. 82.

8. George H. Townsend to his son-in-law G. Gunther Wallen, 13 March 1939, CMM-Davis.

9. J. Barnes Lusby to George H. Townsend, 20 October 1939, CMM-Davis.

10. G. Gunther Wallen to George H. Townsend, 10 October 1939, CMM-Davis.

11. *Rudder*, August 1941, p. 33.

12. Hulbert Footner, "Simple Life at Solomons Now Thing of the Past Due to War," Baltimore *Sunday Sun*, 17 July 1943, page number unknown.

13. "Talk of the Town," *The New Yorker*, 25 January 1947, page number unknown.

Chapter 10

1. *Lloyd's Register*, 1942, Suppl.

2. *Yachting*, November 1927, p. 67.

3. *Rudder*, September 1936, p. 22.

4. *Down Wind* eventually was changed to *Downwind*

5. Jean Dash to the author, 10 October 1986, CMM.

Appendix A

Known vessels built by the Davis family

Vessel	Date	Place	Type	Remarks	Vessel	Date	Place	Type	Remarks
John Davis[1]					Helvetius	1834	Taylors Island	Sloop	
Flying Fish	1804	St. Michaels	Schooner	Bill of sale: $2,186	Cornelia Ann	1836	"	"	Vienna enrollments (MHS MS 2476)
Ariel	1805	"	"	BCC[2]; 85 gross tons	Baltimore	1836	"	"	
Experiment	1806	"	"	Queenstown/ Baltimore packet	Fulvia	1838	"	"	Built for Thos. Hooper & Co.
Director	1807	"	"	Two masts, round stern	T. R. Betton	1839	"	"	Baltimore/Mobile/ New Orleans packet[4]
Betsey	1807	Talbot Co.	"	Owners: Wm. & Thos. Harrison					
Joshua	1808	St. Michaels	"	BCC; "sharp built in bottom"	**Isaac Davis I[5]**				
Hope	1808	Miles River	"	Oxford carpenter's certificate	Eagle	1835	Dorchester Co.	Schooner	Vienna enrollments (MHS MS 2476)
Corsica	1817	Chester River	Sloop	Baltimore enroll-ment book (Mary-land Historical Society MS 2476)	Sally Ann	1840	"	"	BCC; builders Stewart and Davis[6]
					Miranda	1842	Taylors Island	"	45.3' x 20.5' x 6.1'
George Davis[3]					**John Henry Davis[7]**				
Hope	1822	Dorchester Co.	Schooner	Vienna enrollments (MHS MS 2476)	Jamestown	1852	Dorchester Co.	Schooner	BCC
Orizenbo	1822	"	Sloop	BCC	Mohawk	1853	"	"	Note 8
Cicero	1826	Taylors Island	"	BCC: built for James Smith	Frank	1854	"	"	
Caledonia	1826	"	"	Vienna enrollments (MHS MS 2476)	Beloir	1859	"	"	Owner: Marcellus A. Mitchell (builder's brother-in-law)
Louise Jane	1828	Oxford	"	Oxford enrollments (MHS MS 2476)	Corredor	1863	James Island	"	Same owner as Beloir
Lucritia	1830	Taylors Island	"	Bay craft; sharp built	Nellie	1863	"	Brig	Same owner as Beloir

Vessel	Date	Place	Type	Remarks
Thomas W. Moore	1866	James Island	Pungy	Owner: Thomas Moore
Cornelia	1866	"	Schooner	Named for builder's wife
Levin A. Insley	1869	"	Pungy	
John Henry Davis	1869	"	"	
L. C. Spencer	1870	"	"	Note 9
S. F. Kirwin	1870	"	Schooner	Centerboard; 86.66 GT
Augusta	1871	"	"	Note 10; 54.10 GT
Minnie Estelle	1872	"	Sloop	
Mary Francis	1873	"	Schooner	
H. L. James	1875	Todd Neck	"	Built for Zachariah Mitchell
George Howard	1876	"	Bugeye	8.86 gross tons
Joseph H. Johnson	1877	Cambridge	Schooner	Davis & Johnson[11]
Anna C. Burdsall	1878	"	Steam Tug	"
Alwildia C. Eaton	1878	"	Schooner	"
Early Bird	1880	Solomons Is.	Pungy	Built for Thomas Moore
James A. Garfield	1881	"	"	Note 12
Bessie Tankersley	1882	Annapolis	Bugeye	Note 13

Vessel	Date	Place	Type	Remarks
Isaac Davis II[14]				
Zephyr	1871	Solomons Is.	Pungy	Note 15
Isaac Solomon	1872	"	"	
Julia A. Parks	1873	"	Sloop	Built for Thomas Moore
Joseph Zane	1873	"	Steam Tug	Painting at Calvert Marine Museum
Virginia Mister	1873	"	Sloop	
Stephen J. Fooks	1874	"	Coasting Schooner	Three masts
Clyde	1876	"	Frame Bugeye	Note 16
George C. James	1880	Cambridge	Sloop	
Minnie	1880	"	"	
Edwin C.	1881	"	Schooner	BCC
Helen	1881	"	Pungy	BCC
Oliver C.	1881	"	Bugeye	BCC
Thomas R. Powley	1881	"	"	BCC
Wm. H. Dail	1881	"	"	BCC
Barge Bango	1881	"	Unrigged Barge	BCC 348.27 GT[17]
Barge Breeze	1881	"	"	" 354.17 GT[17]
Frank & Murry McNamara	1882	"	Pungy	BCC
Eugie Preston	1882	"	Sloop	Crisfield Carpenter's Certificate (Nat. Arch.)
Carrie & Belle	1883	"	Schooner	BCC; 104.76 gross tons
Sweepstakes	1885	"	Sloop	

Notes

1. Data on John Davis's vessels researched by John G. Earle.

2. "BCC" indicates carpenter's certificate filed in Baltimore, now located at the National Archives, Washington, D. C.

3. George Davis was the probable son of John Davis and uncle of John Henry Davis. The list of his vessels was developed from the National Archives, the Maryland Historical Society, and the records of Marion V. Brewington at the Calvert Marine Museum.

4. Carl C. Cutler's Papers, Mystic Seaport, MS 100.

5. Referred to as "Isaac Davis I" to avoid confusion with Isaac Davis of Solomon & Son and Davis. Isaac I was father of John Henry Davis.

6. It is assumed that Stewart and Davis were James A. Stewart and Isaac Davis. The former obtained a warrant on 18 January 1842 for the arrest of Isaac Davis for non-payment of debt (Dorchester County Historical Society manuscript F-325).

7. Father of Marcellus Mitchell Davis.

8. Information from Brewington archives, Calvert Marine Museum.

9. Pungy, according to John G. Earle.

10. Abandoned in Curtis Creek in 1936.

11. John Henry Davis formed a partnership with Joseph H. Johnson in 1877.

12. Clarence E. Davis informed John G. Earle that this pungy was built by John Henry Davis.

13. John Henry Davis died in Annapolis.

14. Isaac II may have been a son of George Davis, cousin of John Henry Davis.

15. Isaac Davis came to Solomons Island to work for Isaac Solomon. He later became a partner in Solomon & Son and Davis, vessel builders and operators of the first marine railway at Solomons.

16. This may be the first frame bugeye. Isaac Davis was also building two other vessels, identity unknown.

17. Both built for the Lehigh Valley Railway.

Appendix B

Part I.
The Davis Years at Solomons

1880-1881
    John Henry Davis & Marcellus Mitchell Davis
1882-1883
    Marcellus Mitchell Davis
1883-1885
    M. M. Davis T/A Hayward and Davis

1885-1904
    M. M. Davis & Co.
    M. M. Davis was inactive between 1898 and 1900
1904-1936
    M. M. Davis and Son
    M. M. Davis died in 1924
    Clarence E. Davis died in 1936

Part II.
Vessels built by M. M. Davis and his son, Clarence E. Davis[1]

Vessel	Date	Type	Official Number [2]	Remarks	Vessel	Date	Type	Official Number [2]	Remarks
Katie and Ella	1883	Bugeye	14414[3]	BCC[4]	Fannie C. Northam	1886	Sloop	120723	
Fannie E. Hayward	1883	"	120603	Note 5	Volunteer	1888	"	161657	Note 10
Willie H. White	1883	"	81015	Note 6; name board at CMM	Emma	1889	Bugeye	136089	Note 11
Freddie Hayward	1883	"	120639	Note 7	Frank Folsom	1889	"	120789	
					Ivy	1889	"	100449	
Carrie P. Gambrill	1884	Sloop	126328		Elenora Russell	1889	"	136042	BCC
Mattie	1885	"	91842		Willie J. Gibson	1889	"	81230	
Maud R	1885	"	91841						
Little Maud	1885	"	undoc.	Note 8	Florence Northam	1890	"	120803	Later, a yacht; half model at CMM
Raymond	1885	"	undoc.	Note 8					
M. Blanche Hayward	1886	Bugeye	91896	Note 9	J. C. Arminger	1890	"	76892	
					M. A. Roberts	1890	"	92241	
Col. R. Johnson Colton	1886	"	126410	Later, a yacht	M. C. Weber	1890	"	92167	
Claudy May	1886	"	126405		M. M. Davis	1890	"	92182	
Ada C. Shull	1886	Schooner	106546		Thomas G. Duncan	1890	"	145514	

Vessel	Date	Type	Official Number[2]	Remarks
W. J. Lowery	1890	Bugeye	81292	
Annie C. Johnson	1891	Schooner	106831	Figurehead at CMM
George	1891	Bugeye	86167	BCC
Thomas E. Taylor	1891	"	145591	
Gorman C	1892	"	86196	
...ula and Sadie	1892	"	141226	Later, a yacht
William H. Perry	1892	Schooner	81365	
Blue Wing	1893	Bugeye	3596	BCC
Edith Marcy	1895	"	136497	Later, a yacht
Ann E. Maasch	1896	"	107232	BCC
James O. Carter	1896	Tow Boat	77213	Steam powered[12]
...ottie M. Leach	1896	Bugeye	141452	
R. B. Haynie	1896	"	111134	
T. Selecman	1897	Tug	77263	Steam powered
M. Mitchell Davis	1897	"	92824	Note 13
S. Hoskins	1898	"	77319	
Florence	1900	Bugeye	121144	
Alpha	1901	Tug	107661	Steam powered
William H. Yerkes, Jr.	1901	"	81757	Painting at CMM
M. Mitchell Davis	1902	Tug/Tow	93262	
M. W. Adam	1903	Tug	93380	
Cecil	1904	"	201163	Note 14
Edward G. Gummel	1905	"	202052	Steam powered
Ethel Vail	1905	Bugeye	201810	
Captain Toby	1906	Tug	203235	
America	1907	"	204568	
John I. Clark	1907	"	203995	Steam powered
Esther Phillips	1908	"	205432	Engine builder's plaque at CMM
Gadabout	1908	Yacht	undoc.	Steam powered: designed by E.B. Schook(No. 84)[15]
Mary P. Riehl	1908	Tug	205640	Name board at CMM
John Miller	1909	"	206062	
Dispatch	1910	"	208045	
Advance	1911	"	208462	U. S. Navy tug
Catherine	1911	Bugeye	209260	Round stern
Condorth	1911	Yacht, Motor	undoc.	Probably gas engine; designed by E. B. Schook (No. 115/142)[16]
M. M. Davis	1911	Menhaden Fleet	208438	Note 17
Wilbert A. Edwards	1912	" "	209910	
Winfield S. Cahill	1912	" "	210003	
Leroy Woodburn	1912	Bugeye	211624	The last bugeye[18]

Vessel	Date	Type	Official Number[2]	Remarks	Vessel	Date	Type	Official Number[2]	Remarks
T. G. Herbert	1914	Tug	212519	Steam powered	Gadfly	1926	Yacht, Ketch	undoc.	Designed by C. E. Davis
C. W. Hand	1915	Oyster Boat	213158	Gasoline engine[19]	Bonhomie	1927	Yacht, Motor	226638	Diesel powered; designed by the owner, Robert C. Roebling
Takana	1915	Towboat	212941	Steam powered					
Raymond	1916	"	213888						
Tioga	1916	Tug	214230	In 1918, USS Tioga	Seawitch	1927	Yacht, Yawl		Designed by Philip L. Rhodes (#480)[22]
Tioga II	1916	"	229739	U.S.Coast Guard					
Sarah Weems	1917	Freighter	215838	Note 20	USCG AB-24	1928	Icebreaker	-	U. S. Coast Guard
Progress	1918	Tug	216839		West Wind	1928	Yacht, Cutter	undoc.	Designed by P. L. Rhodes (#490)
Artisan	1919	"	217615						
Craftman	1919	"	217939		Windward	1928	" "	undoc.	Designed by P. L. Rhodes (#640)[23]
Custodian	1919	"	218783						
Guardsman	1919	"	218770		Saki	1928	" "	undoc.	Designed by P. L. Rhodes (#690)
Woodman	1919	"	217937						
W. A. Smoot, Jr.	1921	Dredge (Channel)	171421		Mary Anne	1928	Yacht, Motor	undoc.	Designed by Alfred Hansen
					W. A. Smoot No. 5	1928	Dredge (Channel)	171423	
Studwell	1923	Tug	223511		Corthell	1929	Tug	229223	
William T. Covington, Jr.	1923	Menhaden Trawler	223398		Coretta	1929	Yacht, Sail	228792	Bugeye design; designed by Philip L. Rhodes (#1060)
Ballantrae	1924	Yacht, Motor	223842	Designed by C. E. Davis					
John T. Hughes	1925	Tug	224698		Orithia	1930	" "	229570	Bugeye design; designed by Philip L. Rhodes (#1390)
Fidelity	1925	"	224698						
Carcassonne	1926	Yacht, Ketch	undoc.	"Tahiti" ketch; designed by John G. Hanna[21]	Luna	1930	Tug	230263	Electric diesel[24]
					Madeira	1930	Yacht, Motor	230793	Davis-45; designed by Philip L.. Rhodes(#890)
Job No. 122	1926	Houseboat		Name unknown	Lord Jim	1930	Yacht, Schooner	230250	(#476)[25] Designed by John G. Alden

Vessel	Date	Type	Official Number [2]	Remarks	Vessel	Date	Type	Official Number [2]	Remarks
Columbia	1931	Tug	231000		Tejeria	1936	Yacht, Cutter	287504	Designed by Sparkman & Stephens (#102)
Condorth II	1931	Yacht, Motor	231113	Davis-45 (see *Madeira*)[26]	Diana	1936	Yacht, Motor Sailer	234745	Designed by Sparkman & Stephens (#121)
High Tide	1931	Yacht, Schooner	230608	Designed by John G. Alden (#456)	Ko-Asa	1936	Yacht, Ketch	235629	Bugeye design; designed by Henry J. Gielow, Inc.
State Pilot	1931	Freight Boat	231501						
James S. Whiteley	1931	Tug	230794		Puffin	1936	Yacht, Sloop	undoc.	Designed by John G. Alden (#601)
Dog Star	1931	Yacht, Ketch	undoc.	Designed by P. L. Rhodes (#1600)	White Cloud	1937	"	236188	Designed by Sparkman & Stephens (#137)[28]
Nixie	1932	Yacht, Sloop	undoc.	Designed by P. L. Rhodes (#1850)	Manitou	1937	Yacht, Yawl	236528	Designed by Sparkman & Stephens (#99)[29]
Manana	1932	Yacht, Schooner	233021	92 feet loa; designed by Charles D. Mower					
Mimi II	1932	Yacht, Sloop	undoc.	Designed by P. L. Rhodes (#1870)					
Shirley Ann	1933	Yacht	233366						
Aweigh	1934	Yacht, Cutter	undoc.	Designed by Sparkman & Stephens (#24)					
Kiboko	1934	Yacht, Motor Sailer	233412	Designed by Sparkman & Stephens (#37)[27]					
Trivit	1935	Yacht, Sloop	undoc.	Designed by P. L. Rhodes (#390)					
Cheerio Too	1935	Yacht, Motor Sailer	234015	Designed by Charles D. Mower					
Lady Patty	1935	Yacht, Ketch	undoc.	Designed by P. L. Rhodes (#1790)					
Narada	1936	Yacht, Cutter	undoc.	Designed by P. L. Rhodes (#397)					

Notes

1. All of these vessels were built at Solomons, Maryland. No attempt has been made to list vessels built for the U. S. Government in World War I.

2. Documentation number is from the *Merchant Vessels of the United States* (hereafter MVUS) or from the U. S. Coast Guard Documents Office.

3. This bugeye was probably a commission to John Henry Davis by Thomas H. Tankersley who allowed Davis's son Marcellus Mitchell Davis to build it at Solomons after the death of the elder Davis.

4. "BCC" indicates carpenter's certificate filed at Baltimore, now located at the National Archives in Washington.

5. M. M. Davis went into a partnership with George W. Hayward, called Hayward and Davis. Hayward, who was not a ship carpenter, was the son-in-law of Thomas Moore. The last-known vessel built under this partnership was *Maud R* in 1885

6. Still in documentation in 1988.

7. *Freddie Hayward*, *Carrie P. Gambrill*, *Mattie*, and *Maud R* were all built for Thomas Moore or for Hayward. From this it is assumed that the builder was Hayward and Davis.

8. Mortgages were held on *Little Maud* and Raymond by M. M. Davis. This was not an unusual procedure for a builder. Neither is listed in MVUS for 1887.

9. The first owner was George W. Hayward. M. M. Davis purchased lot number 6 in 1885 from Thomas Moore. It is assumed that Davis was on his own after August 1885, and that this vessel was build for his former partner.

10. Contract of sale ($625) with John (Mac) Jones in Calvert Marine Museum archives.

11. M. M. Davis married Emma Norwood.

12. This was the first towboat built by M. M. Davis.

13. This was the second vessel named for M. M. Davis. A second tug, and third vessel named for M. M. Davis was built in 1902.

14. M. M. Davis and his son, Clarence E. Davis, then age 21, formed a partnership as "M. M. Davis and Son."

15. This was the first known yacht built by M. M. Davis and Son.

16. *Condorth* was built for and owned by the Davis family for pleasure and to take visitors to the new shipyard on Mill Creek.

17. Taken into the Navy during World War I; renamed USS *M. M. Davis*, a minesweeper.

18. In 1933, this was a police boat for the New Jersey Fish Commission. In 1987 it was a Port Norris oyster dredger.

19. In 1988, a Bivalve, N. J., oyster dredger.

20. *Sarah Weems* measured 1521 tons gross and was 206 feet in length. She was by far the largest vessel built at Solomons.

21. John Hanna's "Tahiti" class yacht was based on the design of the *Carcassonne*, but not until some eight years after she was built.

22. In 1988, owned in the Virgin Islands.

23. In 1988, owned by the Calvert Marine Museum.

24. In 1988, owned by a foundation in Boston Harbor.

25. In 1988, Canadian owned.

26. *Condorth II* became a Davis family yacht when it became obvious that there would be no sale.

27. In 1988, named *Authur C. Nielson* and owned by Buzz and Diane Hamilton.

28. Clarence E. Davis died during construction of this vessel. In 1988, the owner is Stephen David of San Francisco.

29. Clarence E. Davis died just after the keel of this vessel was laid. In 1988, the owner is the Harry Lundeberg School of Seamanship at Piney Point.

Appendix C

Custom vessels built by M. M. Davis and Son, Inc., George H. Townsend, owner[1]

Vessel	Date	Type	Official Number	Remarks	Vessel	Date	Type	Official Number	Remarks
Spree	1937	Yacht, Motor	undoc.	Designed by Charles D. Mower	Cheerio Tree	1940	Yacht, Ketch	239382	Motor sailer; designed by Sparkman & Stephens (#247)
Virginia	1937	Tug	235904	The last tug built here					
Whitecap	1938	Yacht, Sloop	237178	Motor sailer; designed by William H. Hand, Jr.(#614)	Mike	1941	Yacht	undoc.	Designed by John G. Alden (#718)
					Patrol IV	1941	Patrol Boat	240489	
Awab	1938	Yacht, Motor Sailer	237359	"Crusailer"; designed by Sparkman & Stephens (#227)	Alan	1942	Fishing Trawler	252448	
					Betty and David	1943	" "	253993	
Gray Ghost	1938	" "	237090	"Crusailer"; designer: see Awab	Elsie Jane	1943	" "	249828	
					Laura B	1943	Freight Boat	254881	
Tui-Hana	1938	" "	237708	"Crusailer"; designer: see Awab	Rowe	1943	Fishing Trawler	257498	
Moon Maid	1938	" "	237723	"Crusailer"; designer: see Awab	Ann Bryan	1943	" "	246899	
Down Wind[2]	1938	" "	238712	"Crusailer"; designer: see Awab	Judith Fay	1944	" "	247090	
					North Wind	1944	" "	246887	
Cygnet[3]	1938	" "	237690	"Crusailer"; designer: see Awab	Bessie Ann	1944	" "	246926	
					Choctaw	1945	" "	247399	
Rosa Lee	1938	Freight Boat	237700		Gannet	1945	" "	247549	
Valmer	1939	Yacht, Sloop	undoc.	"Little Sister" class; designed by Philip L. Rhodes (#457)	McClain's Pride No.1	1945	" "	247297	
					McClain's Pride No.2	1945	" "	247929	
Pinard	1939	"	undoc.	Designer: see Valmer	Jupiter[4]	1948	Yacht, Motor	257469	Designed by J. Barnes Lusby
Rosa Lee II	1939	Freight Boat	239090						

Notes

1. No attempt has been made to record the names of all government craft built during World War II. After the war the shipyard built only production craft except for the *Jupiter* and two minesweepers. In 1945 the yard built the first five hulls of the famous Owens cutter.

2. *Downwind*, originally named *Down Wind*, is owned (1987) by Mr. and Mrs. Thomas Dash of Annapolis.

3. *Cygnet*, now named *Antares*, is owned (1987) by Mr. and Mrs. David Grow of Indiana.

4. *Jupiter*, now named *Double Eagle*, is owned (1987) by Mr. A. W. Bayer of Marina del Rey, California.

186

R

Rainbow, 133
Ralph Wiley shipyard, 156
Ratsey sails, 93, 131
Raymond, 26
Reagan, Frank H., 50, 97
Regatta paint, 93
Rekar's Hotel, Solomons, 2, 77
Rena (schooner), 41
Rensselaer, Indiana, 157
Retsilla, 46–47
Revolutionary War, 43
Rhode Island, 39
Rhode River to Gibson Island Race
   of 1936, 129
Rhode River to Gibson Island Race
   of 1940, 115
Rhodes, Philip L., 50, 64–68, 71, 73,
   78–80, 95, 98–103, 109–14, 116,
   118, 132, 159, 162
Rhodes, Philip L., Jr., 103
Richardson, James, 15, 26
Richardson, Webster, 15
Richardson brothers, 18
Richardson, Davis and Company,
   15
"Risdon's Beginning" (farm on
   Taylors Island), 17
Riverside, Connecticut, 53
Robinson, Bill, 83
Roebling, Robert C., 57, 62–63, 97
Rothrock, J. T., 44
Rousby Hall, 6
Rowe, 163
Ruark, Virginia, 98
Rudder (magazine), 49–50, 53, 60,
   95, 98, 105, 122, 135, 154, 158, 161
Rudder Station, 49
Ruff House, 53
Rush (Coast Guard patrol boat), 144

S

The Sailing Years (book by Donald
   H. Sherwood), 64
St. Francis Yacht Club, 137
St. Georges Island, 44
St. John Creek, Solomons, Calvert
   County, 139
St. Joseph, Michigan, 135
St. Mary's County, 4, 6, 9, 25
St. Mary's River, 152
St. Michaels, Maryland, 16–17, 23, 39
St. Petersburg to Havana Race, 122,
   166
"St. Richard's Manor" (St. Mary's
   County estate), 9
St. Thomas, Virgin Islands, 129
Saki, 71, 97–98
Salisbury, Maryland, 45, 54
Salisbury Marine Construction
   Company, 50, 54
Sallie L. Bramble, 45
Sallie Solomon, 9
Sally Ann (schooner), 18
San Francisco, 25
San Francisco Bay, 136–37, 167
Sandy Island, See: Solomons,
   Maryland
Sanford, W. W., 41
Sanford & Brooks Company, 36
Saona, 111
Sara's Ledge Buoy, 88
Sarah E. Walters (bugeye), 43
Sarah Weaver, 36
Sarah Weems, 36
Saunders, J. J., 13, 21, 23, 26
Savarona, 63
Say, Leon, 41
Sayle, Charlie, 27
Schook, E. B., 34
Schooner yachts, 81
Schooners, 15–19, 21–23, 26, 28, 31,
   38, 40, 43, 53
Scows, 36
Seafarers International Union, 152

Seawitch, 64, 66–68, 71, 73, 79, 90,
   97–99, 124
Seely, Blaine, 167
Seven Seas Sailing Club, 95
Shadyside, Maryland, 44
Shamrock, 136
Sharks Tooth, 158
Sharptown Yacht Company, 54
Shelton Clark Trophy in 1946, 147
Sherwood, Donald H., 64–68, 73,
   75, 97–99
Shirley Ann, 120
Shull, John, 26
Silent, 103
Skiffs, 23
Skipjacks, 31, 34, 152
The Skipper (magazine), 60
Slaughter Creek, Dorchester
   County, 17
Slaves Robin and Nan, 17
Sloops, 18, 21, 23, 25–26, 34, 39–40,
   58
Smith, Isaac E., 58
Smith, John (explorer), 54
Smith, Thomas, 8
Smith and Williams, 54
Smithsonian Institution, 163
Smoot Sand and Gravel Company,
   103
Sodus Bay, New York, 96
Sollitt, George, 135
Solomon, Charles, 8–9, 11, 13–14
Solomon, Eloise L. (Mrs. Charles), 8,
   11–12
Solomon, Isaac, 4, 6–14, 17–18, 21,
   23, 25, 139
Solomon, Isaac (ancestor of Isaac
   Solomon of Solomons), 7
Solomon, Joseph (brother of Isaac),
   11
Solomon, Sarah, 7–8, 11
Solomon, William, 9, 11
Solomon & Son and Davis, 9, 11, 13,
   15, 21, 28
Solomon's general store, 9

Solomon's Oyster Cannery,
   Solomons, 4,9, 11, 25
Solomon's Wharf, 71
Solomons, (including Solomons
   Island), 1–2, 4, 6–9, 11–15, 18–19,
   21–28, 30, 34, 36, 40, 43–44, 46,
   48–50, 53–54, 57–58, 65–66, 71,
   73, 76–77, 79, 80–81, 93, 97,
   103–104, 109, 120, 122, 128, 131,
   134, 138–41, 144, 152–54,
   158–59, 161, 163, 165–67
Somers, Sam, 43
Somerset County, 8, 23, 43
Sommervill, Alex, 8
Sommervill, Eloise See: Solomon,
   Eloise L.
Sonsy (Yacht), 54
Sorensen, Charles E., 134–35
South America, 6
South Manitou Islands, 144
South River, 96
Southern Ocean Racing Circuit, 112
Southland (ex-Sarah Weems), 36
Sparkman and Stephens, Inc., 113,
   115, 120, 122–23, 125, 128,
   130–33, 136, 138, 142, 145,
   154–55, 157–58
Sparrows Point, 41
Spencer family, 16
Sprague, Phineas, 95
Spree (motor cruiser), 153
Stanford, Alfred, 117, 162
Stanton, Cathy, 95
"Star Boats" (class), 58, 64, 87, 109
State Pilot, 103
Statue of Liberty, New York harbor, 43
Steamboats, 10
Steers, George, 43
Steinlein, Eric J., 163
Stephen J. Fooks (schooner), 13
Stephens, Olin J., 98, 102, 115,
   120–21, 128, 132–33, 136, 142,
   147–48, 153, 158, 161
Stephens, Rod, Jr., 98, 102, 115, 120,
   122, 131, 133, 136, 138, 141–42

Book design: Dennis Roach
Cover design: Dennis Roach
Layout: PageMaker/Macintosh Computer
Typesetting: Award Publications
Typefaces: Avenir, Linotype Company
               Palatino, Adobe Systems, Ltd
Printing: Science Press
Binding: Advantage Bookbinding, Inc
Paper: Printed on Cougar 70# natural acid
               free paper.